PRAISE FOR WOMEN OF THE ALWAYS

I love this book. It resonated for me over and over. As an 82-year-old grandmother and retired psychotherapist who worked with women's groups for many years in California, often in nature, it feels as though we are kindred spirits.
— MIMI RICH, MA. LICENSED MARRIAGE AND FAMILY THERAPIST & AWARD WINNING AUTHOR OF FEISTY

This is an AMAZING book. It resonates deeply with me and, I believe, will serve as a powerful manifesto for women who are ready to embrace all that being female represents. My edits are only to help create clarity and smooth, effort-less reading, so women are able to focus on the depth and power of your words. I plan to give copies to my daughter and soon-to-be daughter-in-law the moment it is released.
—EMILY SUTHERLAND

Ingrid, thank you for all it has taken to bring Women of the Always into being. This book is a gift to me as it will be for my daughter. I will be giving it to many people and that's not because my painting adorns the cover. My giantess! I will be gathering women and others in circles to continue the work you have brought forth. I am so grateful. Women of the Always actively honors all readers, not just women. You have brilliantly woven together truth telling, story telling, and provocative questioning. The reader is invited to step into the words and think. Your book is a gift. You are a gift!
—KATE JACOBSON, ARTIST

I just started reading your book and I'm already enamored. I absolutely adore the imagery, the questioning, the strength you offer to each reader. Thank you for this gift to the world. I can't wait to get my hands on a published copy so that I can touch it, feel it, and capture my thoughts within it. This book will change your life if you let it. There is no pressuring, no directives, no prescriptions. Ingrid just asks deep questions that lead you to look at your life differently. It's difficult to read this book, really read it, and go back to living the way you always have. You will walk away unsatisfied with the mundane and unwilling to settle for what you have in the past. You will see that there is more to life and you will feel empowered to go in search of it. After reading her book & working with Ingrid I HAD to make changes. I realized I had been numb for so long just to be able to tolerate my life. Ingrid helped me realize I could want more and actually get it! So much of my thought process & my life has been transformed because of her and I am living so much more joyously.
— TRISH C, TECH EXECUTIVE & HEDGE WITCH

A wise and poetic book that eloquently probes the deep meaning of womanhood. Male readers would also do well to heed its message. I wish I'd had this book as a teenager.
— CHRISTOPHER MCINTOSH, BRITISH-BORN HISTORIAN AND AUTHOR OF BEYOND THE NORTH WIND

This is a book I will cherish for many years to come. It speaks to a deep place inside of me. Ingrid's wisdom is unlike anything else I've found. She teaches me to think differently and cut through the noise to remember what's actually true. In our divided and misguided world, everyone needs this kind of clear thinking. — ERIN DONLEY, NONFICTION GHOSTWRITER, EDITOR & BOOK COACH

In a voice that is fierce and tender, and urgently needed, Ingrid Kincaid casts the tale of Women of the Always. She resurrects stories long buried, breathes them back to life, daring us to remember who we are. Her questions cut to the bone. Women of the Always is not simply a book—it's a summons, a ritual, a wake-up call. If you are a woman, if you love women, if you are willing to stand in awe of what it means to be fully alive—this book is for you. — LYNNETTE BROWN, AUTHOR OF YOU DON'T LOOK PSYCHIC

Women of the Always

Women of the Always

Rooted in Wisdom
Sourced from the Dark

INGRID KINCAID

Red Thread Publishing LLC. 2025
Red Thread Books Imprint

Write to info@redthreadbooks.com if you are interested in publishing with Red Thread Books. Learn more about publications or foreign rights acquisitions of our catalog of books: www.redthreadbooks.com

Hardcover ISBN: 979-8-89294-040-5
Paperback ISBN: 979-8-89294-035-1
Ebook ISBN: 979-8-89294-036-8
Cover Design: Red Thread Designs
Cover Art: Kate Jacobson, www.KateJacobson.com

THIS IS A BOOK DEDICATED TO WOMEN
To all the women who did
To all the women who could not
To all the women who dream
To all the women who cannot sleep
To women of the always

Why do we write?
A chorus erupts.
Because we cannot simply live.

–Patti Smith

I want to go home, I whimpered.
But I already was.

–Patti Smith

CONTENTS

Introduction

∾

This book is creative.
This book is destructive.
It was never my intention to write a book that everyone likes.
Why would I do that?
This is a book you can read.
This is a book you can ignore.
This is a book.

It can be a guide, a map, an inspiration, a detour.
You can travel along at your own pace.
You can work through it with a friend.
You might be challenged.
You might be disturbed.
You might become angry, or sad.
 It might feel familiar.
It might feel strange.
It could seem negative.
Perhaps positive.
None of this is important.
This is a book.
Full of truth and full of lies.
Mostly full of questions.

Birthed From a Question

This book was birthed from a question.
But before it was a book, it was a vision.

I envisioned it as a yearlong cycle of discussions. Twenty-six unique, yet connected topics.
I would bring together a small group of women and we would meet twice a month, for a lunar year, following the path of the ever-changing moon through her cycles of 13 moons fully in shadow and 13 moons fully illuminated.
The vision came to life.
I owe a great deal to the brave and inquisitive women who showed up, moon after moon, willing to ask questions, answer questions, laugh, cry, argue, agree and disagree, be vulnerable and be stubborn.
As the discussions gained momentum, the number of women who joined us grew.
I facilitated these gatherings for ten years.
It became clear that these brave and inquisitive women were women of the always and that what we were creating together was valuable for all women, for any woman who was willing to stand in the center of her own life and claim her sovereignty with integrity and courage.
The gatherings were part of a circle, and we had to enter the circle at some point.
I made the decision to start with the topic of Names.
Our identity as women.
Our invisibility.

Our place in a linear, male-dominant, patriarchal, misogynistic world.

This book was birthed from a question. My question. A question asked by a ten-year-old girl.

"Dad, why don't the women in the Bible have names?"

When you read this book, where will you begin?
At the beginning?
At the ending? In the middle?
Which topic will you choose?
Where will you decide to enter the circle–the story?
Will that decision be birthed from a question?

Begin the Journey

It's time for us to remember who we are and to live from that remembering.

Women of the Always will take you on a journey, an adventure, exploring the fearsome, awesome, bewildering power we hold as women.
We are seers, healers, shape shifters and wisdom keepers.
We spin the threads of fate, weave the tapestry of life, as we remember the future and foretell the past.
We bleed with the moon.
We see in the dark.
We give birth.
We midwife death.
All human life comes through our bodies.

We speak our wisdom through mystery.
We are mystics, feared and revered.
We are the Holy Trinity, the triple spiral of creativity, sexuality and spirituality.
We are women of the always.
Fearless. Wild. Wise.
Passionate. Fierce. Courageous.

Women of the *Always* is an experience, a guide, a map. It is a companion for women seeking greater connection with who they truly are. A sojourn of return and remembering.

Women of the Always invites you to embark on an adventure of self-inquiry, exploring challenging and controversial topics, asking thought-provoking, revelatory questions.

You will be encouraged to dig deeply into the fertile soil of women's wisdom where creativity, sexuality and spirituality are firmly rooted.
You may be angered.
You may be troubled.
You may be strengthened and enlivened.
You may not agree, or you may shout the holy *Yes!*

You will be changed.

Are you ready to begin?
Are you hungry for a more passionate, adventurous life, something perhaps you cannot name?
Are you living a life that makes you truly happy?
Are you living someone else's idea of what your life should look like?
Have you reached a place where you feel like your entire life needs to be reimagined or do you long for something small to change?
When one thing changes, everything changes.
Are you courageous enough to live life as an adventure, a work of art, instead of a prison sentence?

You can read this book on your own, at your own pace, taking time to ponder, ask questions, answer questions, create altars or notebooks, burn candles, meditate, engage in activities, do research or additional reading.
Or, you can just read it.

It is designed and written in such a way that it can also be used with a friend or in a group or circle of women.
Imagine gathering with women who are interested in building community, sharing food and stories, asking and discussing difficult questions—women who recognize and live from the place of their own sovereignty, who are committed to truthtelling, and creating lives that are joyful, exciting, meaningful, and truly authentic.

What would you talk about if you weren't afraid?
Afraid of being judged.
Afraid of being embarrassed, made to feel stupid, or even ashamed.
Afraid of being criticized, of being wrong.

What would you talk about if you knew you would be heard?
What secrets, desires, or dreams have you hidden away?
What beliefs and ideas have you never dared to speak?

If you want something different for yourself and your life you must
be willing to do things differently, reevaluate your priorities, and
chart a new course.
Ask yourself this question...

Where in my life do I settle for less because I'm afraid?

Who Are Women of the Always?

We are women who speak our wisdom through mystery.

The mystery of creativity
 We live life from the place of imagination and possibility.
 We take time to play.
 Our lives are works of art.
 We do not save ourselves for retirement.
 We live fully in the moment.
 We refuse to settle.
 We create possibilities instead of making excuses.

The mystery of our sexuality
 We own our own bodies.
 We are willing to transgress.
 We have yearnings and desires bigger than society allows.
 We know how to be alone, in solitude and silence.
 We know how to be in relationship.
 We refuse to believe we are shameful, imperfect, or unclean.
 We embrace the power of our biology, remembering that all
 human life comes forth from the body of a woman.

The mystery of our spirituality
 We do not need a savior, nor do we need to be saved.
 We are not the cause of death.
 We refuse to be part of religious or spiritual practices or orga-
 nizations that are misogynistic.

We courageously walk away from relationships, jobs, life situations, and family connections that are abusive, toxic, or demand silence or submission.

We reject the lie of creation stories that claim that the male is the beginning.

We embrace the dark, honor death, and celebrate our bodies.

"May we all wear new eyes to recognize the changes that will come; a hundred thousand women might be enough to transform the world."
–WEAVERS' ORACLE, CAROLYN HILLYER

A woman of the always is honorable, courageous, and brave.

A woman of the always stands as sovereign in the center of her own life.

She is afraid at times but refuses to live life from the place of fear.

She is a warrior not a worrier.

She is not her trauma. She is not her victim story.

She refuses to live her life based on other people's ideas of who she should be.

Are you a woman of the always?

What is possible for all of us, for any of us, when we remember who we are?

"Ingrid, I may be about halfway through the course now. I haven't counted but I think it's been about six months. The other day I paged through my scrapbook and was astounded at how rich it is! I can't convey enough how powerful this class is for me, in such a quiet, underlying way. I feel so proud of the way that my scrapbook captures my spiritual unfolding, and I can look back through it to center and ground myself. I have a vision of cycling through the themes each moon, year after year, and including my girls as they get older." –SARAH, PARTICIPANT

Who Am I?

I am an old woman, old enough to call myself wise and wise enough to be irreverent.

I have lived a long time.

The sound of Scottish bagpipes in the Highlands makes my heart sing.

The Viking blood of adventure runs in my veins.

I am as stubborn as a rock troll and as mischievous as an imp in the heather.

The smell of wood smoke from a pre-dawn campfire makes me feel at home, safe, and at peace with the sound of wind in the pines.

I have played in cow pastures irrigated with water from the Sacramento River.

I have jumped from hay lofts in the family barn and eaten molasses oats and alfalfa pellets that were stored in grain cribs for the livestock.

I climbed to the top of a volcano that my grandmother watched erupt in 1914, from the veranda of her family home in Northern California.

I walked the path of Hadrian's Wall that crosses the northern edge of England, from west coast to east coast.

I have wandered cobbled streets, prayed in ancient stone churches, explored castle ruins, and strolled atop the walls of a Tuscan city.

I have ridden horses and ridden motorcycles, driven trucks and driven nails, and maybe even driven some people crazy.

I have given birth and given notice, written poems and grocery lists, slept in tents and in the open under the stars, beside a lover and alone.

Wild, stormy weather and silent snowfall both bring me delight, as does sunshine in a mountain meadow and a full moon dropping into the Pacific Ocean.

I am a teacher who loves to read and a reader who loves to write, to travel in search of myself, to find puzzles in the meaning of words.

I have raised children, buried parents, was present at the birth of my only grandchild, and have experienced amazement and awe all along the way.

My degrees in wisdom, intuition, and determination were earned by living life.

Creativity and sexuality remind me that my human body is spiritual and there is no place for me to go. I am already here.

I do not strive for enlightenment, raised vibrations, or higher consciousness.

I seek instead the deeply rooted balance that comes from wisdom sourced in the dark.

I teach, mentor, counsel, and guide, speaking in the voice of my ancestors and my offspring, sharing wisdom that is timeless and ancient, modern and mundane.

I have come to the winter of my life, being more content with solitude and silence. I take naps in the afternoon, write in the middle of the night, smoke a cigarette once in a while and drink whiskey whenever I feel like it.

When I am finished with this life, my wish is that those who knew and loved me will be truthful enough to say I died, not just passed away.

I was not like most children. I always felt a bit different. Maybe even a lot different.

My first word was not mama nor dada.

My first word was *why*.

I have a strong inkling that it will also be my last word.

Time will tell.

Weaving Together
Tattered Edges

This is a weaving together of tattered, frayed edges, of many different paths and many different teachings, a weaving together that honors the fact that we are all from the land, we are all people of the earth, and the differences and similarities among us come from our ancestors, the land they lived on, the choices they made at the crossroads, as well as from the land where we were born, the places we have lived, and the place we are living now.

The terrain, the climate, the plants and animals, the food we eat, what we drink, and the ways we choose to describe the things we experience, all of this and more make us who we are, different and the same.

All things are alive.
The spirit of the rock is different from the spirit of the tree, and the well, and the ripe grain.
There are the spirits of our ancestors, and the spirits of the land, and the gods and goddesses of our own people and of the people whose land we find ourselves living upon.
Some of this you may already know.
Some of it you may not know, but it might feel or seem familiar to you.
Some of it you may agree with.
Some of it you may not.
Some of it might frighten you.
Some of it might embolden you.

It's all good.
It's all bad.
It's nothing and it's everything.

We can choose to honor all the women in our families, those who have gone before us and those who are coming after us, and in so honoring the women, we also honor the men.

For it is through the body of women that all men come forth, those living, those who have died, and all men yet to live.

We can choose to honor all the women who were afraid to speak their truth and live their gifts.

We can choose to honor all the women who were fearless and perhaps lost their lives because of it.

We can honor all the women who have chosen to give birth and all who have chosen not to give birth and all the women who did not or do not have a choice.

As we wind our way along this path, we can call upon them all to be present here with us. We can say to them, out loud or in silence, *come join us if you wish*.

It is not our choice.

It is theirs.

And we can say to them, you are all welcome.

26 Paths to Wander

Names

When Women Remember Their Names

Names hold power.
Names remind us of who we are and where we come from.
They affect how we interact with the world.
They affect how the world interacts with us.
Names carry memories.

Naming is power.
Name giving is power.
Naming yourself is a powerful act of self-assertion.
Your true name is a prized possession.
Remembering your true name opens a doorway to truth.
Hearing your true name empowers you.
Saying your true name can evoke dread and it can also inspire.
Names are the language of making, the words of creation.

What does it mean to you to remember your name?
Does it feel like you have forgotten yours?
Does it feel perhaps like you have known a diferent name all along
but never dared to use it?
Do you know who you are?

I was raised in a Christian home.
We read the Bible.
We studied the Bible.

We memorized the Bible.
My father was a kind and gentle man, loving, with a big heart.
I never knew him to be mean-spirited.
He was the head of the house.
We believed it was his God-given right and duty.
My mother was in subjection to him and submissive, most of the time.
My four siblings and I were the next level down, with perhaps the hint that the two sons were more important than the three daughters.

One day, when I was about ten years old, I asked my father some questions.

> *"Dad, why don't the women in the Bible have names? Why does the man who built the ark have a name, but his wife doesn't? And what about the other women? What were their names, like Lot's wife, and Jephthah's daughter, or the Queen of Sheba, or the woman at the well?"*

My father thought for a moment and quietly said, *"Ingrid, that's just the way it is."*

That might be so, I thought, but that was not a good enough answer for me.
I've spent my entire life asking questions.
I begin this chapter with a question.

Why don't the women have names?

Recorded history, for the most part, has been written by men, in their voice, using their own language and from their own perspective. The stories of women have been mere footnotes or marginalia. In fact, even though we make up more than half the population of the world, very little is known about us. When women have been written about, if at all, many of them have remained nameless. Being nameless makes it easier for us to be discounted, dismissed, disrespected, forgotten, and abused.

There have been times in history when people were reduced to numbers, were part of a mass, and became nameless faces in a crowd.

This has been true for women all along.

Names carry the pride of a family, a clan, a tribe, or a folk. Names carry our history, our identity, our ancestry. We are told to be proud of our names, to live up to them, to not bring shame upon them. But what if our names are only the names of our fathers, or perhaps only the names of our husbands? What if our children carry only the name of the male?

Have we lost the names of our mothers?
Does forgetting the names of our mothers make us nameless?
This namelessness of women has been the case for several thousand years. It happened to our mothers and grandmothers and great grandmothers, to our foremothers.
It's not easy to know who you are if you don't know your name.
It's not easy to know who you are if you are nameless.
When you don't know who you are, it's almost impossible to have a voice, to speak with authority or confidence. It's easy to be forgotten.
How do you introduce yourself?
How are you recognized?

When you have no name, you are referred to in relation-ship to someone or something, or you become a description. Some people rename themselves to hide their identity, perhaps for reasons of safety.

Some immigrants were renamed, often without choice, because their names were too hard to spell or too difficult to pronounce. But there is a large block of us who have given our names away, often without thought.

Even in the twenty-first century, there are still many women who give their names away, who participate in a renaming ceremony when they get married. They may do it willingly, but quite often they do it because it is the custom or it is expected. Perhaps they don't know any other way, or they have never given any thought to what it actually might mean.

For the record, I got married at the age of nineteen, way back in 1968. I gave away my name without giving it a second thought. I forgot to ask the question why.

In the words of my father, *"That's just the way it is."*

I have always loved reading, and when I was about 10 years old, I discovered a book that truly changed my life. *I Married Adventure.* It was written by Osa Johnson. This thick book, whose cover was a beige and brown print of a zebra skin, was one of my favorites. I remember reading it again and again, amazed by the courage and daring of this young woman from Kansas who, at age sixteen, married a photographer many years her senior. Together they traveled the world, visiting exotic places such as Borneo, Kenya, and the Congo, filming wild animals, headhunters, and cannibals. Each time I read it, I came to the end with great sadness. On the last page was a copy of a small newspaper clipping.

> "On January 12, 1937, a Western Air Express Boeing 247 crashed into Stone Mountain, Saugus, California, while attempting a landing at Burbank Airport in the fog and rain. On board were Martin Johnson and 12 other passengers. The thirteen occupants of the plane were thrown in a heap, and one, James Bradebon, Cleveland, Ohio, was instantly killed. Martin Johnson, world famous traveler and explorer, was badly hurt, dying Wednesday morning. He was survived by his wife."

I was sad about the plane crash. I was sad that Martin died. I was sad that Osa lost her husband and best friend. But I also remember feeling angry that even though they had traveled, explored, and risked everything together, wild animals, headhunters, dangerous treks into the wilderness, in the news clipping, she was a nameless woman.

Three more letters, O, S and A would have given her a name.
In the words of my father, *"That's just the way it is."*

Later in life, I came across a book called *Pioneer Women: The Lives of Women on the Frontier*, written by Linda Peavy and Ursula Smith. The cover is a black and white photograph of a dark-haired woman standing in a field of wheat that is almost shoulder high. Unsmiling, a slight wrinkle of a frown on her forehead, she squints as she faces the camera and the sun. The child she holds also faces the camera, unsmiling.

The Preface of the book begins with a question,

> "Who is the woman whose photograph graces the cover and title page of this book? We can tell you the name of the male photographer, Joseph E.Stimson, who waded out into the field, set up his tripod, and slipped under his black hood to frame a single moment in her life. We can even tell you the names of the two kinds of wheat in the field in which she is standing. Yet we cannot tell you the name of this woman. Or how she came to be standing in this particular field on the day that Stimson arrived to document the harvest height of the wheat.
>
> Clearly, the woman and child are little more than well-placed props against which to highlight the height and fullness of a particular strain of wheat, a resilient, experimental strain bred to thrive under conditions too harsh for less sturdy stock. It was the wheat, not the woman, that Stimson was paid to immortalize, yet it is the stark juxtaposition of woman and wheat that has immortalized the photograph itself."

How often does it happen that we are just props, used to hold place for something else? Below are some questions regarding your name. Take some time to answer them.

What was the full name you were given at birth?

Were you named after anyone in your family?

Does the name you were given hold any significance or importance in your family?

Does it have a story behind it?

If you were adopted, was your name changed?

When you were young, did you ever wish you had a different name?

Is your name common or ordinary?

Or is it perhaps considered to be foreign?

Is it difficult to spell or pronounce?

Do you like your birth name?

What name do you use now?

Did you give your name away when you got married?

Have you ever used any other names, such as nicknames or aliases?

Do you have a ritual or spiritual name?

Have you ever thought about changing your name?

Would you consider creating or taking a new name for yourself?

What does the phrase *when women remember their names* mean to you?

> *"For me, it is a transformational statement. When women remember their names, they can heal the sounds of forgetting and of being forgotten. I think of the statement 'when a woman remembers her name' as a singular experience, and it hits me differently than the plural 'when women remember their names.' I think that remembering is a subversive act! Brave, bold, daring. Possibly dangerous. The danger of rejection, isolation, being told you're too big for your britches. I see myself in the action of remembering my name. First comes shame and then confusion. To remember demands heroic action. Now I am beginning to realize it takes time, and maybe the time is now."*
> –SUSAN WEBB, PARTICIPANT

GIVING YOUR NAME AWAY

Taking the man's name in marriage is still the most socially acceptable option in many countries. Why? Why should or would a woman change her last name? A few generations back no one would have even thought to ask such a question. It was just automatically done.

Have you ever considered the idea that putting your name on something implies ownership? Slave owners gave their names to the slaves they purchased and to the children their slaves birthed. The Anglo-American common-law concept known as the law of coverture dictated that once a woman was married her legal existence as an individual was suspended. Therefore, she no longer had a name.

Do some people still believe that a woman is owned by her husband or is his property?

What are some of the reasons why a woman would not want to give up her name?
How might things be different if it was a common practice for the man to take the name of the woman?

What are the implications of the use of the word maiden for a woman's birth name and why is there not a similar word for a man's birth name?
When couples choose to hyphenate, is it because the man is not okay with the idea of giving up his name? Is it possible that what seems to be a compromise might in fact still be about male dominance?
What would it be like if couples created a new name for the family they were forming?
Have you ever been married and if so, did you take your husband's name?

If you did, and you are still married, would you consider taking back your own name?
If your first thought is how hard it would be and how many changes you would have to make, consider the fact that you were willing to go through all the same things when you gave it away.
Why do some women still keep the husband's name even after getting divorced and sometimes even after being widowed?
If you did not take your husband's name, why not?
Did you consider the possibility of him taking your name?

NAMED, NAMELESS, AND INVISIBLE

How do you feel when someone forgets your name, mispronounces it, misspells it?

There is a deep connection between namelessness and invisibility. The work of women so often happens anonymously. When women are politically, economically, domestically invisible it's easy for them to be sidelined and abused.

What are your feelings about the nameless woman and child in the wheat field or the wife of Martin Johnson? Where in your life have you felt like a well-placed prop?

GERDA LERNER AND WOMEN'S HISTORY

Gerda Lerner was a professor, mentor, and director who taught, in 1963, what is considered to be the first women's history course. She established the first graduate degree program in Women's Studies in the United States. She was instrumental in demanding that attention be paid to studying women's roles, contributions, and experiences in society. She greatly contributed to the successes of the feminist movement.

In her own words,

"When I started working on women's history...
the field did not exist. People didn't think that women had a history worth knowing."

"Everything that explains the world has in fact explained a world that does not exist, a world in which men are at the center of the human enterprise and women are at the margin 'helping' them. Such a world does not exist —never has."

"Women have always made history as much as men have, not 'contributed' to it, only they did not know what they had made and had no tools to interpret their own experience. What's new at this time is that women are fully claiming their past and shaping the tools by means of which they can interpret it."

–GERDA LERNER

Below is a quote from an interview with Gerda Lerner titled *Making History Her Story, Too.* The New York Times, 20 July 2002. When asked whether women's studies were still needed, Dr. Lerner laughed,

> "For 4,000 years, men have defined culture by looking at the activities of other men... The minute we started questioning it, the first question we were asked was, 'Well, when are you going to stop separating yourself out and mainstream?' Give us another 4,000 years and we'll talk about mainstreaming."

Have you ever heard of Gerda Lerner?
Have you ever taken a course in Women's Studies or perhaps have a degree in it?
Do you know any women who have?
Do you believe there is value in such programs, and if so, what can be done to encourage more people to study Women's History?
What does this have to do with remembering your name?

JUDY CHICAGO AND *THE DINNER PARTY*

Between the years 1974 and 1979 feminist artist Judy Chicago created a monumental installation artwork, which is a symbolic history of women in Western Civilization. After almost thirty years of difficulties and setbacks and being stored in crates, *The Dinner Party* finally became housed in March 2007 in the Elizabeth A. Sackler Center for Feminist Art at the Brooklyn Museum in New York.

Judy's stated purpose in creating this work was to 'end the ongoing cycle of omission in which women were written out of the historical record.'

t was quite overwhelming for me to read the names of the 1,038 women from history she honored and remembered in the installation. I realized that I knew very little about most of them, and in truth, some of them I'd never heard of. You may find this to be your experience as well.

The multiplicity of lives alluded to in *The Dinner Party* would be impossible to take in except for one over-arching fact communicated through the art: all these remarkable human beings were female.

–THROUGH THE FLOWER, A NONPROFIT FEMINIST ART ORGANIZATION FOUNDED BY JUDY CHICAGO

VANESSA BELL'S DECORATED PLATES

Decades before Judy Chicago created her installation, *The Dinner Party*, Vanessa Bell, Virginia Woolf's sister, created *The Famous Women Dinner Service*, a 140-piece complete dinner service which included forty-eight pottery plates decorated with the portraits of famous females.

Both of these women created works of art that are testaments to women and their lives within the patriarchy. Preparing and serving meals, as well as the hosting of dinner parties, were among the few occasions women could have some autonomy, exert power and influence.

How much has changed during these last forty to fifty years regarding the namelessness and invisibility of women in art and history?

What are your thoughts on the matter?

THE GUERRILLA GIRLS

Do women have to be naked to get into the Met. Museum?
Less than 5% of the artists in the Modern Art Sections are women, but 85% of the nudes are female.

The namelessness and invisibility of women in the art world is highlighted by the words above which were seen on posters on the sides of New York City buses in the late 1980s. The poster was created by the anonymous group of feminist activist artists known as The Guerrilla Girls. They expose gender and racial discrimination in art, politics, and popular culture.

LANGUAGE BIAS

Some of the issues women face around naming and being named have their origins in the Bible. According to a story in the book of Genesis, Adam was named by God himself. After that, Adam named the animals. And after that, he named the woman who was given to him by a male god. Supposedly, she was made from a rib from Adam's body.

Males were the ones who named things.

Woman was one of the things named. Like the animals.

How does that story play out today?

Perhaps it doesn't feel relevant, but remember, there are over two billion practicing Christians worldwide, millions just in the United States, and many of them believe the Bible is the word of God.

Does this naming by men continue to be true in language?

Some of what I share here may only be true in the English language. You may wish to explore similar concepts in other languages.

As women, we face the challenge of being nameless in general language usage. In English, man or mankind is the word used to describe all people. So, in the container of the word *man*, we have *man* and *woman*. Woman is a subset of man.

The word *man* is used to describe humans in general. In these instances, we women are asked to think of ourselves as men.

All men are created equal.

That's one small step for man, one giant leap for mankind.

Man cannot live by bread alone.

We are trapped in male-centered language, trying to express our thoughts and feelings. We are trapped trying to name ourselves. In her book *The Tongue Snatchers*, Claudine Herrmann charges that language is the fundamental means by which women are oppressed. If we wish to truly express ourselves, she states, we must steal language or invent our own.

How can we remember our names when we are only spoken of as subsets of man?

Are there possibly subtle, or not so subtle, ongoing detrimental effects experienced by women because of gender-bias in language?

Is it something we are so used to that we don't think of it as a problem or an issue, or perhaps we don't think about it at all?

We face challenges expressing ourselves in a language that perpetuates women's marginality and lumps us together under male pronouns and generic terms such as human and mankind.

RELIGION AND SPIRITUALITY

How are women remembering their names in spiritual and religious settings in the twenty-first century, when patriarchy is still the prevailing religion of the entire planet?

Even the choices we make around spirituality can cause us to forget who we truly are. We can only begin to experience our own spiritual powers when we remember our names.

Do you find yourself in situations, circumstances, trainings, rituals, etc., where men still dominate or attempt to claim superiority or power over women?

Often, I hear women expressing the idea that we have made progress. They use examples like: Women are allowed to be clergy in religious institutions, or women are allowed to serve in the military, or women are allowed in positions of power in politics.

I encourage you to consider the use of the word *allow* or even the word *let*.

Ask yourself, who is doing the allowing?

Who is letting us in?

The ones doing the letting are the ones who are still in charge, the ones who are still in control and holding the power.

In order for something to really be different, we would need to change the institutions.

Are you still somehow attached to a belief that you need to be saved by a man or that someone needs to intercede for you?

What kind of religious or spiritual communities are you still a part of?

We are ignorant of our own power. We are taught to believe that it comes from someplace outside ourselves. We must remember that we, as women, have the power to create new life inside our own bodies and give birth to it.

How would the world be different if all women remembered that all human life comes forth from their bodies, not from some man's rib?

What would happen if we were no longer thought of as property?

Property of our fathers.

Property of our husbands.

Property of the State.

What would happen if we were no longer stamped with names that are not our own?

Is it possible that some of our namelessness as women comes from religions that teach that the creator is male?

The cords of connection to ourselves have been severed because we have no mothers. Men did not give birth to us, or to anything, for that matter. We were not and are not created by men.

It's time to remember who we are.

It's time to remember our names.

It's time for us to tell our own stories, in our own language, using our own words and our own voices.

It's time to move ourselves out of the margins and become our own stories.

We must stop looking to an outside source of authority to tell us who we are.

We must reconnect with and honor our own deeply rooted wisdom.

And when we do, we can all rise up and give back the names to all the nameless women in history, to all our nameless mothers, grandmothers, and great grandmothers, all the way back through time.

Names Meditation

This story begins in the middle. It is a story about your life but only a part of your life.

To begin this meditation, get comfortable and cozy, then gently and slowly close your eyes and begin paying attention to your breath. Slowly breathe in a long, deep breath and then gently, slowly release it. Take another long, slow, deep breath, then gently release it. Continue doing this, paying attention to your breath and to your body as you begin to relax.

Imagine you are in a dark place that is silent, peaceful, and serene. Imagine you are lying on some sort of bed. It might be a pallet, or a stone shelf, or a cushion of soft moss, twigs, or straw. You are quite comfortable, cozy, and warm.

All around you is evidence that you have been in this place a long time: dust, silken webs, and ancient musty smells.

You are so still it might be difficult for an observer to tell if you are asleep in death or merely asleep

You are lovely, you are beautiful, and you are still.

Your breath is slow and rhythmic.

Off in the distance, you hear a sound. You listen. You hear it again. It is a voice. Someone is calling.

The voice gets louder, not harsh or demanding, just insistent and beckoning. Someone is coming near. You watch and slowly the one whose voice you are hearing appears. She moves toward you and the place where you are resting. She encourages and assists you to rise up.

You begin to breathe more deeply as she leads you slowly to the opening of what appears to be a cave.

As you approach the opening, you see that it is night outside. The moon is shining bright and full. You know the moon. She has always been with you. You know her in your body. She is familiar, and you are not afraid. Slowly, you step out of the cave. As your eyes adjust, you see a gathering, a circle of beautiful women. Some you recognize, some you do not, but you know they are your sisters, aunties, grandmothers, and foremothers. They have come together to witness your awakening and coming forth.

As you emerge from the cave, you breathe deeply, a sigh of love. All the women begin to sing.

> She has risen.
> She has risen.
> She who is glorious and strong.
> She who is loving and wise.
> She who is wild and beautiful.
> She who remembers her name.
> You are not nameless.
> You are not invisible.
> You know who you are.
> You remember where you come from.
> You are a woman who remembers her name.

You enter the circle and join in the song.
You sing about the glory of rebirth and remembering.
You sing until dawn.
You sing the sun up.
And as the sun is rising, the moon is setting.
You feel the sun warm on your face.
You take a deep breath, slowly open your eyes and close them.
Another long, slow deep breath. You open your eyes slowly, then close them.
When you are ready, you open your eyes. With a soft gaze, you look around and see that you have returned to the place where you began this meditation.
Slowly, you find focus.

What is the name you remembered?

Use the link or QR code to listen and download all the audio meditations.

www.ingridkincaid.com/women-of-the-always.html

Meander

Meandering
Wanderers

It takes courage to wander.
Women of the always are courageous.
Meandering is nature's way of slowing things down.
It provides us access to the wisdom inherent in the rhythms and
cycles of life.
It uncovers and exposes the dangers of a purpose-driven life.
Is there value in not knowing where you are going?
Can we dare to stray and wander off the straight and narrow path?

MEANDER

Once long ago, in the beginning, which was also the ending, two
children of the Greek goddess Gaia, Tethys and Oceanus, coupled.
Tethys gave birth to the Titan Meander.
Meander's name was given to a wandering river in the country we
now call Turkey.
It is said that in ancient Greece, lawsuits were brought against the
god Meander, for he was ever changing the course of the river,
thereby forever altering its boundaries.

Can you imagine a lawsuit being brought against you because you
dared to wander and follow your own nature, perhaps crossing
boundaries and coloring outside the lines?
It might not be too hard to imagine such a thing. We are criticized,
judged, and often punished when we decide to break the rules and
change the course of our river.
Have you ever meandered?

Are you a wanderer?

The beauty of being a meandering wanderer instead of living a purpose-driven life is that there is no destination. No rules or instructions. No timelines or deadlines. No pressure. No goals. No obligations. If you relax into it, wandering can free up your mind, inviting creativity, and allow you to slip into your true nature.

There seems to be very little spaciousness in our culture, or economy, for wandering or meandering, for slowing down, savoring instead of rushing. More focus and attention, more praise and encouragement are showered on those who have a goal, a purpose, and are driven or motivated to make something of themselves.

What words come to your mind when you think about such errant behavior?
Unproductive. Wasteful. Lazy. Irresponsible. Poor. Uneducated. These are words often used to describe artists.

Or do you think instead of words such as creative, inspired, free, happy?
Who decides when it's okay to meander?
How do you know when you've been off course too long? When is it time to stop, do a reality check, and get back to work?

THE MEANINGS AND VIBRATIONS OF WORDS
The definition of the word meander, when used as a noun, is a winding course or aimless rambling.
As a verb, it means to do something in an idle, lazy, useless, or ineffective manner.
Do such words apply to the meander of a river?
Several words in the English language are similar in meaning to the word meander.
Rogue, vagabond, extravagant, roam, as well as wander.

Rogue is a word used to describe an unprincipled, dishonest person who may perhaps be slightly mischievous. It is also used to describe an animal that wanders apart from the herd or an individual that varies markedly from the standard, especially someone inferior or possibly a lawbreaker.

A vagabond is described as someone who is without a settled home, a vagrant, one who wanders about aimlessly, idle, irresponsible, with no purpose. Quite often, an element of assumed poverty is attached to the word.

We often think of extravagance as being excessive or showy, exceeding what is reasonable or appropriate, lacking restraint in spending money, costing too much. Its definition can be "to go beyond reasonable limits or to be excessive."

This definition implies that when you are extravagant, you wander off the path or go beyond or outside of what is acceptable.

Roam is another word that means to travel or to wander without purpose or a fixed goal, and it can suggest a sense of freedom and pleasure, coupled with a lack of purpose.

And if you wander, it could mean you have digressed, strayed, lost clarity, or focus.

Adding to all of this, wander can also mean you are sexually unfaithful. In other words, you cheated on your partner.

These words are not neutral. They carry judgments and negative energy. It's no wonder we are surrounded by exhausted, frustrated, angry, disillusioned, disconnected people attempting to live purpose-driven lives.

Do you always need a purpose?

Must you always have a set course or a fixed goal?

Must you always be busy, doing something, or is it okay to be idle at times?

Is it okay to daydream?

Do you dare stray from the fixed path?

Do you dare wander apart from the herd?

Is it ever okay to do nothing, to be unproductive, to meander?

MEANDERING IS NATURAL
According to Peter S. Stevens in his book *Patterns in Nature*

"The bends in a river are predictable. The windings turn out to be surprisingly regular, quite independent of subtle changes in topography."

That's an interesting fact.

The meandering course of a river is natural and predictable.

The natural course of water flowing on a smooth and gentle slope is never straight downhill as one might imagine. Rather, as it flows, it begins to meander, wandering back and forth like a skier on a slope or a sailboat tacking in the wind.

As a river flows, it carries sediment, some coarse, some fine. Things as large as a fallen tree or as small as a pebble cause changes in the speed of the flow. When this happens, sediment gets deposited on the side of the river that is flowing more slowly. This buildup of sediment is called accretion, the gradual accumulation of layers of matter.

As the water slows on one side of the river, it speeds up on the other. As it moves, the faster water begins to erode the bank. The change in the speed of water between the two banks is the beginning of a meander.

This effect gets multiplied because as the bend or curve develops, the slower side of the river continues to get slower, and the faster side speeds up. More sediment gets deposited on the slow side, and more erosion happens on the fast side. The bend gets more and more pronounced.

Eventually, an oxbow forms a U-shaped or crescent-shaped bend in the river. Over time, the oxbow bend becomes an oxbow lake. Erosion on one side and simultaneous accretion on the other creates a body of water that is closed off and lies alongside a winding river.

YOUR LIFE AS A RIVER
The nature of water is to flow. And the flow that exists in the nature of water is a cycle of return. All water flows to the ocean, and the ocean never refuses it. This is the natural unfolding of life, slowing

down, speeding up, resting for a while in the body of a lake, eventually returning to the ocean, only to rise up again and descend. Imagine your life as a river, ever flowing to the ocean. It's not about relentless purpose, or a perpetual drive to reach the ocean; it is the natural unfolding of the cycle of return.

Sometimes the water is crystal clear, mountain run-off from snow melt, rapidly rushing over stones. Sometimes it is lazy, sluggish, brackish water wandering its way through marshland or peat bogs. This is nature. The change in speed and flow, the stopping as well as continuing, and the return. It is all part of a cycle.

This rhythm of flow cannot happen in a life that is out of balance, a life that is freeway-fast, target-focused, and relentlessly driven by some mental force determined to succeed or attain a goal or prize.

Consider the flow of your life.
What causes the meander to form?
Where does the flow speed up?
Do you allow it to slow down?
How do you vary the speed?
What things present themselves in the path of the flow?
Are they large or small?
Are they obstacles that get in the way or opportunities to experience the flow differently?
Are they a necessary part of living your life at different speeds?

Accretion and erosion happen simultaneously.
Destruction and creation happen simultaneously as well.
What is your sediment and how does it contribute to creation?
What is your erosion?
Where is it evident?
Where are your oxbows?
How long did it take them to form?
Have any of them become lakes where the water rests for a while?
How long has the water been held?

Who determines how you live your life?
Do you impose upon yourself the rules and regulations of a society that does not honor or allow for wandering or meandering?

What changes could you implement right now that would honor the value and necessity of leaving the purpose-driven path?

What deep wellsprings of creativity could you access by meandering? What storehouses of wisdom, intuition, and inspiration would open to you if you stopped striving for a goal, looking for a purpose, struggling to find the one right answer, and allowed yourself to be yourself, to naturally unfold, to be enough without the doing?

Do you ever long for or dream about the extravagant life of a wanderer, a vagabond, or even a rogue?

How might meandering slow you down to a pace that is more meaningful, more natural, and perhaps less damaging and destructive to your creativity, spirituality, and even your sexuality?

THE BEST POSSIBLE CHOICE

Meandering is one of nature's ways of slowing things down. Following a meandering path can be a way to move toward the resolution of a problem, dilemma, or decision.

Meandering can take different forms. Activities that are slow and/ or circular. Walking, doodling, weaving, knitting, swinging in a hammock, staring out the window, daydreaming, or watching the clouds.

A slow meander may sometimes be the best possible choice, the best possible way to understand something or tap into your inner wisdom, because wisdom is not just in the mind. It is held in the memory of the physical body, and the body moves at a pace much slower than your thoughts.

Is it possible to be too driven or too intense, trying too hard to attain something or to resolve anything?

The constant focus on performance, goals, or purposeful activities can have a negative or harmful affect upon us. We look to the solutions outside of ourselves, instead of paying attention to our own rhythms and inner guidance.

There must be a natural ebb and flow to life, creation that is simultaneous with destruction.

It is true that there are times in life when we need structure and focus, intention, and form, but to place greater value on such things, believing that they are somehow better, superior, right, or more desirable, is to fall into the trap of imbalance. It is not any different from believing that light is better than dark, or that above is more valuable than below.

SAFE AND ALONE

To truly meander, to wander about without paying attention to direction or location or intention, you need to feel completely safe and out of danger.

You must be able to relax your vigilance.

For most of us, especially women, this rarely happens, whether we are in nature or in public. We must always pay attention, be on the alert, watch for danger.

Because of this, we might need to look for ways to wander while staying in place.

And to truly wander, you must be alone.

Time spent alone is not a frivolous luxury.

It is rather a creative necessity.

Lack of it will impoverish your inner as well as your outer life.

> "Certain springs are tapped only when we are alone. The artist knows he must be alone to create, the writer to work out his thoughts, the musician to compose, the saint to pray. But women need solitude in order to find again the true essence of themselves."
> –GIFT FROM THE SEA, ANNE MORROW LINDBERGH

DISCOURAGED IN CHILDHOOD

It is no wonder most of us have a hard time meandering.

It is discouraged in childhood, at times even forbidden.

From infancy on, we are groomed to follow a schedule that has nothing to do with who we are and what we need.

By nature, each of us has our own rhythm, our own way and time of doing things. The unique nature of each baby is present and noticeable in utero and becomes even more evident at and after birth. Our nature stays with us throughout our lives, whether we acknowledge it or not.

Ideally, a newborn is kept close to the mother's body and nurses and sleeps as is natural and needed. As the infant grows and matures, it continues to develop and embrace its own nature, in its own way, and in its own time.

It is the parent, the system, the culture, the fear that impose time-lines and schedules upon these little ones, not allowing them to develop, explore, and live in harmony with their own rhythms, rarely allowing them to learn how to self-regulate.

Society and economics do not support what is natural. Mothers are forced to wake their children from much-needed sleep, often while it's still dark, get them out of bed, dress them, and deliver them to daycare, or babysitters, or school. This is a sad reality. Our children suffer from it. We suffer from it.

We disrupt our children's sleep instead of allowing them to naturally wake on their own. We have been conditioned to believe they have to go to school. We are forced by the government to make them go. We are told that if they don't go to school, don't learn to follow a schedule, don't become part of the system, they will never be successful. They will fail. They will be failures.

School, at any age, is extremely stressful and damaging, especially for our little ones. They are regulated, controlled, restricted, and at times even punished.

They are standardized and monitored, told when to get up, when to eat, when to nap, when to pee, when to play, when to learn, in a never-ending cycle of control.

They are set up and conditioned to become part of a machine that will most likely determine for them how they should live for the rest of their life.

Once they start school, children are rarely allowed to meander, wander, linger, or daydream. Sometimes it is disciplined out of them, beginning at home, before they even start school.

The focus is on goals and accomplishments, on errors and mistakes, on looking for what is wrong, what needs correction or improvement.

Children are taught that the way to gain approval, to fit in, to be a success, is to look for and find the one right answer.

They are groomed, trained, and conditioned to enter the world and become a cog in the wheel of a system where meandering, and wandering, and daydreaming are certainly discouraged or not allowed at all. These things are looked upon negatively in a society that is all about productivity and under constant pressure to do something, to arrive someplace, to achieve success, produce results.

Then they are told they must have a purpose, a goal, a career.

They strive to determine what this goal, purpose, or career is, and then they must relentlessly work toward the accomplishment and fulfillment of it.

In the face of all this, who would dare to daydream? If you are under such pressure to perform and to be acceptable, watching the snow fall is certainly not allowed.

Is it any wonder we all feel so stressed?

A woman of the always is not a child, yet she is often still operating under the same rules and regulations that were hammered into her from infancy, rules and regulations that are purposely designed to turn her into a good slave in a broken system of greed and power that is not in her best interests.

Do you feel guilty when you do nothing?
Who determines what doing nothing looks like?
Must you have a purpose?
Must you strive to accomplish a goal?

Are you afraid that if you don't have something to aim for you will become lazy, depressed, possibly a vagabond, a rogue, or live a life that is not acceptable?
Who taught you such lies?

What can we learn from nature when we slow down enough to listen, to pay attention, watch, observe, and be amazed?
We have been convinced that we need to have, must have, a purpose.
We are told to keep our eye on the prize, to focus on the goal, the finish line, and then what?
When we arrive at some place, is it the ending or the beginning?

Great harm is done to all life when man interferes with the natural, winding course of any river, the ebb and flow of its seasons.
The plants, the animals, the insects. Birds and fish, marshes and floodplains. The climate.

What great harm are you doing to yourself by interfering with the natural flow and rhythms of your life?
What damage has occurred, what losses have you sustained in your landscape? What has happened to your flora and fauna because you have forgotten how to wander and meander?

If meandering is nature's way of slowing things down, is it valuable, perhaps even vital, for us to wander off the fast track, quit the rat race, and even leave the purpose-driven path?
Is it possible that the purpose-driven life is dangerous?

Must we always seek to find our purpose?
Do we even need a purpose?
Must we always be busy, or can we at times be idle?
Can we dare to stray from the path, the set course, the fixed goal?
Can we dare to wander apart from the herd?

Do you ever long for or dream about the extravagant life of a rogue?

How many people take vacations from work, or go on a sabbatical, but do not allow themselves to experience their time away? Instead, they fill it up with plans, projects, travel tours that have deadlines, schedules, lists of sights to see, places to go, photos to take, buses to catch. Are your vacations just another form of relentless busyness that's not any different from your work life?
Have you ever needed a vacation from your vacation?

What would happen if you took your vacation and did nothing, went nowhere, made no plans, just allowed the time to unfold on its own in a natural, organic way?

What would happen if you stayed in bed all day, perhaps reading, relaxing, napping?

How would it feel to sit outside in the sun and listen to the birds?

How does it feel to imagine doing nothing?

What would happen if you let go of the constant focus and fixation on finding out what your purpose is supposed to be, stopped looking for the next thing you need to do, left the self-help church, and allowed yourself to meander instead of aiming to reach a goal?

TANGLED AND TWISTED

Some of these ideas about purpose and goals can become twisted around ideas of religion, spirituality, and what we believe about why we are here.

We can become tangled up in teachings and beliefs about being sinful, innately imperfect, not good enough, not deserving, needing salvation of some sort, salvation that can only be obtained by following the rules, fulfilling a purpose, staying on the path.

Only you can determine if any of this comes into play when you consider meandering or wandering away from the herd.

We are in nature, and we are part of nature. It's not possible for us to be mere observers or to separate ourselves from it. All the goals and rules and schedules cannot change that, cannot change the unfolding of cycles and rhythms, or change that the nature of water is to flow, or that the ocean never refuses a river.

When we are so fixated on finding our purpose and focusing on a target or goal, we are not present to what is being called forth in the moment. We judge, criticize, regulate, orchestrate, strive, and most often end up frustrated, exhausted, and still asking the questions, *What am I here for? What am I supposed to be doing?*

Perhaps the answer is nothing.

You are not supposed to be doing anything.

You are supposed to be doing nothing.
Life invites you to just be.

A woman of the always knows how to meander.
A hundred thousand meandering, wandering women can transform the world.

Mirrors

Mirrors and Reflections

> "Somebody was hiding in the mirror watching her from the far side of the glass...What empowering memory did some distant sister hide inside that cracked glass?"
> –WEAVERS' ORACLE, CAROLYN HILLYER

What do you believe about mirrors and what they reflect?

Is the reflection you see in the mirror a memory?

Do things get trapped in mirrors?

Are you looking back, or are you peering into the future? Or both?

Have you ever considered that the reflection you see is already the past?

When the past comes toward you, does it stop being the past? Does it become the present moment?

When you see something in the mirror, the image is in front of you, yet if you turn around, you realize that what you are seeing is also behind you.

What do mirrors and reflections have to do with the mystery and magic of women?

What would you like to explore, reflect on, or even reflect back on, as you wander your way through this topic?

NAKED WOMEN AND VANITY

Most of us take mirrors for granted.

They are part of everyday life.

They hang in our homes.

They hang in public places.

They are used in science and technology.
They are used in photography and astronomy.
They are used in surveillance and spying.

Many things, both manmade and in nature, can be used as mirrors.
Windows, the calm surface of a lake, polished metal, and even some
stones. Some of the earliest mirrors found by archaeologists date
back 6000 years. Mirrors make frequent appearances in art, and
they are often referenced in fairy tales and children's stories. They
can represent many different things.

Nude women looking at themselves in a mirror are quite often
portrayed in art. John Berger, a British author known for several
volumes of art criticism, commented on this in his book, *Ways
of Seeing*.

> "You painted a naked woman because you enjoyed
> looking at her, you put a mirror in her hand and you
> called the painting Vanity, thus morally condemning
> the woman whose nakedness you had depicted for your
> own pleasure."

In common usage, the word vanity refers to any act or thing that is
futile, idle, or worthless. It can also imply self-satisfaction, excessive
pride, or conceit, or even something that is lacking or empty.
Have you ever been accused of being vain?
Would your parents have considered vanity as something bad or
undesirable?
Especially for you as their daughter.
From a very early age, girls are taught to survey themselves, to look
at themselves, in a way that is much different from boys. Girls are
often taught that how they appear to men will determine how
successful they are in life. They are taught that every glance is a
judgment, and thus they learn to look upon themselves in a judging
way. And one of the ways they see themselves is with the use of a
mirror. On the one hand, we are encouraged to use a mirror, and
on the other hand, we are condemned or shamed if we do.
We might even be accused of being vain.

NAKED OR NUDE

In the quote from *Ways of Seeing,* John Berger uses the word naked.
Is there a difference between the words naked and nude?
It is quite common to see paintings of women that expose them
in various states of undress or full nudity.
It is quite common to see these women holding a mirror.
Why do you think that is so?

Here are a couple of things to consider.
Naked is how we are born, how we run through the sprinklers on
a hot summer day, or how we take a shower.
Naked is like being in water. You can walk around naked and
actually feel yourself in the air.
Nude is used more often in a static situation, something we do
with choice and intention, such as posing for a painting.
Nudity is considered to be sexual by nature, and when it is viewed
that way in our culture, it can carry a sense of being dirty, wrong,
or immoral.

The Naked and the Nude, by Robert Graves, British poet, historical
novelist, and critic...

> *For me, the naked and the nude*
> *(By lexicographers construed*
> *As synonyms that should express*
> *The same deficiency of dress*
> *Or shelter) stand as wide apart*
> *As love from lies, or truth from art.*
>
> *Lovers without reproach will gaze*
> *On bodies naked and ablaze;*
> *The Hippocratic eye will see*
> *In nakedness, anatomy;*
> *And naked shines the Goddess when*
> *She mounts her lion among men.*
>
> *The nude are bold, the nude are sly*
> *To hold each treasonable eye.*

While draping by a showman's trick
Their dishabille in rhetoric,
They grin a mock-religious grin
Of scorn at those of naked skin.

The naked, therefore, who compete
Against the nude may know defeat;
Yet when they both together tread
The briary pastures of the dead,
By Gorgons with long whips pursued,
How naked go the sometimes nude!

Whether we recognize it or not, many of our attitudes and beliefs about being naked come from the power of the story of the Garden of Eden, in the book of Genesis in the Bible. When the god came looking for the man in the garden, the man said to the god, "I became afraid because I was naked and so I hid."
The woman was blamed in this story for the sin that caused the man to realize he was naked, and her punishment was subservience to the male. He became the agent of the god in her punishment.

What is it about nakedness that would cause the man to hide? Why would anyone feel shame or be shamed for being naked? Young children do not feel shame about their bodies or their nakedness.
Such shame does not come naturally.
It has to be taught.

In art it is the shame of the spectator that shames the object. In numerous famous paintings of Suzanna and the Elders or in the paintings of Bathsheba, King David and the elders join together as men who are spying on the naked women. As women looking at these paintings, we join in with the men who are spying on us, and when we do, we share in the shaming.

In some paintings, the woman looks back at us looking at her. In others, she sees herself as a sight in a mirror. She sees herself looking back at herself as she is being looked at. Many of these paintings that depict a woman holding a mirror are titled *Vanity*. This is what John Berger was referring to in his book, *The Art of Seeing*. This, then, is the double shaming of women.

She is shamed for looking at herself.

She is shamed because others are looking at her, and in some paintings, she is shamed for being naked.

Remember that vanity is considered to be something that is empty, or lacking, or is judged to be futile or worthless. The mirror becomes a symbol of the woman's vanity and, once again, the woman is blamed as well as shamed.

Is there vanity involved whenever we look at ourselves in a mirror?

Does it matter how we appear?

Who determines whether or not it matters?

Who determines what appearance is acceptable and what is not?

Can you look in a mirror and not feel shamed or ashamed?

Can you look in a mirror and not judge yourself?

Can you do it merely for grooming and to make sure nothing is present that might be embarrassing or revealing?

Could we do without mirrors and depend upon those around us to tell us if we need to attend to something?

REFLECTIONS

Mystical powers were attributed to any reflective surface. It was believed that a reflection was the part of your soul that was projected out of your body and onto the mirror.

Because of this belief, mirrors were considered especially powerful, and stories about the use of mirrors and mirror magic were stitched into the fabric of fairy tales and ancient history, written in the grimoires of the past. Mirrors were believed to provide gateways to other worlds. They could protect from evil. They told the truth. They told the future. They were connected to death. Some even believed that you could enter another realm by gazing at your reflection or that you could divine your own future if you saw yourself.

How many fairy tales, fables, and myths can you think of that contain mirror imagery?

MY FACE YOUR FACE

We spend our days looking into the faces of others.

Do we see in their faces a reflection of ourselves, or do we see in their faces a reflection of how they view us?

Mirrors allow us to detach from the crowd and see or inspect ourselves, separate from others. But can we look at ourselves through neutral eyes, or do we see ourselves only as a comparison to what we believe we are supposed to look like?

> "A Man can no more know his own Heart than he can know his own Face, any other Way than by Reflection."
> –ON THE DIFFICULTY OF KNOWING ONE'S SELF,
> JONATHAN SWIFT

Swift is speaking here about something other than simply looking in a mirror. Seeing ourselves is not limited to literal eyesight.

> "Man is least himself when he talks in his own person.
> Give him a mask (not a mirror) and he will tell the truth."
> –OSCAR WILDE

What do you think he means?

Are these men saying the same thing, just differently?

Our face announces our presence. It is one of the ways that others recognize us. By facing outward, it bears a message for others and demands a response.

Ask yourself, what does my face reveal?

What does my face conceal?

Do I have an inmost part or place that is not visible to others when they look at my face?

It is becoming more and more common, as well as acceptable, to have cosmetic facelifts. We see images of movie stars, celebrities, and public figures with faces that have been altered to appear youthful. What happens, though, is we cannot trust the image because the rest of the body does not match up, energetically or otherwise.

There has been discussion around the illusion of aging and the seeming incongruence of how one feels inside compared to how one appears in the mirror, or perhaps more correctly, the meaning attached to how one looks in the mirror.

An interesting comment is made by James Hillman in his book *The Force of Character.*

> "For the good of society, should cosmetic facelifts be prohibited? Are they a crime against humanity? What you do to your visible image has societal implications. Your face is the Other for everyone else."

Trying to find the meaning of the poem, *Break the Mirror,* brings up a lot of questions and a great deal of discussion. Some women say they are jolted or troubled by the expression "save the world."

In the morning
After taking cold shower
What a mistake
I look at the mirror.
There, a funny guy,
Grey hair, white beard, wrinkled skin,
What a pity
Poor, dirty, old man!
He is not me, absolutely not.
Land and life
Fishing in the ocean
Sleeping in the desert with stars
Building a shelter in the mountains
Farming the ancient way
Singing with coyotes
Singing against nuclear war
I'll never be tired of life.
Now I'm seventeen years old,
Very charming young man.
I sit down quietly in lotus position,
Meditating, meditating for nothing.

Suddenly a voice comes to me:
"To stay young,
To save the world,
Break the mirror."
–BREAK THE MIRROR: THE POEMS OF NANAO
SAKAKI, NANAO SAKAKI

What if you decided to stop using mirrors?
What if you decided to break the mirror?
What if you decided to see yourself differently?
What might that have to do with looking at or reflecting on yourself?

"Man should not be able to see his own face. Nothing is more terrible than that. Nature gave him the gift of being unable to see either his face or into his own eyes. He could only see his own face in the waters of rivers and lakes. Even the posture he had to adopt to do so was symbolic. He had to bend down, to lower himself, in order to suffer the ignominy of seeing his own face...The creator of the mirror poisoned the human soul."
–THE BOOK OF DISQUIET, FERNANDO PESSOA

"One day seven years ago, I found myself saying to myself—I can't live where I want to—I can't go where I want to—I can't do what I want to—I can't even say what I want to— (...) I decided I was a very stupid fool not to at least paint as I wanted to—that seemed to be the only thing I could do that didn't concern anybody but myself."
–GEORGIA O'KEEFFE

Is there anything that Georgia said in this quote that you can personally relate to in your own life?
Right now, what could you decide to do for yourself that does not concern anyone else, that would be similar to her decision to paint the way she wanted to paint?
There has been rich discussion around the Georgia O'Keefe quote. "When a woman does the one thing she can do, many of the things she believes she cannot do fall away."

What if you decided to stop using mirrors?
What if you decided to see yourself differently?

It is a common practice in Feng Shui to place a mirror in an entryway.
Do you have one in the entrance to your home?
Do you consider that to be superstitious?
Do you have any superstitions about mirrors or know people who do?

Mirrors reverse images.
This actually allows us to get a different perspective.
When you look in the mirror, are you looking back or looking forward?
When you reflect, looking inside yourself, do you look back or do you look forward?

Because of what we believe about the way light travels, it has been suggested that we are seeing the past when we look in a mirror.
Does that mean it is possible that we are seeing the future at the same time that the light curves back around?

There has been some discussion around Narcissus and why a person who thinks too highly of herself is called by his name.
How might the story of Narcissus and this interpretation perpetuate the belief that looking in a mirror or looking at oneself is vain or dangerous?
You may want to explore the fact that Narcissus is made to appear effeminate.
How does that apply to women?

In English, vanity is the name given to a piece of furniture with a mirror, usually found in a woman's bedroom or dressing area.
Coming from the Old French word *vanite,* it translates to self-conceit. It can also mean empty or excessive pride.
What meaning or significance would you attach to that?

How do you react when you see yourself in a mirror?

Is it different from, or the same as, hearing your own voice in a recording?

How do you react when you see yourself in a photograph?

Is it the same or different when you see yourself in a mirror?

Why do many people say they have trouble with or do not like old or antique mirrors?

Why are mirrors covered when someone dies?

Many women have expressed having feelings of self-hatred, loathing, and depression when they go into the dressing rooms or changing rooms in stores.

Have you ever had this experience?

What do you think might be happening?

Is it possible that the energy of the countless women who have stood in that space and judged themselves in an unkind way is trapped in the large mirrors?

There is no way to see yourself except by means of reflection.

But do we need to look in a mirror for that to happen?

How do you see yourself when you close your eyes?

How do you see yourself when you look inside yourself?

Remember that the true nature of the moon is dark.

She is always there, but we see her only when she is reflecting.

But can we know the moon even if we do not see her with our physical eyes?

Can we know her in other ways?

Who are you, and how do you see yourself when you are truly just being and not mirroring or reflecting anyone or anything else?

SUGGESTED ACTIVITIES

Create your own ritual around a mirror or mirrors and see what experiences you can have with seeing into the past, or the future. Select a woman from either the present or history and begin collecting information about her: images, quotes, information, stories.

This can be an ongoing project for you as you continue through the book.

Create your own story about her.

Knowing that the only way we see ourselves is through reflection, I would like you to explore what you see of yourself reflected back in the life story of the woman you choose.

Olivia, a participant in the year-long course, shared some of her experiences with the other women in the group.

> *"I love the homework suggestion of selecting a woman and writing about her for this course. But I haven't been able to choose anyone yet and here is why. This has been a challenge for me for quite a while when I read stories about the accomplishments of other women. It seems that the traditional stories praising women that I read focus so much on the woman's ability to exhaust herself doing everything under the sun for the good of her family, her community, and so on, and to push and strive to accomplish and prove at all costs. I admire these women so much, in particular the female lawyers who paved the way for me to do what I do today. But that's not me and doesn't represent my values. I would like to write about a woman who stands in her power and doesn't buy into the idea of giving it all away and looking for self-worth through busy-ness and awards and promotions. But it seems those women don't get the spotlight, so I don't find out about them. I think one option would be a writer or other kind of artist. Like Anne Morrow Lindbergh or Mary Oliver. Both are certainly very "accomplished" in the traditional sense, but it seems to me from their writings that they placed the highest value on their creative lives, sovereignty, and solitude. Or I am thinking about whether there is a woman in my family or community that I know personally that I could write about."*

Mirror Meditation

Set aside at least an hour of totally alone time, quiet time, unin-terrupted time.
Do this when it is dark or in a place you can make completely dark.
Create a comfortable place where you can relax.
Be sure to wear comfortable clothing and make sure you are warm enough.
You might decide to do this meditation without clothing.

Find a mirror large enough for you to see your face completely, and make sure you can position it so it is stable and secure. This exercise can take on even more significance if you have a mirror large enough to see your whole body.

Light a candle, sit in front of the mirror, and gaze at yourself. Look at yourself. See what you see.

Can you see beyond your own image?
Can you peer into your own image?
Don't force anything.
Don't try to overthink it or imagine you aren't doing it correctly, or that it should be different.
Just be still and explore the experience.

You might want to have a notebook or journal nearby so, after the meditation is complete, you can take note of any thoughts, impressions, and questions that come during the reflection time.

Be prepared that this experience can be charged with emotions. It may bring up issues of self-worth, memories, feelings, or possibly even physical sensations. Stay with it if at all possible and allow whatever is happening to wash over you.

Be gentle.
Be kind.
Be loving.

To access all downloadable meditations, go to page 48 and scan the QR code.

Blood

Reclaiming Blood Mysteries

I wrote the shortest poem in the world. One word.
One single word that says everything.

Blood Everywhere
Women

I wrote another poem, a longer poem, a poem that says everything
but with more words.

All The Bleeding Women
We women
have always been bloody
we flow on and on
men fear the mystery
a wound that's not a wound
our blood
a wound that never heals
bleeding
on all the men
who are afraid

We are weeping
everywhere
our tears turn to blood
unstoppable
seeping

growing
flowing
continues
We leave a trail
daughters
mothers
grandmothers
sisters
going home
returning
bleeding

Women bleed from a wound that is not a wound, a wound that never heals.
We hide our bleeding.
We disguise our bleeding.
We suffer from it.
We are inconvenienced by it.
We dishonor it.
At times, we celebrate when we see that bright red stain.
At times, we celebrate when it does not come.

Do you consider bleeding sacred, or do you call it The Curse?
If you were to write a poem about bleeding, what would you say?

Mystery is something that goes beyond understanding and explanation.
For the ancients, bleeding women represented a great mystery. Their bleeding was celebrated with ritual. They were revered and, at the same time, they were feared.
How could a woman bleed and not be wounded?
How could a woman bleed on a monthly basis, often following the rhythm of the moon, and not die?
The actual physicality of the female body broke taboos.

It is believed that many rites of passage for men and boys attempted to mimic a woman's bleeding. Men had to cut and pierce their bodies to make them bleed. They had to organize their rites and plan for them.

Our female bodies begin to bleed on their own, as if by magic. It happens naturally, silently, repeatedly, sometimes painfully, and it is always blatantly obvious.

Our bodies bleed, and our bleeding is woven into our ability to create new life and birth it into the world.

This is the mystery of our blood.

We bleed from a small opening, hidden between our thighs. Small indeed, yet powerful. This small place between our legs is the place of giving birth, a messy and bloody experience, a miraculous, magical experience we share in common.

Not because we all bleed.

Not because we are all women.

Not because we all give birth.

But because we all came forth from the body of a woman.

Some of us have chosen to give birth.

Some of us have not.

Some of us cannot give birth.

Some of us have given birth when we had no choice.

Some of us still have our wombs.

Some of us have lost them.

Where are you on this list?

What we all have in common as women is the fact that we are all daughters, and we are here because of the blood of our mothers. Never should we be ashamed of our blood or our capacity to bleed. It is connected to our sexuality, spirituality and creativity, our ability to bring forth life.

Yet many of us have been made to feel ashamed and are often shamed because of the bright, red flow.

SINFUL BLEEDING

In the eighth and ninth centuries, an ascetic, monastic movement in Celtic Ireland, Celi-De, upheld an inhumane attitude toward women. The movement asserted the belief that the cause of passion, which was considered sinful, was the presence of excess blood in the body, and the fact that women bled monthly and did not die was obvious proof that women were sinful. If a woman wished to become holy, her diet would be reduced in such a way that she would become malnourished and starving. This brought on the condition known as amenorrhea (absence of menstruation). She lost her strength, vitality, and sexuality, making it easier for her to fall prey to the abuses of male power and dominance.

Is it hard to imagine such beliefs and practices? Are we shocked? We should not be.

We still see evidence of such disregard and disrespect for women and their bodies in the fashion industry, where young women starve themselves, believing this is necessary to be attractive and beautiful, to look like the models wearing designer clothing featured in fashion magazines and in the media. In many instances, extreme dieting and exercise regimes affect good health and nutrition, causing some women to unnaturally and prematurely stop their menses. Some of these practices also exist in the sports world, where women engage in extreme physical activities and diets that upset their hormonal balance.

Have you ever tucked a tampon or pad into your sleeve or pocket, hoping no one would notice as you hurriedly found your way to the toilet?

Have you ever called in sick to work because you were bleeding and felt you needed to stay home to rest and nurture yourself?

Have you ever told the truth?

"I am staying home because I am bleeding."

Or did you say something like, "I have a headache, or a cold, or don't feel well."

As women, we have been shamed because of our normal bodily function of bleeding. We have been taught to ignore it, discount and invalidate it, hide it, and even joke about it. We have been robbed of the profound spiritual connection that is possible through the reverence and celebration of our bodies. In almost every religion in the world, the menstruating female is believed to be unclean, dirty, defiled, and polluted. Our bleeding is called the curse. God's curse of condemnation.

Bleeding women are outcasts. They defile purity laws. They are forbidden to engage in daily activities, forced to sleep outside, not allowed to enter places of worship, not allowed to pray. They are required to hide their shamefulness. Some religious texts even go so far as to declare it a sinful, punishable act for a man to have contact with the body of a bleeding woman.

These shaming, controlling, fear-based laws are forced and enforced by threat of punishment or even death.

We may not live in such extreme religious environments, but we are still given messages to hide our cycles and dishonor what happens to our bodies on a monthly basis. How is it possible that a natural, bodily phenomenon is believed to make us unclean and impure? This dishonoring causes conflict and disharmony in our uterus, our ovaries, our entire being. Menstrual and reproductive problems and difficulties often begin with stress. Perhaps the stress is simply the stress of being female in a male-dominated world, the stress of being cyclical in a linear ideology. We are taught that we should not see, hear, feel, or smell anything when we bleed.

All is well. All is the same.

Life goes on as usual.

Take pain pills, use tampons, and smile.

Wear white, go swimming, go to work, nothing special is happening.

The deep discontent and disconnect felt by women about their bodies has a direct connection with the loss and absence of honoring and celebrating our birthright, which is our blood right. Bleeding is wondrous, amazing, inspiring. It is messy and shocking, at times painful and inconvenient. It is the magic of human existence. It is not "an error of nature" as pontificated by the German gyne-cologist, Fritz Beller.

Bleeding women are powerful. The power of blood is the power of life and death, and we hold immense power because we create and bring forth life from our bodies.

How is it possible that we live in a time where this magic is ignored, hushed, and spoken of as something shameful, needing to be hidden, and worse yet, something to joke about.

How is it possible that women globally continue to be dominated, raped, and abused by men who believe they have the right to make decisions, choices, and laws about what can and cannot be done to our bodies?

We should all be outraged!

Reclaiming the Mystery of Our Blood

The word reclaim was originally used in falconry. Its meaning was to call back.

Another definition of reclaim is to make wasteland or desert capable of being lived on by the use of water or irrigation. Reclaiming involves bringing something back to its original condition or to a better state.

I like both definitions. It seems that we became a wasteland when we lost our connection to the mystery of our blood, and now we have the chance of calling it back, of being alive again through reclaiming.

Polytheistic, nature-focused, spiritual practices are greatly attuned to the natural cycles of fertility and the rhythms of life. The spread of the desert religions under the rule of a sexless, singular, male god without genitals caused great harm. Women were no longer revered because they carried the divinity of creativity in their bodies. Instead, their sexual, reproductive, creative cycles became the consequence of a curse. They were deemed unclean and dangerous.

We need to create rituals again that honor our blood, that weave a sense of connection with the mystery of our bleeding and reclaim the sacred for ourselves, for our mothers, grandmothers, sisters, and daughters.

Look back on the time of your first bleeding and remember it. Remember how you felt.

Remember the decisions you made about yourself, your body, and your bleeding.

These memories can be painful, frightening, confusing, lonely.

What kind of experiences did your mother have, and your grandmothers?

Have you ever talked with them about their first blood?

Have you ever discussed your first blood experience with your daughters, sisters, cousins?

Have you ever told your mother how you really felt or what the experience was like for you?

Two themes run through the stories I hear from many women. Either their first blood was no big deal, or it was something not to be talked about. They were sent to the bathroom with a pad and told to take care of it. Some of the women remember being told that now they had to be careful around boys and men. It could be dangerous. Such warnings left them confused.

> *"In the class you asked us to remember our first bleeding. It was a Friday. I woke up with a certain feeling in my belly, a feeling I hadn't felt before but knew what it was. When I went to bed that evening my father said, 'You are a big girl now so you must be careful with boys. Do not get too close. It can be dangerous.' No celebration and no ritual, only a warning about danger."*
> –TINAH, PARTICIPANT

WHAT WE HAVE LOST

We have lost our stories.

We have lost beautiful words to name our experience.

We have lost love and respect for our bodies.

We hàve lost pride in our bleeding.

We have lost the connection between the cycles of nature and the cycles of our bodies.

We have forgotten our ancestral wisdom and our knowing.

What things have you lost?

What do you wish to reclaim?

We live in a society that was and still is created by men, for men, and influenced and molded by their ideas, beliefs, and expectations. Perhaps one of the downfalls of the feminist movement is that we as women moved into the linear in an effort to gain equality, whereas what we needed to do was reclaim the cyclical.
Being equal does not mean being the same.

The male body does not menstruate, gestate, give birth, breastfeed, or experience menopause. The female body experiences enormous and powerful transitions and hormonal changes relating to its capacity to create new life inside itself. When this is ignored or denied, we suffer great imbalance. None of this information is intended to discount or ignore anyone who is born intersex or with ambiguous genitalia. How we identify sexually does not change the biology.

Women are keepers of an ancient wisdom that can restore balance to the world. Each lunar cycle we experience in our bodies, on a personal and cellular level, the turning of the great wheel, the cyclic and sacred nature of life. However, there are many women who find it difficult to access this great mystery because they are barely conscious of the mystery in their own bodies.

We can connect through our bodies with the silence and stillness of the earth. When we do, we can enjoy the rest and restoration our bodies need. Being earth-rooted and grounded brings balance to a way of living that is primarily focused on the mind and intellect. Women's bodies hold a unique kind of wisdom. Our spiritual insights, creative surges, and intuition are often avoided and ignored because they are viewed as bad, unclean, or evil.
In a majority of settings, the only way women can work, function, and be accepted in male-dominated areas such as business, religion, and politics is to completely ignore their cycles or treat them as an illness.

Imagine what it would be like to participate in a custom of separation and withdrawal from the mundane, day-to-day activities and gather together with other bleeding women, in a sacred space, spending quiet time resting, sleeping, moving in and out of trance and dreams. Not because we were forced to do so on pain of death or punishment, not because we were sinful and unclean, but because we were honoring ourselves and respecting the mystery of the blood.

Such an experience was written about by Anita Diamant in her novel, *The Red Tent*.

We might wish for such an experience, but in all likelihood, we would struggle with it because of the conditioning of family, society, and religion.

How difficult would it be to push against the norm?

Our power rests in our softness and our strength, our sweetness and our ferocity, our intimacy with the cycles of life and death, our wisdom and our intuition.

This is what we reclaim when we call back the sacred blood mysteries.

"Our time on this earth is sacred, and we should celebrate every moment. The importance of this has been completely forgotten: even religious holidays have been transformed into opportunities to go to the beach or the park or skiing. There are no more rituals. Ordinary actions can no longer be transformed into manifestations of the sacred."

–THE WITCH OF PORTOBELLO, PAULO COELHO

"The function of ritual...is to give form to the human life, not in the way of a mere surface arrangement, but in depth."

–JOSEPH CAMPBELL

Modern medicine and science have seemingly removed the magic and the mystery from our bleeding. It is time for us, as women of the always, to reclaim it, not only for ourselves but for the men as well.

There is much controversy swirling around in the news, in politics, in science and medicine regarding biology, gender, personal rights, and preferences in the demonstration of sexuality.

The mystery of the blood is the mystery of the womb and the ability to gestate new life.

TASKS

- Do some research on the sacred texts of various religions that address the issue of menstruation and its relationship to men, uncleanness, and punishment.
- Think about what you were taught as a child about menstruation. Do you hold any of these beliefs as an adult? The fact is, literally millions of people today still consider these religious texts to be sacred. And millions of women live in fear and shame because of them.
- Read the powerful article, written by Abigail Jones, that appeared in Newsweek, April 20, 2016. *The Fight To End Period Shaming Is Going Mainstream.*
- Create for yourself or with other women a ritual honoring the cycles of your female body. Before your first blood. Your bleeding times. Your menopause time when blood magic is held tight in your aging, wise body. And if you have had your womb removed, whatever the reason, you may wish to create a ritual honoring your loss.
- Do research on the topic Uterine Transplants In Males.

PREGNANT

There is no WE in pregnant.
It is just you.
The female.
You are pregnant.
The male is not.
How dare he try to claim that power.
The only WE is WE WOMEN, and we should be incensed.

This does not discount the fact that a man who is waiting to become a father can be loving, caring, desirous of being supportive and protective of the woman he has impregnated or who has been impregnated under other circumstances.
And there is still no WE in pregnant.

The man is not vomiting daily, sick from the smell of food, or dirty dishes, or toothpaste.

His body is not swelling up to an enormous size, making it impossible to tie his shoes or get comfortable in bed, nor does he need to sleep on his back with his arms above his head so he can breathe. He can still fit behind the steering wheel.

He is not leaking urine or spotting blood or waddling around on feet so swollen he can only wear oversized slippers.

Another human is not feeding off his body, taking nutrients from his hair, teeth, skin, and bones, causing him to have strange and unusual cravings.

He cannot experience the miracle of movement of another being inside his body.

His life is not on the line, and he will not face death during brutal, violent, endless hours of labor.

The head and shoulders, nor the buttocks of a child, will not tear apart his flesh as it forces its way out into the light and air.

He will not lie in a pool of blood from a life-threatening hemorrhage or placental abruption.

Nor will he ever need to have his body cut open so a stranger can lift out a new life.

He will not go into labor.

He cannot.

There is no WE in pregnant.

And no matter how much he imagines he wants to be, he will never be pregnant.

You are.

And no man has the right to claim for himself the miraculous ability to bring forth life from his body. That belongs to a woman and the mystery of her blood.

The idea of male bodies being able to gestate can be found in mythology as well as science fiction. In modern times, it has also been dubbed "medical-industrial capitalism" due in part to the fact that it is funded by the pharmaceutical industry.

A good place to start exploring this topic would be the writings of Natalie L. Dinsdale, Research Associate and Doctor of Philosophy.

"To be very clear, let me say I absolutely oppose uterine transplants into males, regardless of what the man's

gender identity or expression might be. I especially oppose uterine transplants into males that have the desired
outcome of gestating offspring."

To be very clear, I also absolutely oppose uterine transplants into
males. It is an abomination.

Blood Meditation

Find a quiet, comfortable, safe place where you will not be interrupted.

Sit for several moments, just breathing, paying attention to your breath, in and out.

Imagine it is a warm spring evening, the moon is full and you are in a secluded grove of sacred trees, guarded and protected. No harm can come to you. It is safe to remember.

Let your mind wander back in time to when you were a young girl and started your first moon blood.

How old were you?

What did you look like?

What were you wearing?

Can you recall the time of year?

Was it a warm spring day or perhaps a summer evening?

Were the winds of winter howling?

Did you notice it upon awakening one chilly autumn morning?

Was it perhaps in the fall about the time you started back to school?

Did the smell of burning autumn leaves fill the air?

Just allow the images to come. Some of them may be joyous, some of them unpleasant perhaps even sad. You might not have a lot of memories about the time. That is okay.

You may have blocked them out.

What did you do?

What was the reaction of those around you, your mother, your father, your siblings, your family, your friends?

Who did you tell?

What were you told?

What were you instructed to do?

Did anything special happen for you that day or shortly after to mark this amazing transition?

What did you feel?

What decisions and choices did you make about yourself and your body?

Sit quietly and let the experience wash over you as you remember.

Continue to be still, paying attention to your breath.

Pay attention to your body.

When you feel ready, slowly open your eyes, keeping the focus soft.

Slowly and gently return.

To access all downloadable meditations, go to page 48 and scan the QR code.

Breasts

Front and Center

Imagine you are in a room full of women, all sizes and shapes, some young, some old and everything in between. You are all standing proudly together, your chests bare.

I ask the group, "How many of you have ever breastfed a child?" Please step over there.
A large number of the women move away from the group in the direction I pointed.

How many of you were breastfed? Some of the women move. The configuration changes.

How many of you have had breast cancer? The room shifts.
How many of you have lost one or both of your breasts?
How many of you have known someone who has died of breast cancer?

Who has gone topless in public?
Who wears a bra?
Who has burned a bra?
As the questions flow, so do the women, moving silently back and forth across the room, the size of the groups fluctuating. We are all affected by the experience. We are all connected to each other through our bodies.

Sadly, we have become a society of women who are not only unhappy with our breasts, but quite often hate them. We compare them, measure them, criticize them, flaunt them, hide them. We enlarge them, reduce them, remove them.

The commercial world uses pictures of exposed breasts to advertise all manner of things, from car tires to men's cologne, motorcycles to beer.

They are the objects of bad jokes, shame, criticism, and controversy.

They are too big, too small, too saggy, too droopy, too uneven.

Breasts are a source of comfort and they can cause death.

Breasts are a source of pride and a cause for self-hatred.

Breasts can provide nourishment or incite lust.

Good breast. Bad breast. Life-giving. Death-dealing.

Sacred and profane.

Breasts are front and center.

They are a natural part of the body.

They are connected to and associated with food, sex, disease, profit, national pride, inspiration, spiritual purity, immoral sinfulness, and imagination.

Your Breasts

What are your first memories about your breasts?

Do you have any memories of your mother's breasts?

Do you remember her nursing you or your siblings?

What was your experience when you got your first bra?

Who went with you?

Was it fun? Were you excited? Did you feel embarrassed?

Do you ever go braless, either inside your home or outside?

Have you ever gone topless in public? Would you?

Do you think it is okay for women to do it?

Have you ever breastfed?

Have you ever breastfed a child that was not your own?

What are your thoughts about breastfeeding in public?

What has been your personal experience with breast cancer?

Have you lost one or both of your breasts?

Have you experienced breast reduction or augmentation?

Would you consider it?

Do you consider your breasts to be sacred?

Who Owns Them

This is an interesting question, one to which most women have given little thought.

Marilyn Yalom asks this question in her book, *A History of the Breast.*

> "Who owns the breast? Does it belong to the suckling child, whose life is dependent on a mother's milk...? Does it belong to the man or woman who fondles it? Does it belong to the artist who represents the female form, or the fashion arbiter who chooses small or large breasts according to the market's continual demand for a new style? Does it belong to the clothing industry that promotes the 'training bra' for pubescent girls, the 'support bra' for older women, and the Wonderbra for women wanting more noticeable cleavage? Does it belong to religious and moral judges who insist that breasts be chastely covered? Does it belong to the law, which can order the arrest of topless women? Does it belong to the doctor who decides how often breasts should be mammogrammed and when they should be biopsied or removed? Does it belong to the plastic surgeon who restructures it for purely cosmetic reasons? Does it belong to the pornographer who buys the rights to expose some women's breasts, often in settings demeaning and injurious to all women? Or does it belong to the woman for whom breasts are parts of her own body?"

Who owns your breasts?

Good Breast

Throughout most of human history, a mother's ability to produce milk literally meant the difference between life and death for her infant. Substitutes for breast milk are relatively new on the scene. Because of their connection with life and death, the ancients believed that the breasts held magical powers. Shrines were dedicated to them. Figurines and statues were shaped in their honor. Because it is a normal occurrence for lactating women to not bleed, it was once believed that milk was a form of menstrual blood transformed so the mother could nourish the baby.

The good breast was the breast the man was allowed to touch, fondle, suckle because it belonged to the wife he owned.
The good breast was the maternal-function breast, the breast that produced milk, the breast that fed the baby, the breast of the Virgin Mary upon which the infant Jesus suckled.
To the Dutch, the Germans and the English, in the seventeenth century, the good breast that produced milk was the hallmark of a pious, moral woman. This is clearly evident in the art from that time period.

During the French Revolution, the bare breasted woman became a national icon symbolizing freedom and equal access to all.
The German Nazi political party claimed it was a woman's duty to the fatherland to produce milk.
Bare breasts painted on fighter planes during war were used to inspire soldiers to fight for freedom. Breasts gained an additional meaning alongside the maternal and the erotic. Breasts became political and nationalistic.
There was a certain type of poetry written in France in the mid-1500s that was based upon a breast cult. The focus was on the breast from a purely male perspective, as the viewer whose desire was stimulated and as the owner who could proudly claim lactation as being a direct result of his impregnation.

The Cult of Saint Agatha
There is even a cult that venerates the virgin martyr, Saint Agatha, patron of wet nurses and breast-cancer patients. She was martyred around 251 AD because she refused to sacrifice to the Roman gods and resisted the amorous advances and demands of the Roman prefect, Quintianus. Saint Agatha's breasts were violently ripped from her body by pincers, by order of a governor in Sicily. She is portrayed in a painting by Francisco de Zurbaran, fully clothed in flowing dress, a pensive expression on her face, carrying her severed breasts upon a serving platter. Supposedly these served-up

breasts are considered sacred reminders of piety and devotion. The artist certainly did not portray the actual bloody violence of male dominance and brutal mutilation, most likely death, forced upon this woman.

What connection might there be between the story of the removal of the breasts of martyred Saint Agatha and the violence perpetrated today against women and their breasts in the name of medical science and beauty?

Should women who have suffered the removal of their breasts be sainted?

Bad Breast

The bad breast is linked to lust, one of the supreme deadly sins according to Christian doctrine. These sins are moral transgressions that lead to damnation unless you repent and are granted forgiveness. Symbolic images of this vice often depicted women with uncovered and mutilated breasts, and in one twelfth-century church fresco, a woman, representing Lust, is shown in agony, a long spear piercing her body and left breast.

Exposed breasts were associated with prostitutes and courtesans during the time of the Renaissance. Today, they are associated with models, movie stars and striptease, pornography and prostitution, radical feminists and lesbians.

During the time of the Inquisition, women accused of being witches had their bodies searched for signs of an extra teat, called the witches' teat, something on which the devil could nurse. This could be a mole or a wart, and at times, it was possible that a woman had supernumerary nipples that were considered indisputable evidence of her witchery.

Since one in 18 humans has this condition, we can only imagine how many women lost their lives over this extra teat.

Bad breast

How is this treatment of women's breasts by the Catholic Church any different from the torture and mutilation perpetrated by the Romans against Agatha?

America is still influenced by Puritanical beliefs of the bad breast. It is not surprising that the issue of breastfeeding in public is still a matter of controversy and political debate.

In America, we rarely see an exposed breast. There is still controversy over whether or not women have the right to go topless in public as men do. Few women breastfeed in public. Topless sunbathing is illegal, and even in 2023, there was still controversy over whether bare breasts could be shown as images on Facebook. Prohibition in daily settings makes it possible for breasts to be exploited and used as commercial commodities, moneymakers in advertising and entertainment.

The Myth of the Amazons

The Amazons are believed to have been a race of fierce warrior women. Their stories have been passed down to us in myths and legends. It's said that the female children in these tribes would have their right breast seared during childhood, by their mothers, to facilitate their use of the bow as a weapon. These women were viewed as wild, man-hating killers who lived outside the norms of society and civilization. Perhaps their stories were even used as examples of the danger and fierceness of unmarried, untamed, uncivilized women and girls.

According to legend, they had little use for men except for impregnation.

How dare a woman decide what she wanted to do with her own breasts?

How dare she remove one to facilitate the use of a weapon and save the other for feeding her daughters?

Is there a connection perhaps between the story of the Amazons and their self-imposed breast removal and breast removal of today? Is there possibly some strange twist in which we are being punished with the practice of breast removal because we dare to be strong and powerful?

Women compete with men for jobs and at the same time they need to nurse the baby. Is this the modern day Amazon women myth?

Cut, Burn, and Poison

Cancer, any type of cancer, is a volatile, controversial topic with opinions and beliefs living at both ends of the spectrum. The following information about breast cancer may be offensive to some, refreshing to others, and on the topic of breasts, it is vital that we have the opportunity to consider more than one option. Some of us may have lost loved ones to breast cancer, even after extensive and aggressive treatments. Some of us may have been diagnosed with breast cancer and chose to receive treatment, in some cases even having our breast or breasts removed.

Some women who come from a family with a history of breast cancer have opted to have their breasts removed as a precaution. Some have chosen other forms of treatment, things that are considered to be more natural or holistic.

Cut, burn, and poison. This seems to be the most common approach to breast cancer, and to most cancers.

> "Conventional cancer therapy is so toxic and dehumanizing that I fear it far more than I fear death from cancer. We know that conventional therapy doesn't work—if it did, you would not fear cancer any more than you fear pneumonia. It is the utter lack of certainty as to the outcome of conventional treatment that virtually screams for more freedom of choice in the area of cancer therapy. Yet most alternative therapies regardless of potential or proven benefit are outlawed, which forces patients to submit to the failures that we know don't work, because there's no other choice."
> –Ralph W. Moss, Ph.D.

In addition to being outlawed in some situations, I would add that alternative therapies are rarely, if ever, covered by insurance. This means that for many women who might wish to choose an alternative, the choice is financially impossible, so they are left with no recourse other than the conventional route.

Is there a conspiracy here? Drug companies, insurance companies, doctors?

Dr. Charles B. Simone, a former clinical associate in immunology and pharmacology at the National Cancer Institute, stated:

> "Mammograms increase the risk for developing breast cancer and raise the risk of spreading or metastasizing an existing growth."

When you are encouraged, almost ordered, to have regular mammograms, have you ever been given any information about the increased risk of cancer caused by the radiation?

Here is a list of some things that are believed to cause breast cancer. Maybe they do. Maybe they don't. Maybe we do well to consider them.

Wearing bras, especially those that constrict or restrict the flow of blood and lymph.
Metal underwires in direct contact with your body, possibly causing electrical disturbances or energy imbalances.
Antiperspirants containing aluminum, a toxic metal that has been found in high concentration in breast cysts.
Taking drugs to suppress milk production after giving birth.
Toxins, chemicals, and growth hormones found in a variety of foods and meats.

Enormous amounts of money are spent on "find a cure'" research.
Have you ever wondered who is actually benefiting from all the money raised to find a cure?
Does it really help women, or is it being siphoned off by the drug companies?
How much is spent on "find the cause"?

According to historical reports, Leonidas, a leading physician in the first and second centuries, trained in the Alexandrian School, performed breast cancer surgery. He advocated detoxification of the body. Galen of Pergamum, a Greek physician, living about the same time, AD 130-200, believed that melancholy caused women to suffer from breast cancer. Are there possible links between toxins, depression, and breast cancer?

What Do You Believe

What are your beliefs and feelings about breast cancer, its causes, its treatment, and the availability or lack of alternative choices?
How do societal, medical, monetary, and moral pressures and attitudes affect freedom of choice?
Have you given thought to what you might do or the choices you would make should you be diagnosed with breast cancer?
Have you already had to face such choices?
Could the epidemic of breast cancer be indicative of the overall disrespect we have for the earth as our mother?
When we poison the mother, she feeds us poison in return.
Have we poisoned the earth so much that her breasts are toxic, and now, so are ours?

Breast Control

Women have been tormented by barbaric undergarments such as corsets, which were designed to push women's breasts up from below, sometimes holding them in place as if they were on a platform. The wearing of corsets has been linked to shortness of breath, fainting, and organ damage.
The first modern brassiere that was widely used had the basic design to lift the breasts from above and hold them in place by straps of some sort. Created around the beginning of the twentieth century by a New York socialite named Mary Phelps Jacob, her patented invention was sold to Warner Brothers Corset Company for $1500.
We have gone from corsets to the flat-chested look of the World War I era, from the stiff, pointed, cone shape of the 1950s to stretch bras, to no bras, to burned bras, to sports bras to underwires, to the ultimate 24-hour, comfort-strap, full coverage, 'I can't believe it's a bra' bra.
What relationship do you have with your bras?

How do you feel about your breasts?

Happy? Unhappy? Indifferent?

For many women, it is a love-hate relationship.

Their breasts are too big, too saggy, too droopy. They get in the way, affect their posture, cause shoulder and back pain. Such breasts are often seen as objects for milk production—woman as cow.

If they are too perky, too small, or too flat, they can lose some of their appeal as sexy objects of arousal. Small breasts are rarely used to advertise anything.

Breast Mutilation

Many condemn the brutal practice of female genital mutilation, but what about the practice of self-inflicted breast mutilation? Over one million women a year receive breast implants or undergo breast augmentation. Most women are led to believe that this is a safe procedure with very little risk. But this is not the truth. There is more and more evidence that implants can cause debilitating auto-immune disorders as well as numerous, chronic health problems.

Information on the dangers of breast augmentation is not always easy to find. If you are doing a search on Google, you have to go through several pages of searching, past all the ads for doctors and surgeons, to find the pages that speak about the things most of us are never told.

I truly believe it is vital for women to become better informed and to not always trust medical establishments and those who perform these lucrative procedures.

Of course, we can understand why a woman would choose such a surgery based on the breast-shaming, body-hating culture in which we live.

We all carry a collective sadness and grief over such dishonoring. I would add here that there are some women who have chosen breast reduction because of extreme, severe pain, discomfort, and debilitation caused by the size and weight of their breasts. This is a different issue.

BREAST LOVE

How do you experience your own breasts?
How many loving, supportive, honoring words can you find to describe them?
Fantastic. Real. Sensuous. Mine.
What would you put on your list?

Our breasts are naturally sensitive, not only to touch but also to energy. They are prominently positioned around the heart. We need to love them and be protective of them.
Our nipples are extremely sensitive areas of our body. They are fine-tuned to internal and external stimuli. It is not always sexual. They are constantly feeding us energy and information. So the clothing we wear can hinder and suffocate this flow.
Arousal is not always about sex. Creative energy and sexual energy arise from the same place, life-force energy. Our creativity and our sexuality are intertwined with our spirituality as well. Our breasts are spiritual.
A woman of the always would refuse to be in any kind of relationship with any partner who did not truly honor her body, and her breasts, and her scars as the ultimate expression of the sacred, sensual, sexual, creative, life-giving, life-affirming essence of a woman.

Daily touch your breasts, hold them, love them. Practice ways to move the energy from your vagina and your womb up into your breasts and into your heart, and then back again. This could quite possibly begin to heal generations of self-hatred and negativity.
If you are a woman living your life missing a breast or breasts, these practices are still valuable and nurturing.
Creative ideas and dreams can begin to flow, up through our wombs and out through our breasts, out through your heart.

LIFE SUSTAINING

Throughout most of history, breasts have been considered a symbol of nourishment and a source of life. They have embodied the mystery of motherhood and have been part of the sacred identity of women, as well as the goddesses of many cultures.

They are noticeably positioned on the front of the body, in some instances, quite prominently.

They are soft and round and inviting.

They provide a safe resting place.

Infants know them as a place of protection, love, and nourishment.

The nursing baby moves between states of sleep, wakefulness, and bliss.

Gradual separation from the mother's breasts prepares a person for life as an individual.

We remember this in our bodies, not our minds.

A lack of this early experience deeply affects our development as humans.

Love emanates from our breasts, whether we are mothers or not. We all came forth from the body of a woman, and we were all nourished from her body, inside the womb, and quite often outside, from her breasts as well. It is time for us as women to remember that and acknowledge the sacredness of our breasts.

We must develop and cultivate love for them, value them, and honor them.

Good breast.

Bad breast.

Life-giving.

Death-dealing.

How do you view your breasts?

Are they sacred or profane?

Flesh

Your Sexual Sensual Body

> "When it comes to sex, if you can't talk about it, maybe you shouldn't be doing it... I am the ocean with my very own tide every month."
> –THE RED BOOK: A DELICIOUSLY UNORTHODOX APPROACH TO IGNITING YOUR DIVINE SPARK, SERA BEAK

CARNAL KNOWLEDGE

In Webster's New World Dictionary of the American Language, the word carnal is described as meaning "in or of the flesh; bodily; material or worldly, not spiritual; sensual; sexual."

The expression "to have carnal knowledge" means to have sexual intercourse.

Under the lengthier description of synonyms, the dictionary states:

> *Carnal implies relation to the body or flesh as the seat of basic physical appetites, now especially, sexual appetites, and usually stresses absence of intellectual or moral influence (carnal lust).*

According to the above definition, there is a separation between flesh, and sex, and spirituality.

The culture and societies in which we live have separated most of us, particularly women, from our sexuality, which in turn separates us from our spirituality.

What if the greatest spiritual experience a human can have is the moment of orgasm, that powerful, unstoppable moment of creativity and sexuality?

Many words we use to describe extreme religious or spiritual experiences are also used to describe great sex: passion, bliss, desire, and ecstasy.

Have you ever combined sexuality and spirituality in the same bed?

Have you ever had a spiritual sexual experience?

THE WORD WAS MADE FLESH

There are many ideologies and belief systems that attempt to separate us from the truth of the perfection of our bodies, of being human.

In the Bible it is said that god was made flesh and dwelt among us, took our form so we could get a glimpse of his glory.

Could it be the other way around?

Could it be that god was made flesh so he could have the true glory of our human, sexual experience? According to some accounts, the god who was made flesh never had sex. Maybe that's why he must return.

Supposedly, this handsome, beautiful, perfect man never participated in the one, glorious experience that separates us from the spirits and angels of Christianity.

SEX.

Perhaps if he had experienced the pleasure, he would not have wanted to return to the realm of the disembodied.

MAGICAL SPIRITUAL SEX

Throughout history, animistic, polytheistic, nature religions, no matter where they were practiced, embraced sex and sexuality as being positive, magical, and spiritual. And it was believed that one of the most sacred of all sexual rituals was the Hieros Gamos, or the Sacred Marriage. Records of this go back as far as five thousand years. The ritual involved a goddess having sexual intercourse with a god, and from the success of this union came the blessings of prosperity, life, nature, and of the flesh. As history unfolded, chosen and appointed human representatives took the place of the goddess and the god. The sacred act often took place in a secret chamber, observed by members of the ruling class.

You Will Be Punished

Most of the hang-ups and inhibitions that people have around sex have been taught or hammered into them in the name of the monotheistic, male god represented in the three great religions of the world. And when I say great, I do not mean good or wonderful. Nudity is condemned in the Bible and is connected with the story of the disobedience of Adam and Eve. While pagan gods are most often portrayed nude and exceptionally sexual, the desert-dry god of the Bible is shown with flowing robes, always covered, with no evidence of sexuality or genitalia.

When people worship a sexless god, what effect does it have upon their relationship to their own sexuality as well as their spirituality?

Another thing that would color our attitudes around sex is the fact that sexual acts labeled as fornication and adultery were punishable by death and still are, in fact, in some countries of the world. The fear of sinfulness and punishment is felt in our bones.

Carnal knowledge and sexual freedom might well alienate us from the singular god of Christianity, Islam, and Judaism. The gifts such knowledge and freedom bring are a reconnection with the beauty and perfection of our fleshly bodies, the miracle of birth, the wonders of nature, and the earth, as well as the myriads of gods, goddesses, and other unseen beings. They allow us to tap into the joy of being human.

Religious Freedom

There is no true freedom of religion in any country when there is no true freedom of sexuality. We continue to be slaves to a male-dominated tradition that promotes supposed family values. What are family values if they can only be defined through the lens of patriarchal tradition? Even our politics around sex demand an outward pretense of adherence to outdated religious laws.

What interests you more? What is more attractive to you?

Sex-positive spirituality or sex-negative religion.

MONOGAMY AND THE VOW OF MARRIAGE

Monogamy, the custom of having a sexual relationship with or marriage to only one person at a time, is a construct.

And many feel morally superior because they adhere to this construct within the confines of marriage, also known as wedlock.

They use expressions such as:

I am faithful.

I do not cheat on my partner.

I don't have affairs.

I'm clean and righteous in the eyes of God.

And they hold up the banner of truth, "Some animals mate for life."

What is marriage?

What is the marriage vow?

What is vowed and to whom and to what?

Who taught us that a couple is supposed to stay together no matter what?

Would we not be better served by making a vow to ourselves, a vow to be true to ourselves at all times?

What if we vowed to tell the truth to ourselves always and to reaffirm the nature of that truth one day at a time?

That kind of vow would create more honest, loving, committed relationships and partnerships.

What if we vowed to each other to always tell the truth, no matter what?

What exactly is it that we commit to, make a promise or vow to, when we get married?

Why would we believe that a 'until death do us part' vow would be more morally righteous than vowing to be truthful one day at a time?

The Vagina

Life issues forth from the sacred and mysterious female body.
At some point in history, the body of a woman, her sexual desires
and needs, and her magical ability to bring forth life became demonized. The blessed vagina became the evil vagina, blamed for the
temptation and fall of man into sinfulness and degradation.
The spread of Christianity carried along with it the belief that
the female sexual body is shameful, wrong, and dangerous. It's
important to note here that the witch craze focused on the torture
of women by mutilation and violation of their sex organs.

Masturbation

During Victorian times, the care of female sexual and reproductive
health was transferred from midwives to male doctors in male
institutions. It was not uncommon for these doctors to masturbate
their patients as a cure for hysteria and depression.
Masturbation was allowed and acceptable in these clinical settings,
when performed by men upon women, but women could not
masturbate themselves because it was condemned by the Church
and considered evil and sinful.
As I have mentioned numerous places in the book, I'm intrigued
by the origins and meanings of words, and I find the word masturbate to be an ugly word with disturbing vibrations. So I did a
bit of digging around and discovered that its origins are from the
word manu for hand and stuprare, to defile or dishonor (oneself),
which is related to stupere, to be stunned or stupefied.
We do not defile or dishonor our bodies when we pleasure ourselves.
It's time for us as women of the always to find a new word, a more
truthful way to speak about something so beautiful.

Women have been taught to be ashamed of their bodies, forbidden
to explore, arouse, or satisfy themselves. We are afraid or hesitant
to touch ourselves. We fear or are disturbed by our smell, our taste,
and the way our genitals look. Few women are aware of the fact
that they can know where they are in their menstrual cycle by the
taste, smell, and texture of their own vagina and its secretions.

Even in the twenty-first century, many women are ignorant, wholly or in part, of their own body's anatomy and sexual responses. Some still believe that desiring sexual pleasure or asking to have their sexual needs met demeans them.

Does your spiritual practice encourage you and support you in honoring your own body, to embrace the messiness of it, its fecundity, the smell and taste and throb of your own sex?
Sexuality is connected to the earth and fertility. For many of us who live in the city, it's almost impossible to connect to the subtle erotic forces of the earth. Some of us never feel them. Some of us are not even aware they exist.
Have you ever connected your spontaneous sexual arousal to the cycles and rhythms of the earth? Or to certain places in nature that seem to be magical?
Perhaps the first question should have been: Do you ever have spontaneous sexual arousal?

In the language of archetypes, which is a more male-dominated realm than many of us realize, many of the goddesses have been sexually sanitized and often portrayed in benign roles and defined in relationship to the male. What has happened to the angry, fierce, devouring, sovereign female who stands alone in her own power and whose sexual appetites, hungers, and expressions are not controlled by the laws of men?

BARTHOLINS, SKENES, AND AMRITA

Are these foreign words or words foreign to you?
Not many women know that there are glands at the junction of the vulva and the vagina that secrete fluids.
The Bartholin glands are on the anterior wall of the vagina, and their secretions keep the vagina moist.
The Skene glands can be found on the lower end of the urethra, and they also secrete a fluid, often called female ejaculate. It has a name: Amrita, a very old Sanskrit word meaning divine nectar.
Unless a woman knows otherwise, it is easy to mistake the presence of amrita for a loss of urine. It's not urine. This ejaculate substance

can amount to a cupful or more at a time, and the release of it may occur more than once during a sexual experience. It's a normal component of the sexual response of the female. The state of exquisite pleasure sometimes accompanying the release of amrita is designated amritasis.

Interestingly, most women can tell you what the prostate gland is, what functions it serves, and perhaps even know where it's located in the male body. Why do we know more about the male prostate than we do about our Skenes and Bartholins? Is it because these magical, sexual jewels of the female body are named after men? Caspar Bartholin and Alexander Skene. Just imagine what the prostate gland would be called if it were named after a woman.
What if we name our glands ourselves, perhaps giving them names that speak to the magic they perform and the purpose they serve? Doesn't it seem strange that these glands in a woman's body are commonly referred to as the female prostate? Not to be overlooked is the fact that our word vagina means a sheath, and it does not take too much imagination to understand a sheath for what.
Why would women want to refer to parts of their bodies only in reference to male body parts? Once again, women are named and men do the naming.
It might be fun to play with the idea of naming things the other way around.
What names would women choose for male body parts and their functions?
Any ideas that come to your mind?
Even in this small instance, language impedes a woman's knowledge of her own body because of the absence of words she can call her own.

CUNT
Cunt is one of the few words which in ancient writings was synonymous with woman, and according to Barbara Walker in *The Woman's Encyclopedia of Myths and Secrets,* it was not slang or dialect or even marginal. Sadly, this word is now considered to be derogatory, negative, and demeaning. Perhaps it is time for us to reclaim it.

SEXUAL PLEASURE

We are so far removed from ourselves that many of us don't know how to ask for what we want sexually, and what we want may be far removed from what is considered normal.

The truth is, sexual pleasure is normal, a creative and spiritual part of the human experience. There are many ways for a woman to be pleasured that go beyond the penis-in-vagina thrusting. Some women don't find this form of intercourse to be pleasurable, and for others, it's not all it's cracked up to be.

If you're a woman who often fakes enjoyment or orgasm, you might consider the truth about what truly brings you pleasure.

Our sexuality is profoundly connected to nature. Sexual energy permeates all creation.

Ours is a culture whose dominant, spiritual belief systems focus on the ideology that we must lose or shed our flesh in order to gain true bliss, arrive at perfection, transcend the worldly, reach enlightenment, or enjoy ultimate spirituality.

We cannot change the collective, cultural negativity toward sex overnight, but we can be pioneers in our own willingness to reconnect sexuality and spirituality and reclaim the mystery of our own bodies.

BEGIN BY STOPPING

Stop thinking of the female body as sinful, unclean, imperfect, and less than spiritual.

Does the form of spirituality you embrace engage in spiritual bypass? Do you believe your earthly, sexual, sensual female flesh is perfect, or do you consider it to be less than your spiritual self? Is a low vibration inferior to a high one?

The early church fathers thought erotic energy was from the devil. Saint Augustine (354-430 AD) believed that wanton sex was a direct result of original sin.

Saint Jerome (340-420 AD) demonized women's sexuality and taught that women degraded men by luring them into sin.

Who made these guys saints?

The energies of these kinds of beliefs linger in religious and spiritual communities to this day.

There were, and still are, cultures that consider sexual acts to be a form of celebration that honors the gods and goddesses, but of course, this is not the case with Christianity. The Abrahamic religions worship a rather dry, sexless god.

It is quite possible that the more sexually aware you are, the more connected you are with all of life. You might want to contemplate why so many of the ancient gods and goddesses were lusty and active. There are endless lists of the explicit, divine, sexual exploits of the gods throughout history.

Religious paintings, frescoes, and statues portrayed the gods and goddesses with giant vaginas and phalluses, such being representations of the fundamental creative and spiritual powers of the universe. There was no separation of creativity, sexuality, and spirituality.

There is no separation for women of the always.

In her book *Transcendent Sex: When Lovemaking Opens The Veil*, Jenny Wade documents what she calls "one of the best-kept secrets in human history." Ordinary people can suddenly, without warning or preparation, find themselves in otherworldly realms when making love.

Sexual experiences are often some of the most powerful experiences in our lives.

Sex is more than biological. It is an expression of great creative and spiritual potential.

Sexuality, creativity, and spirituality are the Holy Trinity of the flesh.

Whore

Virgin Mother Whore

Some of us are mothers. Some are not.
Some of us are virgins. Some are not.
We are all the same. Nonetheless.
We are all birthed from the body of a woman.
We are all daughters of the women who were virgins, mothers, and whores.

THE VIRGIN AND THE WHORE

In the realm of many religious beliefs, some still prevalent today, the choices we face as women are quite limited and restrictive.
You are a virgin and have never had sex. You are a widow.
You are properly married and having sex, but only with your husband. And the purpose of sex is not for pleasure but to bring forth children.

If none of the above is true, and you are being sexual and not married or having sex with anyone other than your legal husband, you are deemed a whore, a harlot, a fornicator, or an adulterer. What is the connection that exists between religion and sex, spirituality and sex, and the so-called morals of sexuality?

In this chapter, we will explore not only words that are related to women's sex and sexuality, but also the possible origins of beliefs and practices regarding the when, why, how, and with whom of having sex.

When we examine these things, we will find that most of what we believe comes not only from our religious upbringing but also from the moralistic climate of society, both of which have their roots in patriarchal, misogynistic religions.

It's quite possible you will be troubled or challenged by the information and the questions asked. You might get a few buttons pushed.

"Counting money on a bed is taboo in my family. Growing up, I never fully understood why but I suspected it was another one of our countless everyday South American customs that ensured we were in right relationship with the spirit world. The world that allowed us to live a long, healthy life, and that kept the doors of abundance and opportunity wide open. Eventually, I grew up to be a brilliant hooker and to count money habitually, wherever privacy presented itself. Not being able to count money on a bed became a much greater obstacle than I could have ever imagined. I decided to ignore the warnings of my tias that bad things would happen. And the first time I did, I instantly understood that this belief was actually rooted in whorephobia and not our culture."

–UPROOTING WHOREPHOBIA: WHY WE MUST CHANGE THE STIGMA OF SEX WORK, PLUMA SUMAQ

History shows us, through art, mosaics, sculpture, and text, that sex and sexuality played a powerfully visible role in religious practices. To name a few: the carved reliefs on Hindu temples of gods and goddesses copulating, the fresco of Priapus and his enormous phallus at the House of Vettii in Pompeii.

Women, as well as men, were given in service to the fertility gods and goddesses of the land. They served at temples and sacred sites. A pilgrim's visit to such sites might include engaging in sex as a form of worship or honor.

What better way to use the energies that imbue our bodies with the ability to create new life?

Why would we not offer up our sexual energy in a creative, spiritual way?

Sexuality expressed in such a way would be open and inclusive, divine and promiscuous, not at all possessive.

Why would it not be worthy and deserving of respect?

How could it be considered inappropriate?

Sex as a form of worship of the gods is quite different from and at odds with many people's view of sex, and most certainly it is in direct opposition to the Abrahamic religions.

Sex and sexuality are part of being human. They are the energies of aliveness and the ability to create. Sex is intimately linked to our spirituality as well as our creativity.

If we believe we are divine, then so is sex, and if that is true, why would there be so many rules, regulations, laws, and restrictions around the way we choose to express it and with whom?

CHALLENGING THE BELIEFS

It is time to challenge some deeply entrenched beliefs.

> What is the definition of a whore?
> What words would you use to describe such a woman?
> What is your definition of a virgin?
> What words would you use to describe a virgin?
> Is a virgin better than a whore?
> Is a whore better than a virgin?

If you're single, unmarried, or not partnered and enjoy being sexual and engaging in sex, perhaps with multiple partners, perhaps even quite frequently, what words might others use to describe you and your activities?

What would you call yourself?

I realize that currently, this choice of personal, sexual expression might not be shocking to some and might even be acceptable to others. But overall, for the vast majority of the world, such activities would be condemned. In some places, it could cost you your life.

In the Bible, women do not stand alone. In addition to the fact that many of them do not have names, most women are described in relation to men and to their sexuality. Women are either virgins, harlots, or safely married, and quite often they are married to men who have more than one wife, sometimes numerous wives, as well as concubines or mistresses.

Are there any stories about women who have multiple husbands and lovers?

If so, are they spoken of as being righteous and honorable?

The powerful, misogynistic teachings of Christianity associate women with the dangers and degradation of sex.

There is no place in the conceptual architecture of Christian society for a single, unmarried woman to be anything other than a virgin. If she is unmarried and having sex, she is labeled a whore.

It would be difficult to name a single female Catholic saint who is not associated with or defined by her sexual relations or lack thereof. In fact, female saints are esteemed and highly praised for their chastity, purity, and virginity.

Harlot

In the 1200s, the word harlot meant a vagabond or a tramp, a vagrant, knave, or wanderer. When the word came into use, there was no context in society that allowed for a woman to wander out on her own, without the control, supervision, or authority of a man. In this context, if a woman were a wanderer, that would automatically mean she would be having sex with individuals other than a proper husband.

So, by this definition alone, all of us women are harlots if we wander around in life without a man.

The word prostitute implies placing something of value forward in a way that is not appropriate or respectable.

Do you believe your body is something of value?

Do you have the right to do what you want with yourself and your body?

Do you have the right to put your body or the services of your body up for sale?

Why would having sex be deemed prostitution?

Why would selling a 'body-related' service devalue a woman?

What if she sells the use of her hands and gives massages?

What if she sells her voice and sings for money?

What if she sells her breast milk and allows another woman's baby to be fed by it?

What if she sells her mouth and performs fellatio?

Is it acceptable to sell part of the body but not all of it?

If so, which parts are okay to sell, and which are not, and who determines that and how?

Have you ever considered the possibility that many married women could rightfully be called prostitutes because they are selling their bodies for financial freedom and security, or perhaps because they have had a religious belief imposed upon them that degrades and imprisons them and requires them to have sex with the man that owns them?

If a man pays a woman to give him pleasure in any way, say from fondling to oral sex, to intercourse, how is that different from paying for a woman to give him a massage?

Why would one activity cheapen a woman and the other not?

Why are some of these body activities acceptable and others are not?

BECAUSE IT IS DANGEROUS

We can easily get off track and away from the essence of these questions if we go down the road of argumentation that says prostitution is wrong or bad because it is dangerous. There is the danger of violence and the danger of disease. Prostitution breaks up virtuous, moral families and leads good fathers and family men astray.

Some women engage in prostitution because they have no choice and only do it to survive. Some women choose to be prostitutes because it is a way to make more money than they could doing something else.

Neither choice makes a woman corrupt or sinful.

If the argument against it is about safety and violence, should there not be equal concern for the health and safety of women who labor long hours in unsafe factories, or any dangerous work environment for that matter, where they are being pimped and abused by their employers?

How many women engage in work that is dangerous or unhealthy because they have no other choice?

How many women put themselves at risk to make money?

How many women work in situations that are controlled by greedy, corporate males?

How is it that the woman is blamed for breaking up virtuous, moral families when it is the husbands who are seeking out the service?

> *"One day, my friend was in a hair salon doing part-time work, and a prostitute came into the shop. Later that day, my friend discussed with me the option of doing this kind of work because she needed money. I told her NO! Become a Dominatrix instead. It will release you from having to have full-on sex and will be more fun. Long story short, that's what she's been doing now for the last four years...she was able to save her home from foreclosure.*
>
> *I identify most as a virgin, though I have had a lot of sex in my 55 years. I am all those things listed. A virgin, a whore, an illegal mother, a chaste wife, and a promiscuous lover, and I have no shame about any of it; it is what it is.*
>
> *I prefer to have lovers and come and go as I like. Again, casual sex - OK by me. It's the thinking and assigning values that either make it good or bad to some. The judging, the labeling..."*
> – MEGHAN, PARTICIPANT

WHORE

By today's definition, being a whore means to debase yourself by doing something for an unworthy motive.

Is having sex to earn money an unworthy motive?

Is having sex an unworthy motive?

Or is the real issue here the belief that having sex outside of marriage is unworthy, and if so, by whose standards or according to whose definition?

Promiscuous

Promiscuous means the mixing of elements together. This word from early seventeenth century Latin means to mix, which led to the definition of indiscriminate or undiscriminating. So, when the word promiscuous is applied to sexual relationships, it is interpreted as having sex that is unselective or casual.
Is promiscuity bad?
Is it bad to mix elements together in an indiscriminate way?
If so, according to whom?

Sometimes a woman can be accused of being a prostitute or whore because she's dressing a certain way, wearing too much makeup, or standing around on the street corner. Often, women are controlled by men or society in general by being threatened with the possibility of being labeled a whore or prostitute.
Has such a thing ever happened to you?
Did your mother warn you about such things?

Virgin Words

Virgin is defined as something that has not been captured, tamed, or subdued.
Untouched, unused, unexploited, unspoiled, untainted, unpolluted. Pure, uncorrupted, undefiled, unsullied.
The word chaste has a Latin root meaning pure, and it is often applied to not having sex, being innocent of having unlawful sex, or being celibate. Virtuous, righteous, respectable. Pure, moral, upright.
Sex and sexuality are also connected with concepts of morality, proper conduct, and acceptable standards of behavior.
Right and wrong, good and bad.
And having morals implies goodness and rightness in character and conduct.

Why would words such as goodness and rightness be applied to sex?
Goodness and rightness according to whose standards?
Why would someone who has not had sex be called virtuous?
Does the mere act of having sex somehow make a person unclean?
Is it possible to have unlawful sex?
Does unlawful sex imply that there is lawful sex?
Is there anything unchaste about marital intercourse?
Is sex clean or unclean?

Take some time to answer these questions. Exploring your feelings around them will open you up to insights around your own beliefs and behaviors.

VALUABLE VIRGINS

Why is a virgin considered valuable?
The concept of virginity has nothing to do with sex.
It has everything to do with purchase and ownership.

For some, the idea of having sex with a virgin carries a thrill, like buying a new car, a new house, or the pride that comes because you can have something that has never been used by anyone else. You can afford it, claim it, and own it.

The idea that a sexual virgin is so valuable comes from whose perspective?
When someone uses the expression, "She saved herself for her husband," have you ever thought to ask, "saved herself for what?"
For his benefit? For his bragging rights?
Who is he in relationship to her body?
Does sex always have to be in the context of someone with whom you are in a relationship?
Can sex ever be casual and not be judged?

There are still many people who believe that you should only have sex with someone you are in a legal contract with. Translate: married. When slaves were purchased, they became the property of the one who bought them, and they were forced to take on the name of this new owner.

That owner had the right to do what he pleased with the slave's body.

How is that any different from the concept of marriage?

Your body now belongs to someone other than yourself, and, as is often the case, the man claims the woman by putting his name on her.

This leads right into the question, Who owns your body?

Ownership

Do you own your own body?

Do you have the right to use it as you see fit?

What is at stake if you choose self-ownership and individual freedom?

Do you believe that a male god gave you life and, therefore, that male god is the only one who can determine how you get to use your body and your life?

Is this a religious or a spiritual belief?

Does a woman have the right to sell herself if she wants?

Does she have the right to use her body any way she chooses as long as it isn't doing harm to anyone?

And harm according to whom?

This takes us back to the self-righteous, family-values-man who comes seeking the services of a prostitute.

Adding Mothers to the Mix

Here are some more things to ponder on the topic, including thoughts about mothers and mothering and their relationship to virgins and whores.

One definition of a virgin is a maiden, a woman, especially a young one, who has not had sexual intercourse.

The word virgin often suggests something untouched, unmarked, pure, and clean.

Think virgin snow.

Virgin can also mean unused, untrodden, undiscovered.

Think virgin forest.

What is it about the act of having sex that would make a woman unclean or impure?

In order to have a baby and become a mother, a woman must have sex. Some might argue that this is not true, given the modern practice of artificial insemination, but even that requires that a woman's body be entered and be in contact with fluids that are sexually produced in the body of a male.

So, does becoming pregnant automatically make a woman impure? Does giving birth automatically make a woman unclean?

The word pure implies free from sin or guilt. Free from anything that adulterates or taints.

Chaste implies moral excellence, someone who is virtuous, modest, not indecent.

Once you become a mother, do you automatically become unchaste, no longer virtuous, unclean, and impure?

What a terrible thought!

It would seem that the only way open to a woman would be for her to be wed-locked or sworn in matrimony. That way, she could become a mother and avoid all the uncleanness.

Or she could choose to never have sex and could become a saint.

MARRIAGE

Why is marriage considered a holy sacrament?

Why do we use the expression holy matrimony instead of holy patrimony?

When was it decided that a woman had to be married before she could rightfully become a mother?

If an unmarried woman decided to become a mother, she would no longer be a chaste and pure virgin. She would become a harlot, a woman wandering around without the protection of a man.

That, of course, would make her dangerous, a threat to the order of things. And that would make her children illegitimate.

Of these three words, which one do you relate to the most?

Virgin
Harlot
Mother

Which one is the most acceptable?

Why?

All three refer to the sexuality of a woman.

Does our sexuality always have to be in the context of our relationship to and with men?

LEGITIMATE OR NOT

How do we refer to children who are born to mothers who are not married?

Do we still use the word illegitimate?

Or perhaps born out of wedlock?

What about words like bastard?

If society and religion truly honored and respected motherhood, there would be no need to ask such questions, and there would be no need for such words.

Why would a woman need to do something to make her motherhood legal?

Does being a mother have anything to do with legality?

Who or what determines whether or not a woman's child is legitimate?

The word illegitimate means "not recognized as a lawful offspring or not sanctioned by the law."

How can a child be unlawful?

WHO IS MY MOTHER?

Misogyny is a disdain for and denigration of women. It is still alive and well in cultures all around the world. In fact, patriarchy is the prevailing religion of the entire planet.

Unwed mothers are rarely honored, and yet, motherhood is often forced upon women because they are denied access to birth control and abortions.

A mother is always sure a baby is hers. Her body fed it. Her body breathed for it. Her body carried away its waste. It came into the world from and through her body.

For a man, there is always the shadow of a doubt.

That's why he is forced to seek out a paternity test.

Most likely, that's why, in the past, men demanded their bride be a virgin and required her to be monogamous.

He wanted to be as certain as possible that all her children were his.

Thus, the virginity and fidelity of a wife became a fundamental, patriarchal requirement for claiming ownership.

ALIVE AND WELL

"Recorded history, remember, only began approximately five thousand years ago. In this narrow 3 percent slice of the life of our species, patriarchy and misogyny have been the dominant norm in most major civilizations and through nearly every historical period... perusing the daily news confirms that patriarchy and misogyny persist in every major contemporary society. From the Taliban in Afghanistan to Japanese men's repression of women, from male pro-life fanatics in the United States to the practice of bride burning in India, evidence for these insidious twins abounds. Wide swaths of Africa and the Islamic world still practice female genital mutilation, and forced prostitution is rife among the former Soviet Union Republics. Sex slavery is an ugly fact of life from Saudi Arabia to Thailand. Humanity staggers on like a person who has suffered a stroke that left half of the body paralyzed."

–SEX, TIME AND POWER: HOW WOMEN'S SEXUALITY SHAPED HUMAN EVOLUTION, LEONARD SHLAIN

Such information is sobering to say the least. Things will not change until we, as women, are willing to change.

Do your beliefs and actions contribute to and support the perpetuation of the denigration of women, their bodies, and their sexuality?

Do you have attitudes and judgments about women who believe differently than you do?

What do you consider yourself to be?

A virgin

A whore

An illegal mother
A chaste wife
A promiscuous lover

How can you claim wholeness for yourself without setting aside the beliefs, rules, standards, and morals of patriarchal, women-hating religions, governments, and social structures?
What words can you use to name yourself that do not carry the stigmas, condemnations, and labels of judgment?

"...the crucial question of *why* it makes us so uncomfortable. As it turns out, intimacy, sex and sexuality not only activate some of our deepest fears, but also some of our deepest woundings. The immense silence surrounding the sex industry is symptomatic of our society's phobia of sexuality, the taboo of women as sexually powerful, a fear of intimacy stemming from violence and trauma, and the circulation of misinformation. Our homophobia, transphobia, femmephobia, erotophobia, and fear of prostitutes ensures that we remain silent, pushing these issues to the bottom so that we cannot resolve them, so that we cannot heal from them. The fear of prostitutes is so loaded because it drags with it the chains of desire, disgust, judgment, morality, guilt and shame. It is loaded with things we are too hurt and too wounded to recognize; we only recognize it as something to fear and therefore something to stay away from. Never does it occur to many of us to take a closer look because there is no hiding from it, because only by taking a look at an impossible bridge can we ever imagine we will cross it. The crime of prostitution is that we would rather not look deeply at our own pain. Prostitution presents us with a reality that is sometimes too emotionally painful to unravel because as we attempt to do so, we begin to realize that it is our reality too."
–A Disgrace Reserved for Prostitutes: Complicity & the Beloved Community, Pluma Sumaq

"The campaign that some feminists have undertaken to ban prostitution as a uniquely degrading, violent activity is self-defeating. Singling out sex work as especially degrading contributes to devaluing and blaming the women who practice it, without at the same time providing any clue about what options women really have. We have sold our bodies in marriage. We have sold ourselves on the job. We have sold ourselves in universities, other cultural institutions, and the movie industry. And we have engaged in prostitution in support of our husbands. Let's be abolitionists, but not only with respect to sex work. All forms of exploitation should be abolished, not just sex work. Our task as feminists is not to tell other women what forms of exploitation are acceptable…"
–BEYOND THE PERIPHERY OF THE SKIN, SILVIA FEDERICI

Whore Meditation

Imagine you are wandering along a lovely sunlit path in a park that you know well. It's a warm summer day. As you wander along, you begin to realize that you are also wandering back in time, slowly, gradually. The longer you walk, the farther back you go, and at the same time, you begin to realize that the path is unfamiliar. Yet you know someplace deep inside yourself that you have been here before. You continue walking, wandering, and you are surprised that you are not tired. You feel rested and at peace, and your wandering has taken on a sense of quiet determination. You begin to know that you are no longer just wandering; you are on a journey.

You are seeking the first woman, the mother of us all, she who gave birth to all who live, she who always was, who always is, and who always will be. You begin to walk faster. You cross a lush valley with a sparkling stream and then a green meadow with wildflowers and birds singing.

You see in the distance steep mountains covered in snow. You continue to walk. You walk along the seashore and at the edge of a vast desert. You find yourself in a deep forest and a thick jungle. You are not tired. In fact, you are gaining energy and vitality as you continue walking. You feel a sense of excitement and anticipation. Finally, you arrive at the exact place where you knew all along you would find her, the first woman, the mother of us all. She is there, waiting for you, waiting to welcome you. She knew you were coming. She holds out her hand. You take it. You embrace. She invites you to sit with her, for she knows you have many questions. But first, she wants to tell you the truth about the great mother. She knows you have come seeking the truth.

You stay by her side, listening, resting, being comforted by her love. As she speaks, you realize that as her story unfolds, she is answering all your questions before you even ask. Forever passes by in a moment of time. You fall asleep in the arms of the great mother, content and satisfied.

When you awake, you find yourself back where you began, back in the same place. As you open your eyes, you realize that you have not been dreaming; you have been in the presence of the Ancient One, and you have brought back with you the truth about what happened to her, the mother of us all.

To access all downloadable meditations, go to page 48 and scan the QR code.

Truth

If I Really Tell
The Truth

If I really tell the truth, I'll stop being nice and start being real.

HONEST SPIRITUALITY

As women of the always, our spirituality must be real.

It must be based upon the truth of who we are, and how we feel, what we long for and desire.

It must be rooted in our ability and willingness to speak truthfully and with integrity.

It cannot be a practice that is only in our heads, based upon rules and regulations that feed us guilt and shame and teach us that we are defective and need to be saved.

We need to be able to meditate, fast, or pray if we want, as well as smoke a cigarette, swear, eat meat, drink whiskey, and feel spiritual about doing all of it. We must be able to engage in the so-called guilty pleasures of life and not feel guilty.

It is vital that we are in love with ourselves, our bodies, our sexual appetites, and our need for sensuous luxuries.

It is vital that we tell the truth about this.

This may look like rebellion and irreverence, decadence and obsession.

But for us, it is the holy trinity of creativity, spirituality, and sexuality woven together in perfect harmony, in the incredibly beautiful female body.

We cannot thrive when we feel virtuous about deprivation.
We cannot thrive when we are constantly trying to please others, keep quiet, be nice, not make waves, be helpful, and be of service. The list goes on.

We are women.
We are intense and noisy.
We are messy. We bleed.
We create life from our bodies, and we drip milk.
We are fierce, wild, undomesticated, alive, and real.
We are not the cause of sin.
We are not problems that need solutions.
We do not need to be fixed.
We do not need to be tamed.
We are order and chaos, mostly chaos, and we can see in the dark, even when we are afraid.

TRUTH TELLING

The essence of this chapter is truth-telling. The material grew out of a daylong workshop I teach. Stop Being Nice. Start Being Real.

The focus is truth-telling.
How to be honest with integrity.
How to live a life that is authentic and real.
This is not an easy thing to do, especially for women.
Our lives are at stake.
We must learn to speak our truth, learn to use our voices in powerful, honest, and meaningful communication.

How often have you been told to be nice, to be silent, or to be invisible?
Did you grow up hearing the words, 'If you can't say something nice, then don't say anything at all?'
I did.
Do you hold back from speaking truthfully for fear of upsetting someone or making them angry?

Have you ever been told you are too big, too loud, too unladylike, too opinionated, too judgmental, too bitchy, too much?
How often do you say yes to things when you really want to say no?
How often do you say yes to things when you need to say no?
Do you hesitate to ask for what you truly desire or really want for fear of being called selfish or demanding?
How many times have you remained silent because you feared the consequences of saying what you really wanted to say or saying what really needed to be said?

Would you be in danger?
Could you lose your job?
Would your family shun you?
Would your partner leave?

What would happen if you stopped trying to be nice and started being real, and truthful instead?
What effect would this have on your spirituality, your sexuality, and your creativity?

How do you know when to speak your truth and when to keep silent?
If you cannot say something nice, is it wise to follow the common advice and not say anything at all?
Is it possible to be kind and compassionate without sacrificing honesty?

If you really tell the truth, are you able and willing to handle the consequences?
Is it possible to say an honest yes to someone if you cannot just as easily say an honest no?
Have you ever felt resentment or regret about a situation because you were not truthful in the first place?
Have you ever been afraid to set boundaries because you were not sure you could or would take the action necessary to enforce them?

What would happen in your life if you really told the truth?

In what areas of your life do you find it the most difficult to say no?
    Family
    Work
    Relationships
    Friends
    Clients
    Living situations
    Something not mentioned here

DANGEROUS THINKING

We are taught to be nice, helpful, loving, open, generous, and compassionate.

We are admonished to stick things out, see them to the end, or even try harder because we have a lesson to learn, or it is our karmic path.

We are not taught how to say no, and worse yet, we are told it is more acceptable to just be nice.

Have you ever heard it said that the things you do not like in someone else are your own issues, the things you do not like in yourself, or things that are wrong with you?

Have you ever thought about the dangerous implications of believing that is true?

This is another example where religious ideology and New Age spirituality jargon encourage us to turn on ourselves and perpetuate the belief that there is always something wrong with us. That we are the problem.

Think about children. Would this belief apply to them as well? They have an instinctive response to people, situations, and things they do not like. It might not make any sense to us as adults, and because of that, we often try to make them explain why or justify their reaction or response. In fact, we often try to convince them that what they are experiencing is not real or valid.

We teach our children early on that they cannot trust themselves. We often instruct them to override their instinctive response, telling them to be nice.

If a child does not like someone or something, does that mean they are merely responding to the same issue inside themself?

How ridiculous is that! And dangerous.

And how does such early childhood conditioning make it easy for us as adults to believe the ridiculous ideology mentioned above?

How are we encouraged to not tell the truth?

We are animals. We have instinct and gut responses. We don't need to make up some story about why we don't like something. It's enough that we don't like it. And we certainly don't need to turn on ourselves and try to figure out what is wrong with us. This is fertile ground for abuse. It is not uncommon for those who are being abused or have been abused to feel somehow that everything is their fault, or they are doing something to deserve it.

BEING SELFISH

Where in your life right now, in what situation, commitment, obligation, or relationship, do you feel overwhelmed, resentful, stressed, angry, frustrated, or just plain done?

Are you trying to convince yourself that somehow there must be something wrong with you because you have these feelings?

Have you ever considered the possibility that the reason you feel this way is because you are not being selfish enough?

You need to say yes to yourself more often than you say yes to others.

Some might call that selfish. No worries. It is.

Saying yes to self is selfish and necessary.

Life is not a popularity contest.

Stop trying to please everyone.

You are sovereign in your own life, and the only way to rule and govern well is to take care of yourself first.

It is integral self-interest to be selfish enough to be self-protective.

Being self-protective may not always appear to be nice.

Being nice is not nearly as important as being authentic, truthful, and real.

If you are not, you cannot be trusted.

When we are who we truly are and say what we truly mean, we stop shouldering the responsibility for everyone else's emotions and feelings and become accountable for our own.

Honesty has to start with each of us as individuals.

Being honest with yourself allows you to have honest connections with others, connections that are grounded in mutual respect.

When we artificially and dishonestly accept or say yes to people and circumstances, we become resentful and ill tempered. We simmer, get cranky, and perhaps even hostile.

How can we give an honest YES to anyone if we are not able to give them an honest NO as well?

Clear, honest, truthful communication is fundamental to happiness, wholeness and intimacy. We all benefit from it.

In our efforts to be nice, keep the peace, not hurt anyone's feelings, or cause problems, we disconnect from our own feelings and emotions and stop being truthful, not only with others but more importantly with ourselves.

We are taught from a young age that it is best to keep emotions stuffed inside, that crying is taboo, that showing anger, hurt, or sadness is a sign of weakness. Pretending to be nice, happy, and positive seems to be preferred.

Some of us are people pleasers who seem to always say yes. We don't like to make waves, and we avoid confrontation at all cost.

Some of us are bold and uncensored in our communication, so much so that others find it hard to be around us.

Speaking freely, without projections or attachments, allows us to articulate what we want to say and be confident in our communication.

When we are too nice for too long, we stop being nice at all.

AUTONOMY

Are you living any part of your life based on "I should and I have to"? Do you carry the burden of the guilt and shame of religion, the righteous moralizing of society, or other people's ideas and expectations of how you are supposed to act and what you should be doing?

What would it feel like to live fully from a place of joy, creativity, and autonomy?

What would it feel like to live from a place of your own truth, from the place of your own deeply rooted, innate, inner wisdom?

NICE VERSUS KIND

Is there a difference between nice and kind?

True kindness comes from a place of genuine self-confidence and heartfelt goodness. This allows for setting clear limits and boundaries and being assertive as well. A kind, self-confident individual is not a people pleaser, nor do they worry about whether or not people like them.

When someone is always trying to be nice, constantly seeking approval, they are easy prey for all sorts of unpleasant situations, co-dependent relationships as well as being used or taken advantage of.

Are you constantly trying not to offend people?

Do you often ignore or deny your own needs because you focus on others first?

Do you stuff your emotions because you don't want to appear negative?

Are you afraid to ask for what you need?

Interestingly, people who are always nice quite often end up being angry, resentful, frustrated and passive aggressive.

Is truth telling the foundation of your life?

How difficult is it to speak the truth when you are trying to be nice rather than real?

How often do you say no?

How often do you say yes when you mean no?

Just imagine what could happen if we all practiced speaking the truth with integrity.

Just imagine the upwelling of potential in every aspect of life when all women accept the sacred obligation of truth-telling and preface what we say with, "If I really tell the truth..."

CLEAR INTENTIONS EXERCISE

Honest communication is fundamental to happiness, wholeness, and intimacy.

We all benefit from it.

One of the challenges we all face when speaking the truth is being brutally honest with ourselves. This exercise provides a great opportunity to explore our underlying agendas when communicating.

Before asking yourself the following questions, take a few minutes to quiet your mind, remove any distractions. Do not rush. Check in with your body and your breath and feel your way in.

Am I speaking with integrity?

What do I believe is my intention?

What is my intention underneath that?

Do I have a hidden agenda?

If I tell the truth to myself first, what is it?

What outcome do I want?

Am I monitoring, modifying, or manipulating my communication to get a certain or desired response or reaction?

Am I doing this to be right?

Am I doing this to be in control?

Am I doing this for shock value?

GOING INSIDE EXERCISE

This exercise is a tool you can use over and over again. It's a great way to center yourself, get in touch with your feelings and not be led solely by your mind.

It can support you in taking action that's truly in alignment with your integrity.

You can apply it to any situation or encounter where you would like to gain more clarity and make difficult choices.

Where do I feel this situation in my body?

What is the story I have made up about it?

What do I think I should say?

What do I think I should do?

What would I like to say about the situation?

What would I like to do?

What do I think other people will think if I say what I truly want to say?

What do I think other people will think if I do what I truly want to do?

What is my biggest fear?

What is the worst thing I imagine could happen?

Could I live with that?

What is the best thing I imagine could happen?

Could I live with that?

What price am I willing to pay for remaining silent?

What price am I willing to pay for remaining true to myself?

These questions support you in exploring what you already know to be true and then taking action that is in alignment with your heart.

IF I REALLY TELL THE TRUTH EXERCISE

This is a great writing exercise you can use when you want to go deep and get to the root of something.

What are you really feeling?

What would you say if you spoke from your heart?

Where are you holding back because you're worried about hurting someone's feelings or making someone angry?

Will you be in danger if you speak truthfully?

Will you feel relief?

Set aside at least a half hour of uninterrupted time. Get a notebook, tablet, or sheets of paper, and a pen or pencil. Get a box of tissues. Make sure you are in a quiet place where you will not have any distractions or interruptions.

Turn off your cell phone and computer.

You are not available to anyone except yourself.
No matter what you write, you are not going to keep it.
Write from your heart, openly and freely, knowing that you will crumple it up at the end and throw it away.
You might even decide to burn it.
No one is going to read this.
You are not going to read it.
Feel completely free to write whatever comes up for you.

Start each sentence with the one of these prompts:

    If I am completely honest with myself...
    If I really tell the truth....
    What I have been afraid to say is...

Finish each sentence with whatever comes to your mind first, no judgment, no rethinking, no analyzing. Just write whatever pops into your mind and finish the thought.

Write the prompt and finish the sentence.
Write the prompt and finish another sentence.
Then do it again. And again. And again.
Do it 100 times.
You will repeat yourself.
You will contradict yourself.
You might write things that seem stupid, ridiculous, unrelated.
You might write things that are profound, deep, have been hidden away, or forgotten.
Do not judge.
Do not edit.
Just write.

If you use this exercise to explore a specific obligation, situation, or expectation, such as participating in holiday celebrations or work activities, you could name it that way.

    If I really tell the truth about the holidays...
    If I am completely honest about my relationship...
    If I tell the truth about my beliefs...

I use this practice all the time. It keeps me honest and on track.
I'm always in awe of the power of such a simple process.

I love using yellow, lined notepads. I don't feel bad throwing the sheets away.
I keep tissues close by.
This practice might not be easy.
You might get frustrated.
You might get bored, or angry.
You may laugh or cry, or both.
You might argue with yourself.
You might even get mad at me.
It is profound and powerful.
It is a great way to gain clarity.

You will discover how often you say yes to things when you really want to say no or need to say no.
It is a great tool you can use over and over again.

One courageous woman from class was willing to share some of what she wrote when she did this exercise. She requested her name be withheld.

> "If I really tell the truth I am angry. I'm so fucking mad. I'm angry at... well, maybe angry isn't the right word. I feel defeated. Betrayed. Exhausted. If I really tell the truth I am tired. I am so tired. I have done all the things I was supposed to do. I went to college. I got a graduate degree. I married a man and had a kid. I wanted to buy a house. I was supposed to buy a house. And there was not enough money...I still tried. I tried to be successful. To hold down a 9-5 job and make enough money to pay off my debt and buy a house and travel. And still it didn't happen... Somewhere in my mind, I thought that if I did all the things I was supposed to, I would not struggle. If I owned a home and had enough money and played by the rules it would pay off... If I really tell the truth, this is all much more work than I thought it would be. This being a human. It is incredibly hard just to exist some days. At the same time, it is so beautiful. If I really tell the truth, I am often able to hold both these at the same time. The terribleness and the beauty in the world... If I really tell the truth I am afraid I will die before I figure it out."

Spinster

Spinners and Weavers

Spinster.
A single woman.
An unmarried woman.
An older woman beyond the usual age to marry.
A stereotype. A negative stereotype.
Pitiful. Unwanted. Childless.
Prissy. Repressed.
Spinsters are also referred to as old maids.
Old maid. A prim and nervous woman who frets over inconsequential details.

WOMEN AS SPINSTERS

In pre-modern societies women's work was not simply housework. Women were the spinners and weavers. They controlled or had a direct hand in textile production. The very nature of this work bound them together with all aspects of life.
Birth. Death. Fate.
Most stereotypes of spinsters are hostile or derogatory. They include references to sexual and emotional frigidity, lesbianism, ugliness, frumpiness, depression, astringent moral virtue, and overly pious religious devotion.
Or, a spinster can even be a woman who sets her standards too high.

What if a woman chooses to remain unmarried, perhaps as a way to reject the social expectation that all women should, or at least should want to, marry. Today this might be considered an empowered choice. However, in the not-too-distant past, such a choice was considered dangerous.

Before the spinning wheel, the spinning of fibers was done by hand, and this activity was a constant in women's lives. Most adult women and young girls were engaged in some form of textile production daily. Translated into actual hours, providing the bare minimum of yarn necessary to weave enough fabric to make clothing for a six-person family would require seven hours of labor daily, every single day. This is just spinning. It does not include weaving and sewing.

How is it possible that the record of this intense, crucial, vital, daily work is pretty much invisible in descriptions and representations of history?

VIKING SHIPS

History glorifies the Vikings and the ships they built. Their ships relied upon sails. Sails were made from fabric. Fabric was made from thread. Thread was spun from wool or flax.

It is quite likely that it took longer to make the sails for a ship than it did to build the ship.

It took one year of eight-hour days of spinning fiber to make enough thread, to weave enough cloth, to make a single sail. The sails on a fleet of Viking ships represented 10,000 work-years of spinning, not to mention the actual weaving and sewing.

Who glorifies the women who made the sails?

Women were producers, not just the men, and their work as spinners and weavers was essential to daily life.

How is it possible then that spinster, a woman who spins, became a negative, contemptuous word?

Does the word bachelor carry such negativity and judgment?

THE NORNIR AND THE VÖLVAS

"He went to that bower and looked in through a window slit…and saw that there were women inside, and they had set up a loom. Men's heads were the weights, but men's entrails were the warp...a sword was the shuttle, and the reels were arrows." –Njals Saga, an Icelandic epic written in the thirteenth century

---

The women described in this epic are Norns, a group of shadowy beings, who communicate secretly, passing judgement on the fate of men, weaving the threads of war and death, presiding over destiny, even of the gods. There are many Norns but the most famous in Norse mythology are a trinity, often referred to as the Nornir. Urd, the one who twists and turns, the being that revolves. She is what happened.

Verdandi, the one who is becoming from the twisting. She is what is currently happening.

Skuld, the one who shall come forth out of necessity. She is what should happen.

The Greeks had a similar trinity of females who engaged in spinning, measuring, and cutting. They are known as the Fates.

The Völvas were Germanic seeresses, skilled in the arts of prophecy and sorcery. Women of great spiritual authority in tribal Europe. The Völva was she who carried a wand or distaff. She who sang incantations over the web of life. She who lived independently, forsook her family, wandered the countryside, resolved legal issues, and gave rulings over dangerous or important matters. She who had ties to textiles and all women who were spinners and weavers. The distaff for spinning and the loom for weaving were the tools of power for the Völvas. It was said they could stop an entire army simply by tying a knot.

The Christianization of Nordic and Germanic societies brought an end to most pagan practices. The Völvas began to be persecuted and killed. The Norns have been forgotten. The memory of their power and place in society has all but died out.

A Magical Practice

Spinning, done with intention such as chanting, singing, or twisting the spindle in a specific direction, cast spells, created magic. It relaxed the spinner's mind, allowing her to go into a trance-like state. Thread spun in such a way could be used to weave magic into the cloth that was being created. The distaff and spindle were symbols of creation and power. They were tools of sorcery. It is no wonder that at various times in history it was decreed illegal to spin in public. Men in power were afraid of women's magic.

Our foremothers understood the mystery of spinning. It's no wonder the task of spinning shows up in fairy tales and folklore, stories about never-ending tasks of drudgery, supernatural helpers and magic. Spinning itself was a magical act, making something out of what seemed to be nothing. This mimicked the ability women had to create new life from their bodies.

It is time for us to reclaim the power that was evident in the spinning and weaving of cloth.
It is time to reclaim the chants, the songs sung while spinning.
It is time for us to find our way back to trance states, presiding over the fates of men and the gods as we sit at the loom and weave.

> *"Many hours I have spent looking in awe at the magic of things made for the sake of making, made of love and breath and time... each one filled with rhythm. Spinning is rhythmic, weaving is rhythmic, planting, sewing, carving, cooking, chopping. All of life is rhythmic. The act of creating contains breath...we breathe, we hum, we sing. This is what unites me to my ancestors. It is a long lineage of makers, of spinners and weavers, of storytellers and listeners. When I slow down to create, I create with the soul of nature."*
> —SUSAN, PARTICIPANT

SPINNING

Spinning by hand was tedious work. Women's work, most likely done daily, even during free time. In many folk and fairy tales, it was associated with morals, ugliness, being lazy, being industrious. Finding ways to get out of it was a plus, but not wanting to do it was considered a negative.
It would seem that there was no way to win.

It was a blessing and a curse.

Women of the always are spinners. We become the whirling movement of creation. If we spin around in the direction called counterclockwise, supposedly opposite to Father Time, might it be possible that we free ourselves from the spell of clocks and time, deadlines and timelines and become the mothers of time?

Could spinning allow us to meander, rather than always moving forward, aiming for a target, striving for a goal?

As spinning women, could we become wanderers?

Women were threatened and intimidated by being warned that the only respectable option open to them was marriage or becoming a nun. The other roles were prostitute or mistress. Or spinster.

If a woman remained unmarried or was widowed, she could engage in spinning as a respectable way to earn money. She was allowed to stay in her father's home, her brother's home, or the home of her married sister. But in all these instances, she was under the control of the male of the household, and any money she earned, by law, belonged to either her father or the male family member who was responsible for her care and upkeep.

Far into the twentieth century, some states in the United States required that a woman buying property be designated as either a spinster, a married woman, a divorced woman, or a widow because a woman's rights to make contracts, retain her earnings, and own property were directly affected by her status under *coverture*, a legal term used to describe the status of a married woman. No such laws have ever existed for men.

DISTAFF

A distaff is a tool used in spinning. It is designed to hold unspun fibers such as flax or wool so they would not tangle and would be easier to spin. The word comes from Low German, *dis* meaning a bunch of flax and *staff* being a rod of some sort. All spinning was done this way until the invention of the spinning wheel in the fourteenth century.

The term distaff is used in English as an adjective to describe the female branch of a family, the mother's side. It refers to a person's mother and her blood relatives. Developed in English-speaking communities where spinning was common, it became a symbol of domestic life.

The term distaff was used in horse racing up until 2007. The American Breeders' Cup World Championships Race for fillies and mares was called the Breeders' Cup Distaff. Now it's referred to as the Ladies' Classic. The term Distaff Division is still used in martial arts to describe the Women's Division.

MYTHS AND LEGENDS

Habetrot is a spinning goddess of the Celtic tradition, with connections to wool, the spinning wheel, and spiders. It is said that the fiber she spun had magical healing properties and that anyone who wore clothing she made would never fall ill.

In Egypt, Neith was the goddess of weaving. The gods went to her for wisdom.

Spider Woman, according to some Native American legends, created the world with her web.

The Greek Fates were daughters of the goddess Necessity. Together with the Sirens, they kept the stars and planets revolving, spinning around the earth. Clotho was the spinner of the threads of life. Lacheis was the disposer of lots. Atropos cut the threads at death.

Why would Necessity give birth to the daughters of Fate, spinners of the threads of life?

SPIDERS

In many stories, spiders are connected to creative power and the ability to weave the web over and over again. Spiders are also connected to aggressiveness, evident in the way they deal with what is caught in the web and the way they protect the egg sac. In the case of the black widow, her killing of the male after mating, and her sitting in her web, are symbols of her being the center of the world. Spider Woman and Grandmother Spider are symbols for the cosmic mother. Her aggressiveness is her protectiveness.

She knows magic words and is credited with the creation of the alphabet. Some tales need to be unraveled so we can go beyond the patriarchal telling of the myth and find a deeper, older message, favorable to the female.

CHARLOTTE'S WEB

Radical feminist philosopher, theologian, and author, Mary Daly, spun on her heel and took a look, through different eyes, at a popular and well-loved children's story, *Charlotte's Web* by E. B. White.

The hero of the story is a young pig named Wilbur. Wilbur was destined to be killed because he was a runt. His life was spared through the aggressive efforts of a little girl, Fern. He was continually helped by a wise ewe who lived with him in the barn.
This is an old theme, a familiar story.
The hero is helped and saved by females.
The focus of the story is Wilbur.
Not the little girl.
Not the ewe in the barn.
Not Charlotte the spider.
Wilbur is eventually saved by Charlotte, a spider who performed a miracle by weaving words into her web, capturing the attention of the farmer and people from miles around.
Wilbur gains the reputation of being "no ordinary pig."
Only the farmer's wife was wise enough to recognize that the praise belonged to Charlotte. She stated,

> "Well...it seems to me you're a little off. It seems to me we have 'no ordinary spider.'"

Yes, the story is well written.
Yes, it clearly shows that Charlotte is creative and aggressive.
Yes, it gives, once again, the message that the males are the amazing, shining heroes.
Reinforcing the age-old expressions "behind every man there is a good woman..." and "a good woman is the power behind the throne."

The story ends with this statement.
Charlotte dies alone.

As women of the always, how long are we willing to be content
with being behind the scenes?
How long are women going to be content with saving the male,
who then becomes the hero?
How long are we going to be the nameless wife of the big game
hunter, Martin Johnson, who died in a plane crash?

Is there any significance in the fact that the internet is referred to
as the World Wide Web?
Can we use the web to write a different story?
Or will you be a nameless woman, holding a child, in a field of
wheat?
Who will be there when you die?
Will you die alone like Charlotte?
What are you spinning and weaving in your life right now?
Are you willing to write a different story?

TEXT AND TEXTILES

The words text and textile have the same root. Latin *texere* means to
weave. Sometime during the late fourteenth century, the word text
came to mean the wording of anything written. It came from the
Latin word *textus*, which meant the texture of something woven.
We began to spin tales or yarns and weave stories. Thoughts began to
be referred to as threads. The written page began to be called a text.
Storytellers and poets became spinners and weavers.

Is the cloth or fabric of your life actually the unfolding of a story?
When you tell your stories, are you a weaver?
Does your ability to write connect you with the myths and stories
of the spinners and weavers from the past?
When you weave texture with your words, does the page become
the fabric of your life?
What pattern are you weaving today with your words, both written
and spoken?

NECESSITY

Life. The necessity of movement, from birth to death and back again. The twirling of the spindle, the back and forth of the shuttle on the loom. The weaving of the threads. The texture of the fabric. The cutting of the thread that releases the newly formed fabric from the loom is a ritual. The cutting of the umbilical cord is a ritual. It releases the mother from the baby she has just created in her body and brought forth into the world. And the cutting of the cord releases the baby from the mother so this new being can live apart from and because of the necessity of life.

All these symbols of thread, and loom, and distaff, and weaving are realities that speak of our life as humans. To weave is to join together different realities and to create new stories, cycles, endings, and beginnings of life, nature, humans, nations, peoples, and the universe itself.

Throughout time, spinsters have created the world. And we have done it, no matter what. In silence, locked away in towers, in dark rooms, nameless, unacknowledged, forgotten.

Spider Woman. Grandmother Spider. Spinsters.

We create from our own bodies.

TASKS

- Wander around the World Wide Web looking for themes of weaving and spinning in myths, legends, folklore, and fairy tales. Look for messages, hidden and obvious. Ask yourself how the story represents women and the work they are expected to do, or are forced to do? Who has the power? Who is portrayed in a negative light?
- Read *Charlotte's Web*. Write your own version of the story. Try putting Charlotte in the starring role or turning the pig into a female.

Spinster Meditation

Notice your breath. Slow and steady. In and out. In and out. Continue to breathe, slowly, deeply. Imagine it is very dark. The void. All is silent. You, the beginning, the great cosmic spider, grandmother of all creation, you are alone in the center of the nothing. And you begin to slowly, ever so slowly, turn, and twirl and move, round and round, and as you do, you begin to bring forth from your own body the most lovely, delicate, fragile silken threads, shimmering, glowing. As you continue to turn and twirl and spin, these delicate, fragile, silken threads float silently through the cosmos. After some time, you begin to move along your own silent threads and, using your legs, you gather and connect them. Back and forth, back and forth, you move along the silken threads, tying, knotting, connecting, weaving, all the while continuing to spin magically and silently from your own body. And as you do, the universe begins to take form, and symbols and signs begin to appear, shapes and letters, then words. Sacred, magical.
So it is.
You are the great cosmic mother spider spinning silent webs from your own body, webs that shape the universe.
Back and forth, round and round, twirling, spinning, weaving.
You, the first spinner, the first weaver.
You have created the world from your own body.
You have created words and language.
Feel the void around you filled now with the magical, shimmering threads you brought forth from your own body. Notice your breath. Slow and steady. In and out. In and out. You continue to breathe, slowly, deeply. When you feel ready, open your eyes and, with soft gaze and amazement, you acknowledge and appreciate all that you have made.

To access all downloadable meditations, go to page 48 and scan the QR code.

Creativity

Living Creativity

We are women of the always.
We live our wisdom through mystery.
And part of the mystery is creativity.
We know creativity in our hearts.
We know creativity in our bodies.
We create through our bodies.

WHAT ARE YOU WILLING TO PAY

Creativity is inextricably woven and intertwined with our spirituality and sexuality. Losing our connection to creativity shows
up in a variety of ways. We feel caught, stuck, trapped. We lose
our sense of imagination, possibility, and adventure. We may feel
hopeless, rather like a circus elephant, endlessly plodding round
the ring as people clap.
Setting creativity free always demands a price.
What are you willing to pay?

Creativity is not just about art; it's about life and living life as
a work of art. Setting it free can inspire us to quit jobs we hate,
change careers, end relationships, buy and sell houses, write books,
compose music, make videos, bake cakes, arrange flowers, and
travel to foreign countries.
When creative adventures are embarked upon, dreams are
manifested.
Creative freedom can truly change and quite possibly save your life.

Creating can be a radical act, a subversive act, a mysterious, magical,
deeply personal act.
It is rebellious and courageous.

It requires faith and vulnerability.
It connects us with our spirituality, and our spirituality connects us with the mystery of our sexuality.

"The artist's experience lies so unbelievably close to the sexual...that the two phenomena are really just different forms of one and the same longing and bliss."
–RAINER MARIA RILKE

ART AND CREATIVITY
What is art?
What is creativity?
Is there a difference?
Do you consider yourself an artist?
Do you think you are creative?
Are they important?
Are they necessary?
What part do they play in your life?

Creativity is not always about making art. Creativity allows us to think outside the box and give voice to possibility.
We can imagine things, and we can live with ideas, but that is not enough.
In order for things to change and for something new to come into form, we must move out of our heads and into our bodies.
We can only create using the instrument of our physical, tangible, sexual body.

Have you ever explored the connections that exist between creativity, spirituality, and sexuality?
Is making art spiritual?
Is making art sexual?

We often suppress what we don't understand. This is true for sex as well as creativity.
We rarely stop to consider that sexual energy is creative energy, energy that is coded in our bodies. When we learn to play with

the creative nature of sexual energy, we become wild, succulent, erotic, whimsical creatures. Our creative power becomes a force to be reckoned with.

When we rise up and embrace this energy, it will flood over into every aspect of our lives, our families, our relationships, our finances, our spirituality, what we dream about, what we long for, and what we manifest for ourselves as well as others.

Fall in Love

Sadly, there are many of us who have lost touch with creativity. The fires have either gone out or have burned down to ash, with just a few warm embers.

Our wells have dried up, or the water level is so low that the rope we have tied to our bucket is not long enough to reach the water. We need to fall in love and be in love in order to reconnect with our creative essence. We must be in love with all of life, with the beauty and the beast of it. This gives power and momentum to our creative expressions.

This is how we rekindle the fire and refill the well.

We also need to open ourselves to joy. It lives on the inside. It does not come from the outside. We often think that when we get the new job, or find our soulmate, or live in the perfect house, or live off the grid, we will be happy.

None of this is true.

Creativity brings us joy, not from the things we make but from the connection we have with the flow of life that moves through our bodies.

This is spiritual.

This is sexual.

This is creative.

"It is the love of something, having so much love for something—whether a person, a word, an image, an idea, the land, or humanity—that all that can be done with the overflow is to create.

It is not a matter of wanting to, not a singular act of will; one solely must."
—WOMEN WHO RUN WITH THE WOLVES, CLARISSA PINKOLA ESTES

Being creative requires the dark and the light.
The sky rests in the dark so the stars can be seen.
The earth rests in the dark so she can flourish.
If you want to be creative, you must be comfortable with the dark because creativity lives there.
In a world that values work and productivity over art and creativity, we must be willing to make sacrifices. Sacrifices. Not in a punitive sense or from a place of lack or loss, but from the essence of the meaning of the word, to make something holy, to offer something up as being valuable, special, important.

MEMORY GIVES BIRTH TO CREATIVITY

I've taught creativity classes for almost 40 years. I've seen tears of joy and tears of sadness. I have watched faces light up with memories, seen frowns as well as smiles, and been privileged to witness hundreds of women remembering who they are by reconnecting with their creativity.

In Greek mythology, the Muses were a sisterhood of nine goddesses of creativity. They went forth each day to inspire the gods. Their mother was Mnemosyne, the goddess whose name means memory. Each night, Mnemosyne required her daughters to return to their home on Mount Helicon. There on the mountain, they could frolic and play, refresh, and renew in the springs and fountains, lakes, and rivers.

Memory is the mother of creativity. When we create, we are remembering. We call upon our foremothers. We call upon and connect with those who have gone before us. We create from the place of remembering, remembering that we are women of the always, remembering that we are creators, that we have the capacity to make new life, and it comes through our bodies.

Before art can come forth, we must merge with the divinity that exists in our humanity; we must weave together our sexuality and our spirituality with our creativity. This merging may well be what the Greeks understood when they spoke about the Muses, the daughters of memory. This sisterhood of creativity is ever present, hovering around us, whispering, inspiring, breathing the spirit of remembering into us. The Muses, daughters of memory, inspire us to make art.

MUSEUM AND THE MUSES

The museum in the ancient city of Alexandria, Egypt was said to be a religious shrine built for the glorification of the Muses. They presided over music, poetry, dance, and literature. Its religious purpose was combined with its dedication to teaching and debate. It contained lecture halls, laboratories, observatories, living quarters, a dining hall, a garden, a zoo, and of course, the shrine itself. The museum even had ambulatory colonnades. These structures consisted of rows of evenly spaced columns that were designed to provide a sheltered walkway so men could walk about while having discussions.

Imagine how the Muses felt being housed and confined in a shrine. Imagine old Greek men walking between the pillars of a colonnade, discussing the nine sisters of creativity.

Have you ever had an ambulatory discussion in a colonnade?
How would this serve you and your creativity?
Would the defining columns restrict somehow the essence and freedom of creativity?
Are the Muses served by being discussed?
Do you walk around talking about creativity, or do you create?
Can you be truly creative when confined within a structure?
Without the structure and the colonnade, what might be possible if we allowed the muses to overtake us and create through us?
What might happen if you were to wander off, away from the evenly spaced columns and allow yourself to meander?
Have you ever had a personal experience with the Muses?

Do you have anyone or anything that truly inspires you, breathes spirit into you, moves you to make art?

Have you ever wanted to color outside the lines?

Have you ever felt like the lines were too restrictive?

Are you afraid to break the rules?

Sometimes you need to follow your own creative impulse and do something different.

Maybe you need to turn the paper over and draw your own picture.

DISCONNECTION

A blessing and a curse of modern living is the mass production and easy availability of seemingly endless amounts of goods and products, things we need or think we need for day-to-day living. Often, things that are mass-produced are purely functional, ugly, lacking in beauty and form, missing the small touches that add character and aliveness.

Think plastic food containers. Think cheap clothing.

Imagine a hand-carved wooden bowl given to you by your grandmother. Imagine a hand-stitched quilt made from scraps of fabric from your grandfather's work shirts.

Most modern, mass-produced products lack soul.

Mass production and ease of acquisition create a climate where we rarely experience deep connection with what we own and have around us.

Are you more willing to discard something when you have no deep connection with it?

Do you show honor and respect when you repair something?

Can aliveness exist in things that are mass-produced?

What happens when you don't know where things come from, don't know who made them, or even what they're made from?

What would it be like to only wear clothing that you made yourself or that was made by someone you know?

What would it be like to sleep with blankets that you have woven yourself, using wool that you spun, and dyed using plant and mineral substances you collected?

What if the wool was sheared from a sheep you had raised, fed, and cared for?
Would you have a more intimate relationship with that blanket?
Would you care for it differently?
Would you throw it away?

Do you throw away socks when they get a hole?
Would you do that so quickly if you had knitted the socks yourself?
Is it possible to create relationships with your possessions?
Do you have anything in your life right now that is similar to the blanket described above?

FINDING TIME

What we all have in common is time.
The difference is how we use it.
Sometimes we are so stressed by ordinary, daily tasks that we cannot imagine having time to create, much less imagine what we could create.
We live in a world that values deadlines and goals, work and productivity.
Do you believe that art and creativity are just as valuable and necessary?
What would you be willing to offer up, let go of, in order to find the time to create?

THE CHALLENGE

> "If you feel stuck in your life or in your art, few jump-starts are more effective than a week of reading deprivation." –THE ARTIST'S WAY, JULIA CAMERON

Julia Cameron wrote those words in 1992, more than 30 years ago. Since that time, there has been an exponential increase in technology, information, and input.
I invite you to accept the challenge, for at least a week, to experience a vacation, not just from reading, but from input.

Stop watching television, movies, and the news.

Stop playing games on your phone or computer.

Stop reading books, magazines, and articles for entertainment or relaxation.

Do this consciously and with intention.

How much time can you free up for creativity?

What would it be like to live your own life creatively instead of watching or reading about someone else living their life?

This challenge is not suggesting that something is bad or good. It is an opportunity to pay attention and explore how much or how little time you spend with yourself, being creative.

CREATIVITY SEXUALITY SPIRITUALITY

The patriarchal, monotheistic religions place great value on impregnation and birth. In fact, most religions do.

Is it more acceptable for a woman to be pregnant and raising children than it is for her to be an independent, self-oriented, non-gestational artist?

Must we find ways to be artists while still being the acceptable mother, the selfless caretaker, or loving nurturer?

Can we do both?

Do we need to choose?

Do you use your sexual energies when you create?

Can you be spiritual, sexual, and creative all at the same time?

If memory gave birth to creativity, did she also give birth to sexuality?

Did she give birth to spirituality?

Is it possible that when women lose touch with their sexuality, they also lose touch with their creativity?

Has religion caused women to lose touch with their creativity and their sexuality?

Is the fact that so many women have difficulty manifesting wealth tied up somehow to our disconnection from female creative energy?

Is there something deeper and more profound hidden in the story of creativity, memory, and the Muses?

FIRE AND WATER

"The artist must create a spark before he can make a
fire and before art is born the artist must be ready to be
consumed by the fire of his own creation."
–AUGUSTE RODIN

What sets your soul on fire?
What fans the smoldering embers so they burst into flame?
What fuel do you need to keep the fire burning?
Sometimes the fires of creative passion are all-consuming.
When that happens, we must return to the mountain, just as the
Muses did.
We must return to the well to be filled up again, to rest, so we can
go forth another day and create.
What is the source of your water?
When do you take time to refresh and restore?

ACTIVITIES

Creating is the bringing together of disparate things in order to
make something that did not exist before.
While you are taking a vacation from media, set an intention to
create something.
Bring into form something that didn't exist before.

Write a poem or a song.
Paint or draw.
Make food from scratch, not from a box.
Bake a loaf of bread.
Set the table in a beautiful way, perhaps include a centerpiece,
flowers, candles.
Work with clay, glass, or other materials from nature.
Knit or crochet something.
Make an article of clothing or a piece of jewelry.
Mend or repair something.
Gather flowers and create a display.

Arrange dried leaves on your windowsill.
Turn your altar into a work of art by positioning items in new or unusual patterns.

Use your imagination and see what happens.
You decide what you call art.
You decide what creativity is.
Watch how you talk to yourself about it or how you judge your efforts and the results.

YOUR HEART

Creativity is cradled in our hearts, and many of us have lost heart. Lost our sense of home, of who we are, and where we belong. We have confused velocity with accomplishment. We run ourselves ragged. We are tired, we are weary, distracted, angry, depressed. Perhaps even afraid.

One way to connect with creativity is through walking. Repetitive and silent, no earbuds, no frantic jogging. Just walk. Listen, smell, sense. Creativity thrives on inspiration, and to be inspired, we must breathe in. Walking allows for rhythmic breathing.
Walk.

We need silence. Long periods of silence, not necessarily formal meditation. Just be quiet. Stare out the window. Watch the clouds. Look at the stars. Rock in a chair.
No radio, no TV, no music or conversation, no reading, no computers, no cell phones.
Just silence.

Creativity is not about logic. It's not about thinking things up or using your mind. It's feeling, sensing, and allowing. Often, when things begin to bubble up or surface, we get anxious, restless, even depressed, and we escape. Meaningless conversations. Binge watching or reading. Any activity we can use to distract ourselves. When we fill our lives with compulsive activity and don't take time to explore the creative impulse, we become cranky and crazed.

We cannot descend into our deep, inner waters if we never allow ourselves to be still and alone.

TASKS

- Do you have a creative desire that is a lifelong yearning? Are you working toward it?

  What is stopping you?

  Make a quick list of all the reasons you are not being as creative as you would like to be. One simple and inexpensive way to start being more creative is to make, buy, or find some sort of box or basket. Start collecting things to put inside. Images from magazines, greeting cards, pencils, pens, glue sticks, ribbons, things from nature, such as feathers or leaves, anything that catches your eye or sparks your imagination. Include a sketch book, watercolor note cards, a book or journal where you can draw, doodle, write, collage. Keep it close at hand. Be spontaneous. Be playful. A basket with a handle can be fun and easy to use. Take it to a friend's. Share ideas. Create together Get your juices flowing.

  Creativity is bringing unrelated things together, acting on them, and bringing something into form that never existed before. Anything you make is original because you are the source of its origin.

- Imagine a stranger coming to your door. What could you hang on your door that would let them know who lived there? This could be a great collage exercise to do alone or with a friend. You might even exchange with each other. You make one for her door and she makes one for yours.

- If you love doing research, you might consider exploring the history of the Museum of Alexandria and what happened to it.

- You might want to make a date with yourself and visit an art gallery or museum.

One of the women from the Creativity class shared her feelings about safety.

"I loved, loved, loved this exploration. Every day, I created some-thing —a drawing, a meal, with my kids or on my own. I thought a lot about how in order to let creativity flow —as with mean-dering and so many of the other topics we've studied— one must feel safe. And it's cyclical, because creativity, in turn, makes me feel more safe. So it's a matter of dropping in to even the smallest whispered invitation to create, rather than remaining tight and closed and unable to hear it. (...)Thanks Ingrid for this class. The work lies quietly below everything I am doing —not always top of mind but working magic in the background." –S.H.

Money

An Abundance of Wealth

For many people, it's easier to speak about abundance than it is to talk about money.
So let's begin in the difficult place.
Money.
Money is never neutral.
When you talk about it, you are discussing the history of your family as well as your personal life.
Personal stuff.
Family stuff.
Relationship stuff.
It is rather like sex.
It can be fun and enjoyable.
Sometimes you have it.
Sometimes you don't.
And sometimes there is shame and guilt and secrets lurking in the shadows.

What do you think about, and how do you feel when you hear words like wealth, cash, affluence, rich?
What about opulence, extravagance, luxuriousness?
What are some of the expressions and sayings you grew up with about money and wealth?
Look for places where there are seeming contradictions.

> *"I think my issues around money are probably envy and jealousy… there I have spoken my truths. I hate that I feel that way from time to time but I do. The fairness issue. Are my closets and pantry now stuffed to the brim? Yes. Do I envy those who are able to travel on a regular basis to faraway beautiful places? Yes."*
> –Christie, participant

How often do you hear people criticizing the rich?

What kind of rich people are usually criticized? Business entrepreneurs? Sports figures? Movie stars? Bankers?

What about expressions like *filthy rich or terribly rich or laughing all the way to the bank?*

Why would people use expressions like *loaded* or *making a killing* when they talk about money?

During my childhood my mother was always struggling to pay bills. She would say she *was robbing Peter to pay Paul*. That was confusing to me. I didn't know who Peter and Paul were and the idea of my mother being a thief for sure didn't sound like a good idea.

I was also told that money did not grow on trees but that it could rain pennies from heaven.

What expressions or sayings would you add to the list?

A good question to ask yourself regarding your relationship with money is found in the book *The Woman's Book of Money & Spiritual Vision* by Rosemary Williams.

> "Do I make automatic choices about money that are based on old messages?"

JUST ENOUGH

Have you ever considered the possibility that someone who is struggling financially just to get by is actually more materialistic than someone who has an abundance of wealth?

Many people struggle with money issues, especially women.

Have you personally had money struggles?

What are your thoughts about whether women generally face more challenges around money or have a harder time than men?

Sometimes I hear women say, "I don't want a lot of money. I just need enough to get by."

What does that mean? How do you feel about that?

At times, I get the sense that there is an undercurrent of implied goodness or righteousness that goes along with that statement, maybe even spiritual superiority.

Imagine saying the same thing about energy.
"I don't want a lot of energy. All I need is just enough to get by."

I just want enough energy to drag through the day taking care of absolute necessities so I can fall into bed at night, used up and exhausted. And then get up the following day to do the same thing. It's okay with me to just barely be able to take care of my own needs. I'm too depleted to even think about doing something fun or extra or helping someone else.

Imagine, instead, having an abundance of energy, so you could enjoy life to the fullest and have plenty to spare. Imagine going to bed at night tired, but not exhausted, and getting up each morning excited for another day. Imagine having enough energy to do the things you love and still have energy left over.

Have you ever seen a tree laden with fruit? Orange trees are a good example. I had a prolific tree at my home in California. It was healthy and thriving, covered with bright orange spheres filled with juice. I can't imagine going to the tree each day and saying, "You are just too much. You don't need to have so many oranges. That's wasteful and greedy. Your opulent abundance takes away from other trees. You only need to produce a couple of oranges; actually, a seed from only one orange is necessary if you want to reproduce yourself."

If money is simply manifested energy, energy that has come into form, like oranges, why would you want to have just enough to get by? Imagine all the possibilities available to you when you have a lot of money, an abundance.

WAITING TO RETIRE
Another conversation that comes up around money is about retirement. I hear people say that they can't do something or afford

to do something until they retire. Or they say they have to keep working in order to save for retirement. And very often, this is said by people who, when they really tell the truth, don't like their jobs, are exhausted and burned out from them, or they're just plodding along like a donkey pulling a heavy cart. Perhaps they enjoyed their work in the past, but it no longer makes them happy. Or worse yet, they are doing something they never loved, but they keep doing it because they're good at it and are afraid to quit.

The sad thing about such a situation is that people spend some of the best years of their life doing something they don't enjoy, hoping somehow they'll have the time and money to do what they love later, without thinking about the fact that when later comes, they are often too tired or too ill to do it.

Or, if they're hanging on because they fear they will not have enough money if they quit now, what they fail to consider is the truth that the fear does not go away. In fact, fear grows bigger and stronger the older we get. If there is fear of not having enough now, most certainly the fear will still be there later and so will the worry.

Money is neither good nor bad. It just is. It can be a tool or a weapon, a gift or a curse. How anyone views it depends on their attitude, feelings, and beliefs.

What kind of relationship do you have with money?

Money and Spirituality

Rarely do I hear discussions about the natural connection that exists between money and spirituality. If you view money and the use of money as part of your spirituality, then you would want to align your beliefs and use of money with your core values, intentions, and spiritual practices.

What are your personal beliefs regarding money and spirituality? Is money spiritual? Can it be spiritual?

The need or desire to evaluate the congruency between your spiritual beliefs and your money beliefs often arises in your life when you feel trapped doing a job or pursuing a career you hate or one that does not bring you joy. This feeling of being trapped, unable to quit, or take a different path, often comes because you're afraid you could not support yourself if you leave.

Some women express a deep-seated belief, one that is strongly attached to fear, that if they quit their job they will become a bag lady and have to live under a bridge.
What happens inside you when you think about major life changes such as divorce, death, needing to move, menopause, and growing old? Do you immediately go to bag lady under the bridge?

Is this a hidden belief you harbor? What would you do if you were fired from your job or given notice that you no longer have a job? The answer I hear most often is, "I'd go out and look for work."
Why do we believe that if we quit we will not be able to survive but if we are fired or laid off we will somehow find a way?
Is there a difference between your response when something is done to you versus when you choose to do something for yourself?
Is your fear of failure deeply rooted in a belief that if you follow your heart, you will not be able to make it in the world?
Deep down inside, do you hold the belief that you need someone or something to save you because you cannot do it on your own?

As women, we have the miraculous ability to create life in our own bodies. We are the ultimate manifestors. What has happened to us that makes us doubt our ability to make an abundance of money and do things we truly love outside the system that is considered to be the norm?

Countless women stay in toxic, dangerous, or soul-draining relationships with partners they do not love, like, or even trust, because they carry the belief that they cannot earn enough money to take care of themselves.
Sadly, this situation is all too true for countless women.
Have you ever been in such a relationship?
Do you know of anyone who is?
It is a sobering reality that the issues women face around money and the fears they carry are valid. We live in a world system that seems intent on keeping women imprisoned by impoverishment.

Have you ever considered using the power and creative energy you hold in your body to bring forth an abundance of money?
Have you ever approached manifesting money from the place of creativity, sexuality, and spirituality?

TASK

• Go to the bank and get a crisp, new bill, the largest denomination you can manifest at this time. See if you can stretch yourself here, out of your comfort zone. It is really wonderful if you can get a new $100 bill. They seem to hold special magic. This exercise is about trust. Place the bill on your altar or sacred place, visible and accessible. Leave it there.
Check in with yourself as you consider it each day. What mind chatter goes on? Observe your habitual thoughts and fears.
In addition, begin to put money in the pockets of your coats, jackets, and sweaters. Tuck bills away in the zipper compartments of your bags and wallets. Place them in drawers and on shelves. Treat them as if they are fresh flowers or special decorations.

What judgments or concerns do you have about doing this?

"It has been years since I have had cash in my wallet. While working with this Money topic I went to the ATM and withdrew more money than usual, and stashed it around in my purse, pockets, etc., as you suggested. Again, a simple change, but a very real feeling of abundance." –MELANIE, PARTICIPANT

THE TROUBLESOME ALTAR

As I shared earlier, this book was birthed from a year-long course I taught in person. Each time the group gathered, I would create an altar that represented the topic we would be discussing.
For the Money topic, I created a simple altar, all items meaningfully placed on green fabric: a jasper frog for abundance, the Fehu rune, a symbol for movable wealth, and my special yew wand with its citrine crystal. The altar drew a lot of attention,

and several women were noticeably concerned, not because of the items I just mentioned, but because I had also placed ten crisp $100 bills on the altar. Most of us are not used to seeing so much money left out in the open, easily accessible, obvious. Undoubtedly, most of us have things visible or on display in our homes that are worth more than $1000, but there is a different energy present when it's cash.

I must admit that working with money in this way was a new experience for me. I was raised with the "just enough to get by" motto. A lot of buttons got pushed. I had to be willing to practice what I preached. It was an enormous step for me to carry around a $100 bill in my wallet with the intention of not spending it. It wasn't there to use for shopping. It was there to remind me of abundance. Gradually, over the years, things have shifted for me. And it wasn't always easy. The $100 bill is now tucked into my wallet with several others, and my altar is decorated with cash along with fresh flowers.

If money is just energy that comes into form, then it's true that there is always an abundance of money. It is always flowing and passing by. Coming into form, going out of form. If you hold onto it too tightly, you form a fist, and a fist is not open to receive. Money is an illusion. In fact, the money circulating today is backed by nothing. It is based upon nothing. It only exists as small numbers on pieces of paper and, in some instances, not even on paper. Just numbers that exist only on the screen of your computer.

LIVING WITH ABUNDANCE

According to the dictionary, the word abundance can mean "a very large quantity of something" or "the state or condition of having a copious amount of something." It originated in Latin, *abundare*, meaning to overflow.

Is it possible for a person to experience an abundance of poverty or lack?
Is it possible to be in the state or condition of an abundance of struggle and difficulty?
Have you ever thought about the word in that way, or do you always think about it from a positive perspective?
When you say you want abundance, are you specific about what kind?
Have you ever said you want an abundance of money?

What does the word abundance mean to you?
What does it look like?
How would it be evident in your life?
Would you say you are experiencing abundance right now?
Can you do the work you are called to do in this world from a place of limited money?
A place of worry and struggle?
Can you have abundance and not have much money?
What have your experiences been around the connection between money and spirituality?

TASK

• Make a list of at least 20 things that make you feel luxurious, abundant, and rich. They can range from the expensive to the inexpensive, and they can even be free. After making the list, select at least one thing you will treat yourself to during the coming week and then do it! Select something new for the next week, and the next, and the next.

Some things that make me feel abundant and luxurious are:
    Fresh flowers in the house, even if they're field flowers or flowering weeds

Clean sheets that hung on the line to dry in the sun
A big, comfortable bed with lots of pillows and 100% Egyptian cotton, high thread count bedding
Beeswax candles in every room, used all the time, not just for special occasions
A manicure, pedicure, facial, or all three
A full-body massage for more than an hour
Leather luggage
Flying first class
Having my car professionally detailed and polished
Candles on the table for dinner, not just for looks, but lit
Fresh raspberries and real, thick cream
Sitting on a rock and dangling my feet in a cold stream, not worrying about work
Camping in the forest or at the beach
Coffee on the porch, early in the morning, just as the sun comes up

What's on your list?
Take time to savor and enjoy this experience. After making the list, go back and get as detailed and specific as possible. Be surprised. Be extravagant. It might take you some time to warm up and exercise your luxuriousness muscles.

Take my example of coffee on the porch in the morning as the sun comes up. If I get more detailed, I might say I boiled pristine water in my electric kettle. The coffee was my favorite roast, freshly ground beans, brewed in a French press, with the perfect amount of fresh cream.
I push a little more. I am at an Italian villa, and my lover/partner/boyfriend is serving me the coffee. I am in a luxurious silk robe, classical music is playing softly in the background, and one more thing, I am looking out over the shimmering blue waters of the Mediterranean.

If you could choose or create a symbol of abundance, what would it be?

SIMPLE ABUNDANCE

According to Sarah Bahn Breathnach in her daybook, *Simple Abundance,*

> "There are six principles that act as guides and six threads that when woven together produce a tapestry of contentment."

Those threads are:
    Gratitude
    Simplicity
    Order
    Harmony
    Beauty
    Joy

Take a look at each one of these threads and consider where they are present in your life and how they contribute to your abundance.
What does the tapestry you are weaving look like?
Poverty of any sort appears in the soul, first, and then shows up in the pocketbook.
What are your feelings about that statement?
Do you believe that?

Here are some thoughts Sara shared in the group.

> *"So with what seems to be a full and abundant childhood on the outside looking in, the loss of both my adoptive parents as a child, along with the dysfunction before they died, were so disruptive that they plunged me into a state of poverty throughout most of my life. Interesting, the idea that an inner poverty manifests outwardly... If our thoughts create our life which I believe they do, then yes, an inner emptiness surely won't result in great wealth outwardly."*

The Bible says the love of money is the root of all evil.
George Bernard Shaw said the lack of money is the root of all evil.
Which one of these statements is true?
Could they both be true at the same time?

Margaret Young, a popular singer in the United States during the 1920s, made this observation:

> "Often people attempt to live their lives backwards: they try to have more things, or more money, in order to do more of what they want so that they will be happier. The way it actually works is the reverse. You must first be who you really are, then, do what you need to do, in order to have what you want."

The following was written as part of an editorial that appeared in *Ladies' Home Journal 1932* during the dark days of the Great Depression.

> "The return of good times is not wholly a matter of money. There is prosperity of living which is quite as important as prosperity of the pocketbook. It is not enough to be willing to make the best of things as they are. Resignation will get us nowhere. We must build what amounts to a new country. We must revive the ideals of the founders. We must learn the new values of money. It is a time for pioneering—to create a new security for the home and the family . . . where we were specialists in spending, we are becoming specialists in living."

Is money spiritual?
How would you answer the question now?

Bees

When the Hives are Full with Honey

I do not believe in God
Because I've never seen him.
But if God is the hive
and the honeybee,
pollen and nectar and sun and moon
then I believe in her
and I believe in her at every moment,
and my life is a prayer
and a celebration
and a communion with the eyes
and through the ears,
I honor her by living spontaneously,
as a person who opens his eyes and truly sees,
and I call her the hive
and the honeybee
and pollen and nectar
and sun and moon
and I love her,
I think of her by seeing
and hearing, and tasting
and I am with her.
—Alberto Caeiro

Do you believe in her, the hive and the honeybee?
There is a beautiful love relationship that exists between the flower
and the bee. The bee sucks up nectar and covers itself with pollen,

gaining sustenance and nourishment from the parts of the plant pulsing with sexual, reproductive energy.

The gift of this love-making is honey. It holds the power of creation. It is prized and valued. The mystery of sexuality, creativity, and spirituality. Bees take us to the sacred, those places in life that should not be violated. Bees are a vital part of the mystery of life, art, and medicine.

Honey is divine. The living element of the sexual power of a flower is contained in honey. When eaten, it creates sensual pleasure and activates the connection that exists between sexual power, mind, and emotion.

Bees are tightly woven into European folk memory and mystical practices. Looking at images from ancient civilizations, bees are depicted as often as serpents. Coming forth from small, dark places at certain times of the year, they bear the gifts of sting and venom, as well as sweetness and intoxication.

HYMEN

Throughout time, women have been in service to the bees. Melissae is the ancient name given to women of the hive. Bees are part of an order of insects that have two pairs of membranous wings. Hymenoptera.

Few women know that a beautiful connection exists between this naming of the bees and the name of the thin piece of membranous tissue that surrounds or partially covers the vaginal opening. Hymen.

One of the sacred obligations of women is to be in service to the bees. We can call upon the same energies used by our foremothers. Chanting, overtone singing, and humming mimic the hum and drone of bees.

The drone of the bees in flight and the music of the hive can alter states of consciousness, as can the beat of a drum and the rhythmic gallop of a horse.

The next time you gather with a group of spiritual, earth-connected women, stand in a circle, hold hands, and hum like the bees in a hive. Keep it up, individually and as a group, loud and soft, fast and slow. Feel the vibration. Sense how quickly you, as well as the group, enter into an altered state. Allow yourself to travel through the worlds in the sacred dance of the bees.

SYMBOLISMS

Various ancient texts, the Bible included, make reference to "lands flowing with milk and honey." Both of these substances played a prominent role in ancient cultures and the expression carries distinct sexual overtones. Milk and honey are symbols of fertility and sexuality, the milk flowing from the body of the mother, and the honey from her sacred, venerated vagina.

Milk and honey speak to the prosperity of the land: healthy crops and thriving livestock. The well-being of the people. The health of the ecosystem. Good soil. Good water. Clean air. Green meadows. Abundant wildflowers.

Copious amounts of honey.

Milk was the symbolic and literal embodiment of nourishment, flowing forth from the goddess. Honey was called "the nectar of the goddess." When the land flowed with milk and honey the people were truly blessed.

Legends and stories tell us that in Britain, Ireland, and northern Europe, bowls of honey, as well as bowls of curds and cream, the richest parts of the milk, were placed outside the barns and dwellings as offerings to the fairies and the land wights.

THE MIRACLE OF HONEY

It takes approximately 550 worker bees, gathering nectar from two million flowers, to make one pound of honey. A single bee can travel up to six miles in one trip, visiting 50 to 100 flowers. Honey is the only food that is produced by insects and consumed by humans. It is a natural food made without destroying any form of life. It contains vitamins, minerals, amino acids, antioxidants, and enzymes. It does not spoil. In fact, honey found in Egyptian tombs is still edible.

Have you ever tasted single-flower honey? The honey most commonly sold in supermarkets is blended, heated, and filtered. It is consistent in color, texture, and taste. It lacks personality and uniqueness, like most of the food we consume today. Generic and sadly lacking in individuality.

The same is true of olive oil. Commercially produced oil is blended and lacks distinctive character. If you have ever had the good fortune of tasting oil that has been pressed from the olives of a single tree, then you know how different it is to taste a unique and singular olive oil. Several years ago, my friend and I visited an ancient man in a small village in Italy. He was the owner and guardian of an equally ancient grove of olive trees. He shared, with deep respect and delight, that he knew his trees so well that he could tell you which tree the olives had grown on simply by tasting the unblended oil. This same experience is true with single-flower honey.

Although honey bees visit many different species of flowering plants, they also exhibit floral fidelity, which means that a bee visits only one kind of flower on any given foraging trip. Floral or flower fidelity makes honey bees special. While many pollinators flit from one plant species to another, honey bees pursue flowers of a certain species. An entire foraging trip by a single bee will be spent on that single flower type. In fact, individual bees are likely to keep collecting the same pollen for many days.

The amazing result of this fidelity is single-flower honey, each one with its own unique flavor. Single-flower honey comes in a range of colors, textures and tastes. Acacia honey is almost clear. Buckwheat honey is dark brown. Light honey is usually more subtle in flavor and dark honey tends to be more intense. Single-flower honey can be thick to thin, granular or liquid, solid, clumpy, or chewy.

Whenever I teach the Bee class, I bring several jars of single-flower honey for the women to taste. At one class, a woman ate an entire jar of Manuka honey. For whatever reason, once she tasted it she became almost obsessed and couldn't stop until it was completely gone.

Female Sexuality

Honey has a sexual-spiritual connection with women. It is another name used for vaginal secretions.

Many stories found in folk lore and fairy tales allude to the fact that hallucinogenic and mind-altering substances were used not just in rituals but in everyday practices as well.

It is believed that women who served at the bee temples would insert into their vaginas substances such as herbs and salves that once absorbed into the bloodstream, would alter their state of consciousness. These ointments were made from hallucinogenic, psychoactive, or narcotic plants. Some of the herbs commonly used were henbane, belladonna, mandrake, datura, black hellebore, opium, and cannabis. Wolfsbane was also used. At the same time, the presence of these substances would alter the state of consciousness of the men who came to worship at the temple, because worship included oral sex with the priestesses; thus they consumed the honey of the goddess.

Legend tells us that witches could fly. It's possible that this belief came from practices such as those described above. These witches then could truly fly just like reindeer are said to fly after eating Amanita muscaria mushrooms. These mushrooms, with bright red caps that look like they've been sprinkled with rock salt, are hallucinogenic. Images and figures of flying reindeer and Amanita mushrooms are commonly prevalent at Christmastime.

Mead

Mead, an ancient fermented, alcoholic elixir, is both magical and sacred. Called ambrosia, nectar, or drink of the gods, it was most often reserved for the elect and initiated. Drinking it was believed to bestow the gifts of immortality and hidden knowledge. No wonder the gods sought after it.

In Norse mythology, mead was honored as a magical beverage that, when consumed, gave the gift of wisdom and poetry, and a connection to the gods. According to one of the sagas, Odin transformed himself into a snake so he could sneak into a cave where the giantess Gunnlod guarded the mead of poetry. He impregnated her, stole the mead, and fled.

Ancient spiritual practices commonly used natural substances to alter states of consciousness and attain levels of awareness and knowing. We still long for and seek altered states in order to connect with the deep things of life.

BEE PRIESTESSES

As women in service to the bees, we play a part in ensuring the fertility of the land and all that dwell upon it. We retain autonomy and control over our own sexuality and reproduction, including our blood. We carry into our hives the magic that lives in the flower, and this is contained in the honey we create. The consumption of honey creates a connection between sexual power, creativity, and spirituality. Therefore, the holy trinity of women can be found in the honey of the bees. It is no wonder that the bee is worshipped as a goddess.

Have you been called at this time to be in service to and in relationship with the bees?

Are you open and willing to accept such a possibility?

If you were in service at the temple of the Bee Goddess, what gifts would you offer up, not only to the bees, but also to those who came to worship there through you?

How would you use your body and your sexuality in service to the fertility and aliveness of the land?

Does the land you dwell in flow with milk and honey?

Do you have a special relationship with the number six and the hexagon, the shape of the honeycomb?

Artemis was called a bee.

Demeter was known as the pure mother bee.

Gunnlod was the guardian of the sacred mead.

Deborah was a bee priestess, a prophetess.

What name would you choose for yourself to honor your service to the bees?

THE QUEEN

Bees communicate with each other through dance. They navigate by the sun. Their presence and existence are vital to all life on Earth. A small hive can be home to as many as 20,000 bees. A larger one can house as many as 80,000. Hundreds of drones. Thousands of workers. But there can only be one Queen.

The drones' work is to mate with the Queen and each drone dies after mating. One of the jobs of the worker bees is to drive out drones who have not been in service to the Queen. They too die, outside the hive.

What is your hive?
Where is it?
Are you the queen?
Who is in service to you?
Who needs to be driven out to die?
If you are not the queen, how do you gather nectar?
What flowers are you gathering from now?
Which ones have you gathered from in the past?
Who are the drones, the workers, the larvae?
What is your honey and is your hive full?
Are you also the wax, the propolis, the royal jelly, or the pollen?
What feeds you through the long winter?
How do you become intoxicated?
What is the condition of your land? Does it flow with milk and honey?
What do you offer up to your gods?

Various women who have participated in the creation of this book and explored its questions have graciously shared some of their own musings, wonderings, and answers about the bees.

> *"What is my hive? Is it the place of buzzing harmony and throbbing problem-solving I seek/find as I explore my creative work? Is my hive my family? If I am the all-mother to myself, to my work and to my family, what gifts do I offer up? The gifts of my presence, accessibility and boundaries. Are these attributes of my honey? I have certainly worked hard to get to a place I can offer them with*

authenticity and in my truth. There is a piece of the hive life that I want to include here. The death of the drones. There are parts of me that are no longer needed to serve the greatest good. Now that I am using and learning boundaries, I am ready to sweep the bedraggled drone of fear out of the food stores in order to nourish the new birth of holding my place. I claim ownership of the last of my life. I am the author, the sovereign, buzzing and dancing with the all-mother of my life." –SUSAN, PARTICIPANT

"The questions and notes of this topic gave me a beautiful insight. By taking care of bees, I am not only serving the bees but through them I am taking care of our food and thus the people, the community.
I never saw it this way. The bee-centered approach of how to work and live with bees hadn't shown me, up until now, that I, as a bee priestess, take care of the people, too.
What I'm doing for the healing of bees is a healing of the land and all our relations here on planet Earth." –TINAH, PARTICIPANT

Are you a woman in service to the bees? Perhaps all of us should be. The number of honey bee colonies has dropped significantly since the 1970s. This is alarming. About one-third of the human diet is derived from insect-pollinated plants, and honeybees are responsible for 80 percent of this pollination.
The decline in honey bees has a direct and potentially disastrous effect on our food chain, hence all life on earth. We do well to pay attention.

TASKS

- Purchase some single-flower honey that is raw, unfiltered, organic if possible, and local. The best place to find this kind of honey is in a small natural food store, a local food cooperative, or if you are fortunate, there might be a local bee farm in your area.
- Buy some mead and see what it tastes like. Mead is one of the first fermented beverages, most likely older than beer. Commercial mead as sold in large stores is often heavily sweet-

ened, uses poor quality, diluted honey that contains added sulfites and lacks uniqueness. Look for mead made at small, artisan meaderies.

- Do some research on flower fidelity and how it affects the health of the bees.
- Do research on the health and medicinal benefits of honey.
- Gather information about the death of the bee population and learn how to protect and preserve them and their hives.
- Stories from times past, closely link bread with milk and honey. Milk is given. Honey is found. Bread is formed. You might wish to explore the significance of these three things in relationship to yourself as a woman and your relationship with your own sexual abundance.
- Are you being called to serve the bees? Do you resonate or hum with the name Melissa? This calling often happens to writers, poets, singers, women with the gift of knowing. Explore spending time out in nature by visiting places where bees are busy making love to life. Watch them as they visit each individual flower. Make time each day to hum. Eat honey daily.
- Create order in your home and life as a reflection of the beehive.
- Do research on the unregulated sources of honey as well as unregulated transportation and storage. Two disturbing facts. The global honey market is unregulated and cheap honey imported into the United States, mainly from China, is often diluted with sugar syrups. Honey is being transported in enormous metal tanker trucks where cross-contamination with possible toxic material can occur. Be sure to carefully read the labels regarding country of origin.

Water

Holy Water Sacred Wells

Wells are timeless, sacred places, full of legend and symbolism. The world over, sacred wells and springs are places of beauty, peace, and healing.

Water that flows from deep within the earth has always been considered a gift from the mother. It's a common, universal concept that wells are gateways to the spirit world, to the realm of the other-than-human, to the more than human.

What do you believe?
Are wells and springs gateways to other realms?

Water is part of an endless cycle of return.
All water returns to the ocean.
There is no beginning. There is no ending.
Vital.
Necessary.

When we forget that water is sacred, we forget how to live.
Water connects us to every living thing upon the earth.
We dwell in water inside the body of our mother. We are birthed into the world with a gush of that water. Our bodies are made up of more than sixty percent water.

We form in water, live in water, are birthed from water.
Once born, we cannot live in water, yet we cannot live without it.
It connects us to our spirituality, our sexuality and our creativity.

LOST CONNECTIONS

We have lost touch with our sources of water. For most of us, it is piped into our homes from places unknown where it is sometimes recycled and reused, over and over again.

Our water is no longer alive.

Imagine how your life would be different if you got your water from the village well or the local river or stream.

Imagine if you had an intimate relationship with the source of the water you use daily.

I recently attended a gathering of Grandmother Wisdom Keepers in the village of Helvoirt, in The Netherlands.

A question was asked from the audience.

> *"It used to be that almost every village and town in Europe was centered around a stream, a river, or a well, but now that is not true. Most of these water sources have disappeared. How can we reconnect with them, bring them back?"*

One of the elders from northern Sweden, Laila Spik, a Saami reindeer woman, answered.

> *"Plant trees. They know how to find the water that is hidden or has gone underground. Plant trees and then sit with them and let them tell you where the water is."*

THE CHALICE WELL

The magic and power of the Chalice Well in Glastonbury, England, has been documented for thousands of years. Due to the high iron content, the water from this well is reddish in color and is considered the blood of the mother. It is fed by a deep aquifer. Archaeological evidence present in the area suggests that the well has been in use for at least two thousand years, most likely longer. The flow of the Chalice Well is around 25,000 gallons daily and it remains constant through drought years, as well as years of abundant rainfall. Its temperature is a constant fifty-two degrees Fahrenheit.

Just consider what amazing conditions have to exist below the surface of the earth for such mystery to exist. Truly, it must be the magic of the spirits of the sacred well.

Have you ever visited the Chalice Well?

In recent times, Christianity has claimed it for its own, ignoring the ancient legends and stories that link it to the worship of the goddess. I cease to be amazed at how often and how easily people of British Isles and Northern European descent are led away from the wisdom, truth, and beauty of the old ways present in the land. Instead, they latch onto the legends and stories originating from the myths of the desert god brought to them by the conquerors. They disrespectfully rename the ancient, sacred, goddess sites.

SACRED WATERS OF THE WEST

Those of us who live in the Western States of the United States–Washington, Oregon and California–do not need to travel far to find sacred wells and springs. They are right here among us, numerous and scattered.

Goldmyer Hot Springs, Washington, is a beautiful, hot spring welling up from inside a cave. The water at the source is 120 degrees Fahrenheit. The springs are located at an elevation of 1800 feet and are guarded by an ancient forest with trees more than 800 years old.

The hot springs at Breitenbush, Oregon, were created thousands of years ago when the two great forces of volcanos and glacial ice met. These springs have long been used by natives in the area for healing and ritual purification.

Vichy Springs, California, is fed by naturally carbonated water that bubbles up from 30,000 feet below the earth's surface. The water from the springs maintains a temperature of around 90 degrees Fahrenheit and is said to be glacial water that has been there for more than 6,000 years.

What natural springs or wells are in your area?

Have you ever visited any?

AQUIFERS

Much of the earth's underground water is contained in aquifers, areas of permeable rock, or sand beds. The Ogallala Aquifer of the central United States is one of the world's largest. It underlies portions of eight states and contains primarily fossil water from the time of the last glaciation.

During the past few decades, rapid polluting and emptying of the waters from our underground aquifers have caused much concern.

The presence of glacial water in these wells and aquifers indicates that glaciers have melted in the past. Global warming and freezing are equal parts of vital earth cycles.

Is it possible that the earth, in all her wisdom, is causing and allowing global warming at this time so the polar ice caps can melt and refill these aquifers?

Water seeks its own level. Are some of the earthquakes and other global disturbances caused because we are emptying these reservoirs at an accelerated rate?

Is the ice melting and the earth shifting and adjusting in order to restore balance?

OFFERINGS TO THE WATER

People all over the world and throughout time have come to sacred wells and springs to be blessed, to be healed, and to make offerings to the gods, goddesses, and the spirits of nature. These offerings were sometimes in the form of small votive figures and, interestingly, the figures that have been found are always female.

What do you imagine is the significance of that finding?

In times past, things such as special stones, coins, jewelry, and weapons were offered up to the water in the wells. These items were not throw-away junk. They were valuable, costly, and special. The giving of offerings to sacred water is still practiced today. One well-known example of this is the tossing of coins into Trevi Fountain, located in the center of Rome, Italy, at the intersection of three streets.

Why would people toss things into wells, fountains, or springs?
Have you ever tossed anything into a well?
What significance did it hold for you?

THE SPIRIT IN THE WELL

"An old English folklorist told me once that nature spirits would live in a well, a spring, a lake or a grove of trees only so long as they were remembered and addressed respectfully. If the spirits were neglected, they'd leave the place; the land would feel soulless and dead henceforth. Remembering this, I dropped a pin into the brown water of Dupath Well. The well-house stands near the work-yard of a farm; I could hear the traffic of the roads nearby and yet somehow the spot still seemed quite peaceful, timeless, magical . . . and very much alive. I felt a little foolish saying "Thank you" right out loud — and I couldn't even tell you now who exactly I thought I was addressing there: a nature spirit, a well faery, a Celtic goddess, or the earth itself. And yet, as I turned to go, I'd swear that someone was listening."

–WOMEN AND FAIRY TALES, TERRI WINDLING

Wells, springs, and pools of water are associated with the Muses in Greek mythology. They were the goddesses of creativity, arts, and science. Their mother Mnemosyne was the goddess of memory. Memory gave birth to creativity.

In Norse mythology, a triple female being dwells beside three sacred wells hidden and protected by the roots of the World Tree. This ancient being, known as Nornir, is keeper and guardian of memory that bubbles up to inform the present. An active force of life lifts the sacred waters that hold all that is known and has been carried out in the past, filling the wells that inform the present.

Water holds memory. Frozen water, ice crystals, preserve and protect memory. As glaciers melt, stored memory is released back into the present. No matter the cause of the melting, long held wisdom is being released.

Much is written about holy waters and sacred wells in Celtic mythology, as well.

ONDINE'S CURSE

Undines or ondines are water spirits or water sprites. The word comes from Latin and means "a wave." In a German tale, known as *Sleep of Ondine,* a water nymph falls in love with a human and marries him. She discovers he is unfaithful to her so she uses her powers to place a curse upon him. This unusual spell does not allow him to rest. If he ever falls asleep again, he will cease to breathe. He is doomed. He must choose between sleeping or remaining alive.

Ondine's curse is a term used for a congenital syndrome which is a serious form of sleep apnea that can actually cause death. In medical literature, the term has been applied to numerous conditions involving breathing dysfunction.

It might seem like a stretch, but is there a connection between the current increase of people diagnosed with sleep apnea and our unfaithfulness to water?

Why are so many people prevented from sleeping?

If *undines* are water beings, is it possible that they combine to form water and, if that is the case, when we drink water are we consuming these beings, interacting with them as if taking communion? If this is true, how might this knowledge affect your relationship with water?

Could such a possibility open you up to new awareness and insight? How might this belief fit in with Masaru Emoto's belief that water responds to human suggestion?

Do the personalities and intelligences of these water beings actually *dwell in* or *are*, in fact, water? Do they *create* the crystals or are they the crystals that Masaru Emoto sees coming into form?

YOUR OWN SACRED WELL

Now is a perfect time to explore the meaning and presence of sacred wells and waters in your own life.

Explore the imagery and actuality of water as a keeper of memory and therefore a keeper of creativity.

What would it mean for you to go to the water to discover your own personal sense of meaning, aliveness and passion?

What is your sacred well?
How deep is it?
Is the water dark, clear, sweet, bitter? Full of silt? Polluted?
Does it bubble up or do you drop a bucket down?
What is the source of the water in your well?

By connecting with the waters that source our creativity and inspiration, we can begin to create lives that are in deeper attunement with our own needs, with our inner wisdom, and with our ancestors.

What are your primary sources of inspiration?
What kind of experiences do you find most fulfilling?
Can you think of a time in your life when you felt completely fulfilled?
Are there any experiences you would welcome into your life now?
Is there anything you would like to explore?
What would you say has been your greatest creation?
How do you access the waters in your sacred well?
Do you have a deferred dream, something you have been wanting to try, do, learn, or experience that you have been putting off, hiding, or denying yourself?
What is it?
Go to the water. Make an offering.

"This topic has more than anything given me a sense of wonder, and deep gratitude for something as simple as water welling up from the ground. How perfect our Earth is for life! How many wonders are kept beneath the ground but bubble up to the surface for sustenance... so incredibly beautiful...a topic to revisit and think about for a long time to come..." –LAUREN, PARTICIPANT

TASKS

- Write a story in which you imagine yourself living in a place where you collect your water from the well located in the center of the village. A gathering place. A communal space. A sacred place of water.

  Who are you in the story? Who do you meet at the well? How often do you go there? What do you talk about?

  What is your life like as a result of living in a community that formed around a central source of water?

- Set a goal that, sometime during the course of the next year, you will visit a sacred well or a sacred spring. Perhaps plan a trip or retreat around the journey. See what you can learn about the history of the waters there. Go beyond the usual tourist-type information. Dig around in different sources of information and look for clues. What were these waters called by the native people who honored them? Go there with the intention of meditating and connecting with the spirit of the waters. Be open to receiving the wisdom that is in store for you.

  What intuitive information, sensations, or experiences come to you?

  If it is impossible or a hardship to travel, then choose a sacred well or water source to research and explore as you can, then create a meditation around it.

  Create an altar or sacred space to honor the gift of water.

  Invite the guardian of the well to visit you and share her wisdom.

- Place bowls of water outside in the sunshine and place bowls of water outside in the moonlight. See if you experience any difference in energy, as well as taste, between them and compare them to water that comes from the tap inside your home.

- Do research on the source of the water in the town where you live.

- Dig around in the history of the Chalice Well. Explore possible names and legends prior to it becoming Christianized.

Water Meditation

Find a comfortable place to sit, either in a chair or on the floor or pillows. Remove everything from your lap.

Close your eyes gently and begin to breathe slowly and deeply, paying attention to your breath. In and out. In and out. With each breath you will feel more and more relaxed.

As you continue to breathe you will notice perhaps that there are sounds outside the room. You may notice that there are sounds inside the room. You may notice that there are sounds even inside your body. Just notice. And continue to breathe.

It is a warm spring day. The birds are singing. The flowers and trees are just beginning to bloom. You wander your way through a grassy meadow just behind your home. You follow the path to one of your favorite spots, the old well that is tucked away under the copper beech tree. You love this place. You have spent many hours at the well, and many magical and ethereal things have happened to you here.

You remember from early childhood that your grandmother spoke to you of the magic of the well under the copper beech tree. She had many stories to tell, not only from her lifetime but also the stories she heard from her mother and her grandmother.

This well is very special. The water is crystal clear and perfectly still, and when you sit beside it and gaze into the depths of its darkness, you can see.

You can see the past.

You can see the present.

You can see the future.

At times, you can even see the face of the guardian of the well, she who is looking back at you as you are looking down at her.

Today, you have come to the well with a special question, one that you have been pondering for a long time. You are ready now to stop thinking about it and allow, instead, the answer to rise up out of the well, from the depths of the water, and from the wisdom of the ancient guardian who dwells within.

You take your seat on the well-worn stones. You listen to the birdsong. You smell the sweet grass. You gaze. You allow your thinking mind to rest a bit, and you gently fold yourself into the magic of the water. You look with the eyes of your heart, and you listen with the ears of your inner knowing, and you wait. Finally, the answer you have come seeking bubbles up out of the water. You sit in silence, taking in the gift.

You remember. When the ancestors give us a gift, they always ask for something in return. You thank the keeper of the well and ask what gift she desires from you. You listen. You make your offering. You are content and at peace with what you have received, sourced from the dark, held safe in the water, and now gifted to you.

You find your way back along the path, back to your home, back to where you began. You have returned with wisdom from the sacred well. When you feel ready, open your eyes and return fully to your place.

To access all downloadable meditations, go to page 48 and scan the QR code.

Left

Two Left Hands

Ambidextrous.
Someone who can use both hands equally well.
Do you know anyone who is *ambidextrous*?
An interesting word of Latin origin.
Literal definition: right-handed on both sides or having two right hands.

If a person can use both hands equally well, why wouldn't we say the person has two left hands or was left-handed on both sides? The word for that is *ambisinistral*.

Does that word sound rather *sinister*?
It is, because the word *sinister*, also from Latin, means left, or on the left side.

Does this language bias rest in the belief that the left hand is somehow negative, bad, or of lesser value and importance?
Why is the left side of the body assigned to females?
Why are there so many negative expressions used to describe things that are left?
What does left have to do with women of the always?

LEFT-HANDED IN A RIGHT-HANDED WORLD

Do you know anyone who is left-handed? Perhaps a family member, a child of yours, a friend or even your partner.
Are you left-handed?
I'm not but I know firsthand some of the challenges and difficulties that lefties face. I have four siblings, two of them are left-handed. We often had to rearrange seating at the table to avoid a clash of elbows.

I grew up very much aware of right-handed scissors, right-handed can openers, right-handed power tools, and training manuals that only made sense if you were right-handed. Both my sister and my brother always complained about these things.

About ten percent of the population is left-handed, and although it can be advantageous in some situations, most of the time it causes difficulties. We live in a right-handed world. Most of us never give that a second thought, unless we happen to be left-handed.

NEGATIVE AND OFFENSIVE LANGUAGE
In addition to the practical challenges, there exists negativity and offensive meaning associated with left and being left-handed. It is written into our everyday language.

For example, being *dexterous* means you can do something skillfully; you are clever and adept.
What is not so obvious is the fact that the word *dexter*, coming from Latin, actually means 'of or on the right side.' The ability to do something skillfully is associated with the right hand.

The word *adroit*, is also Latin and means to lay straight, to keep straight, not deviate. According to the dictionary, a synonym of *adroit* is *dexterous*, which brings us back to the right hand.

Maladroit. The opposite of *adroit*. It means clumsy, bungling, ineffective, not right.

Gauche is an English word that means clumsy or socially awkward, lacking ease or grace, unsophisticated. The same word in French, *gauche*, means left.

Sinister is a word that makes most people shudder. *Sinister* gives the impression that something harmful or evil is happening or will happen, something wicked or criminal. In French *sinister* means left, or on the left side. Another negative word that means left.

Bend sinister is a term that is not very common. Most of us are not familiar with it. When used in heraldry, on shields and coats of arms, it is a band or thick line drawn from the upper left side of a shield, from the perspective of the shield bearer, down to the lower right side. A *bend sinister* on a man's shield meant that he did not have a father who claimed him, so he was claiming the right to his position by virtue of being his mother's son. This term is intriguing because it gives us a glimpse into how the word *sinister* is associated not only with the left side but with females as well. Not to be forgotten. *Ambidextrous*. Having two right hands.

Clumsy, Stubborn, and Awkward

Many are the stories told by individuals who were born left-handed and forced, maybe even shamed, into using their right hand in school, and often at home, as well. One woman in the *Two Left Hands* class shared her story with our group of women of the always. She was shamed by her teacher on her first day of school. She was made to stand in front of the class as an example while the teacher, with anger and venom, stated, "There is no such thing as a left-handed person."
This woman made a decision about herself, while still a child, that affected her most of her adult life.

Left-handed children are often called clumsy.
Of course it would appear that way because so many activities lead with the right hand, such as playing a musical instrument or sports. Left-handed children are often called stubborn, difficult, and uncooperative. Why wouldn't they be, considering they are being forced to use their right hand.
They are called awkward because they have difficulty writing within a system that favors the right hand.
They are singled out as problems because they must be given special attention for seating in the classroom as well as at the lunch table.
It's also said that left-handed children are slow to learn.
Would you want to go to school if you were terrorized, shamed, or even punished for being your natural self?

Or, even worse, what if you were told, as was the women mentioned above, that you do not exist.

It was a common practice in some religious schools, well into the 1960s, to tie children's left arms behind their backs, forcing them to function in a way that was unnatural to them.

BIAS FROM THE BIBLE

The Bible favors the right hand over the left hand, just as it favors the male over the female. And we must not forget that the Bible is still read by millions of people globally and believed to be the Word of God.

Jesus is said to be seated in the heavens at the right hand of God. When the day of judgment comes, it is said that the sheep will be placed on the right and the goats on the left. The sheep gain everlasting life. The goats are sent off into destruction. The right side indicates a place of favor and privilege. The left is associated with negativity and punishment. According to tradition, there were two thieves crucified alongside Jesus. The good repentant thief was on his right. And no surprise, the unrepentant, wicked one was on his left.

The right hand is associated with God and the left with the Devil, both in religious art and religious education. During the European witch hunts of the sixteenth and seventeenth centuries, being left-handed was considered damning evidence of demonic possession. And even within modern witchcraft and Wicca, the left-handed path is associated with so-called black magic and dark practices.

In his book, *The Dragons of Eden,* Carl Sagan states:

> "In the worldwide associations of the words 'right' and 'left' there is evidence of a rancorous conflict early in the history of mankind. What could arouse such powerful emotions?

ARTISTS AND SHAMANS

Based on archaeological evidence found in cave art, it is believed that a high percentage of ancient artists were left-handed, and it is quite possible that these artists of the past were shamans in their communities, spiritual leaders, magicians, or medicine healers.

If it is true that these individuals tended to be left-handed, then it is not a surprise that the conquering Christians would capitalize on this fact, using their left-handedness as just another way to malign their beliefs and rituals as being from the devil.

THEORY OF EIGHTS

In his book, *Sex, Time and Power*, Leonard Shlain posits a thought-provoking argument he calls the Theory of Eights. He states that consistently, in the male population, about eight percent are left-handed, which represents roughly one out of twelve men. He believes that this trait, along with two others, represents a constellation of genetic adaptations that enhanced the success of the original male hunting bands.

It's a thought-provoking discussion. I highly recommend the book. What unique purpose did left-handed women serve in these ancient societies?

The author didn't explore that question.

BEFORE CLOCKS

Once upon a time, before clocks, before the expressions clockwise and counterclockwise, people spoke of turning to the right or to the left, using the body as a reference point.

In the Northern Hemisphere, if you face the rising sun and track its arc across the sky, you would turn to the right. Even though it is rarely used today, the word deosil (or deiseil) means southward, sunward, or to the right. The word widdershins means to go in a direction opposite to the usual, the usual being the apparent course of the sun. The opposite to the usual means you would be turning to the left.

Some of you might be familiar with these words, as they are often used in the pagan community.

The term left-hand-wise was connected to the country folk, the heathens. According to the Christian church, these folk went in the opposite direction, the direction that belonged to the Devil. In fact, the actual left hand was considered to be unclean and turning to the left came to be associated with bad luck.

All of this turning sunwise changes if you live in the southern hemisphere, south of the equator, say in Australia. Turning to the left would be turning in the same direction as the sun because the movement of the sun across the sky, from east to west, is a northward curve when you live south of the equator. Sunwise is not always to the right, nor is it always clockwise.

Some cultures, both ancient and modern, begin their day with the setting of the sun. They also begin their year at harvest, during the fall rather than winter. And they write from right to left, hence beginning their books from what we might consider the back. Life for them, in general, is pretty much counter to the right.

THE PHYSICAL BODY

The body is asymmetrical on the inside. For example, the heart is on the left side of the body and the liver is on the right.
There are differences between the left side of the body and the right, the left side of the brain and the right. And it is a pretty common practice to describe the right side as male and the left side as female. This has apparently been the case for centuries, because we can see in ancient art that male symbols, such as the scepter, are held in the right hand, and female symbols, such as the orb, are held in the left.

Have you ever given thought to the possibility that associating maleness with the right side and femaleness with the left could perpetuate abusive and negative attitudes toward women?
What might be some dangers inherent in using male and female to describe the two sides of the body?
Could we find a better way to speak about the left and right?

No matter how you feel about it personally, the fact remains that bias exists around the left, in language, society, religion, and culture. And, if the left is still considered bad, negative, evil, unclean, etc., why would we connect it to female?

To The Right

What does it mean to you to go to the right?
To turn to the right?
Or to go in the right direction?
Why do the words correct and right mean the same thing in English?
Do you, or have you ever, thought of right as a direction in relation to the sun?
Why do clock hands circle to the right?
Do they turn to the right in relation to us as the observer or do they turn to the left in relation to the clock?

What do you do in your life that could be considered the right direction?
Is there any direction you are headed now that you would like to change and do something opposite, or just different?
Would you like to go to the left?
Are you on any detours, or have you deviated from a course or path?
What norm in culture, society, life, or religion are you going against or turning from in the opposite direction?

Day-to-Day Changes

Doing things differently can feel awkward, strange, clumsy, or even wrong, yet it is a simple way to experience some of the challenges faced by left-handed people.

Here are a few suggestions of simple things you might try to experience a turn to the left.
Drive or walk to your usual places using a different route.
Sit in a different seat at the dinner table.
Move the furniture.

Put your silverware or cutlery in a different drawer.
Put your clothing in different drawers.
Change the uses of various rooms.
Back into places instead of backing out of them.

Make a list of things you already do in your life that you consider to be left.
Non-traditional religious or spiritual practices
Controversial political beliefs
Non-traditional sexual views and activities
Alternative health care choices
The way you earn money
Housing options

Consider some things you might be willing to try that are different from your usual way of doing things.
Go on vacation alone, without your family.
Stop celebrating holidays with your family.
Stop celebrating holidays altogether.
Buy gifts only for yourself at Christmas, things you really want.
Wear shoes or socks that don't match.
Spend part of a day, or all day, using your non-dominant hand.
Attend a different church.
Eat dessert first.

Name one thing you might be willing to try that is extremely opposite from your usual. This doesn't mean you will do it, just that you might consider doing it. Thinking about such a thing might cause anxiety or, perhaps, a bit of a thrill.
What would it take for you to do it?

The biggest challenge we face when we discuss and explore the provocative and stimulating topics in each chapter is how to integrate what we are learning and discovering about ourselves into our daily lives.
How can we use it?
How can we live it?
How can we talk about it, or do we talk about it at all?

Are you stretching yourself?

Do you question yourself about the *why* or *why not* of things you are doing?

If things remain comfortable, safe and familiar, then it is quite possible nothing is changing, or at least very little.

Do you take anything for granted?

Do you do things a certain way because they have always been done that way?

Do you answer questions in a certain way because you are repeating what you have heard?

Embrace the idea of going in a different direction, whatever that means for you, and see what can happen in your life when you are willing to go against the accepted norm and turn in a way that is not right.

Ask yourself what you want your life to be or look like in five years. Remember, if you plant corn, don't expect carrots. Expect corn. If you want your life to be different, you must go in a different direction and be willing to do things differently.

FINDING BALANCE

Women do not fit in.

We do things differently.

We are mysterious, puzzling, and difficult to understand.

We may be viewed as uncooperative, stubborn, or even clumsy.

All of this comes from a right-handed, male-dominant perspective.

Is being left-handed similar to being disabled?

Is being left-handed comparable to being female in a male-fixated world?

A suitable question might be, do we want to fit in?

We currently live in a society where enlightenment and higher consciousness are upheld as the ultimate experiences, things to strive for and attain, a society where light is considered good and godly, better, and more spiritual.

It is no wonder then, that those of us who are sourced from the dark, who find nourishment and connection in the depths, and wisdom in death and the underworld, have difficulty fitting in.
We are women of the always living left-handed in a right-handed world.
It's a challenge to be a woman in a world that has forgotten who we are.
We are brazenly turning in the wrong direction no matter what hemisphere we live in.
We are doing things differently.
We live a circular life in a linear world.
We live a lunar life in a solar world.
Women of the always are *ambisinistral.*
We have two left hands.

TASKS AND EXPLORATIONS

- Select something you would be willing to do in the opposite way or take in a different direction. Write it down. Include the date you are willing to start. If you are working through this book with a friend or a group, you may want to share with each other what you are willing to change. Speak about the difficulties or challenges each of you might face.

- Think about a direction you're going in which you feel you can't do anything differently because of limitations, or limiting beliefs, a place where you say "I can't" or "it wouldn't work." Consider the story you tell yourself about why you can't change. Create a new story. Commit to doing something new and different.

Grey

Shades of Gray

IN THE MIDDLE

When it comes to hair, turning gray is usually a gradual process. We might have heard stories of people whose hair turned white or gray overnight due to fright or shock, but in all likelihood, that's not possible.

For most of us, turning gray looks like this...

At first, a few gray hairs appear. They can be pulled out one or two at a time. I am pretty sure most maturing women do that at least once or twice, but after awhile pulling out the gray ones could cause you to go bald. Going gray, for me, was a slow and subtle process, probably because my hair was blonde. It started when I was in my early forties. It was happening during a time in my life when I was in the middle, not young, not old, just in the middle. Maybe that was a shade of gray!

Being in the middle.

How many times have you been in the middle?

While developing this topic, I asked several women what they thought shades of gray meant.

One woman said, "Indecision. Shades of gray is about not being able to make up your mind."

Another said it was about balance, "The willingness to be in constant motion between one extreme or the other." She added, "I think it might be possible that shades of gray means you don't have the answer and that what is right or wrong, good or bad, always depends on the circumstances and perspective."

What do you think of when you hear shades of gray?
How do you define gray?

TWO SIDES TO THE COIN

There's a common saying, "There are two sides to every coin."
However, this viewpoint tends to be extremely limited in scope.
Invariably, there's another alternative. A third way. This alternative
was well represented in ancient times by the image of the triple
goddess. The hag sat at the crossroads and reminded travelers that
there was a third way.

Do shades of gray only exist between established opposites?

Is the so-called gray area actually the third way?

Is the third way the one so often overlooked in solving problems,
finding answers, and making decisions?

EXERCISE

Take a situation you're currently facing, one that requires making
a choice or decision.

Write out briefly what the situation is.

Then write down one possible choice or decision you could
make.

Next write down a choice or decision that would be the opposite
of the one you just wrote down.

Then select a choice or decision that is the opposite of the
second choice but not the same as the first choice.

Write that down.

Doing this exercise can be difficult. You may have to stretch yourself, be creative, go beyond your usual way of thinking. You may
find that the third choice is one you might not have considered
before doing the exercise.

Did the exercise take you into a gray area or into a shade of gray?

OPPOSITION AND DUALITY

The word opposition comes from French via Latin and means
to set against.

It can be defined as the act of opposing or resisting, the condition
of being in conflict or antagonism, or even something that serves
as an obstacle.

Western culture, for the most part, is founded on fundamentals that are basically dualistic. Dualism is a system of good-bad, hot-cold, right-wrong, black-white. It is a system of opposites, a system of *either-or* that is not very accepting of *as well as,* or *in addition to.* Is it possible that sometimes there is no right or wrong but a full spectrum of possibilities? The word spectrum is a good choice here. It means a broad range of varied but related ideas or objects. Think about hot and cold. In theory, we know that hot and cold are opposites, with the extreme edges being boiling and freezing. But when does *hot* become *hot* and *cold* become *cold*?

The answer is relative.

The same is true when mixing white and black paint together.

At what point does the mix become gray?

The answer is relative.

If you do the exercises suggested below with a group of people, you will get all kinds of answers to the questions, "What is gray?" or "What is warm?"

IN BETWEEN OPPOSITES

In two large containers, pour in room temperature water until both of them are half full. You could say they are both halfway filled with gray. If you start adding boiling water to one of them, at what point does the water become hot? If you have your hand in the water and I also have my hand in the water, we might not agree on when it becomes hot.

Try the same experiment with the second container, but this time pour in ice-cold water. At what point does the water become cold? This exercise offers a good example of shades of gray.

Try the same exercise by mixing black paint and white paint together. You can use watercolors, acrylics, or oil paints.

On a large piece of paper place a blob of black paint on one edge and a blob of white paint on the other.

Take a brush and begin slowly mixing the black paint into the white, or the white into the black.

At what point have you created gray?

How did you determine that?

I have used this experiment in numerous classes, and each time we create as many different shades of gray as there are people doing the task.

AMBIGUITY

Shades of gray is that place of uncertainty between black and white, or hot and cold.

Ambiguity means uncertainty or inexactness of meaning. It can indicate a lack of decisiveness or commitment because of an inability to make a choice or decision, or refer to something that is vague or obscure.

Some people have a high tolerance for ambiguity. This tolerance is often connected to creativity, psychological resilience, and tolerance for diversity.

Other people may have a low tolerance for ambiguity. They tend to be characterized by precision, efficiency and slowness to change a rule.

We can make lists of characteristics that tend to divide these differences in tolerance, and at the same time, we need to consider all the variations that exist in between.

Consider situations in day-to-day life where high tolerance would be preferable to low tolerance, or vice versa.

How do you view your tolerance for ambiguity?

Are women more or less tolerant of ambiguity than men?

What experiences influence your answers?

ONE RIGHT ANSWER

The idea of having one right answer is a dangerous way of thinking, including the idea that all the other answers are wrong or incorrect.

Here's a simple exercise you can use to explore what this looks like.

What is half of thirteen?

I've used this question many times when teaching classes.

The usual answers are quick and simple.

Six-and-a-half, which can be written out in words, or look like 6.5, or 6 ½, or 13 over 2.

Then things seem to come to a halt.

But I continue. What if half of thirteen is four?

Is that possible?

If we spell the word out with letters, then T H I R T E E N has 8 letters, and half of the word thirteen is four letters.

You might have assumed I meant half of thirteen using numbers, but I didn't specify.

The answer depends on our perspective, assumptions, or expectations.

Were we looking for numbers or were we looking for letters?

Depending on who was asking the question, your answer could have been right or wrong.

Think about children. They're creative. They rarely assume things. They like to explore.

There's still another possibility.

Half of thirteen is four, but it is also eight.

Have you heard of Roman numerals?

Have you ever seen them or do you use them yourself?

In Roman numerals, the x is ten and a single vertical line is one.

So, thirteen written in Roman numerals is XIII.

If you draw a horizontal line through the middle of XIII you get VIII. V is the Roman numeral for five so the upper half of XIII is VIII, which is eight.

Simple example. Yet how often do we say we believe something is the truth, or the right answer, or we repeat something because we believe that whoever said it had authority?

It is always good to ask questions.

Could the same story have different meanings?

What perspective could I step into that would allow me to see differently and step away from the belief that there is only one right answer?

The *one right answer* conditioning is what we have been taught in school, at home, and through religion.

It is written in the book.
It is carved on stone tablets.
It is the truth.

Where in your life do you look for the one right answer?
When are you willing to mix the black and the white, the good and
the bad, the up and the down, the sacred and profane?
What is your shade of gray?

GRAY AREAS

Some of the material that follows will bring up questions and issues
of morality, politics, and religious beliefs. Some of the questions
and suggestions might make you angry or indignant.

How often do you stop to consider if your response to a situation
or your belief about something is really yours, or if it just automatically comes from what you have been taught is right and wrong,
or good and bad?
How much of what you believe to be acceptable is based on your
position within your family, your community, your culture, race,
or country?

The intention of this discussion is not to decide what is good or
bad, but rather to stir the pot and see what rises to the surface.
There is more power in the questions than there is in the answers.

Countless scenarios can be put forward that represent extremes
or certainties, and the questions allow for consideration of the
multitude of options that exist in between those extremes.

What if your actions would cause the certain death of one person
but would save the lives of many?
What if your inaction saved the life of one person but caused the
death of many?
What are all the options in between?
How do you choose?
What would you consider?

How do you know when to do nothing and when to do something?
What if your choices were not in agreement with someone else's?
Who gets to decide who is right?
What shade is your gray?

Either-or thinking contributes to separation and division when we become positional and in opposition to one another. Being willing to explore gives us insight and flexibility.

In matters of life and death, good and bad, sexuality, healthcare, religion, and spirituality, are you able to be flexible? Where are you intolerant?

OWNERSHIP

There is power in owning property, having money, and social status. There is also responsibility and accountability.
Is it acceptable or morally right for parents to pass their wealth and property on to their children as an inheritance?
Is there a conflict with human welfare when the rich get richer and the poor get poorer?
Should wealth be reshuffled?

For instance, if you bought a home and then later sold it for a good profit, should you be allowed to keep the profit or should you be forced to share that money with others?
Is this the concept behind communism?

How would you feel right now if the government came to you and said you had to move out of your home into a smaller place because your current dwelling was too large for you and your family? Or what if the government told you that you could stay, but you had to have another family move in and share the space with you?

What if this happened even if you owned the home?
What if this happened even if you worked hard to have such a place to live?
Where do you draw the line?

TOO MUCH

The issues around shades of gray often come into play around money and wealth.

It's not uncommon to hear people rail against the wealthy. They have too much. They have more than they need. They should be giving it away, doing something noble with it, sharing it...

Is there a right and a wrong here?

What are the extremes and who decides what is gray?

I often bring up this kind of issue in a class setting. I ask the women to tell me how many pairs of shoes they own. I have never heard anyone say only one pair.

I then ask how many pairs can be worn at one time. The answer is always one.

If you have more than one pair of shoes, you have more than you need. And for sure, having only one pair means you have more than many people who have none.

Imagine now that I come to you and say that, because you have more than you need, you are required to give them away, and I even tell you which pairs you have to let go of and who you have to give them to.

How is this situation any different from you deciding that someone has too many houses, or too many cars, or too much money?

Is it possible to have everything?

Is it possible to have nothing?

Who gets to decide what is too much and what is too little? Is that person you?

How comfortable are you with having or owning things?

How comfortable are you with the truth that you will always have more than some people and you will always have less than others?

Does that make you a shade of gray?

PARASITES, WOLVES, AND DAMS

Do you get angry at the parasites in the world, whether it's cockroaches, viruses, welfare fraud, or drug dealers?

Are you any different or are we all the same?

Are you a parasite on the mother we call earth?

Do you participate in her destruction by using resources that are obtained in harmful, damaging ways?

Do you generate toxins, waste, or garbage?

Do you participate in activities that bring you gain, but cause harm to others?

Is it acceptable to kill wolves and mountain lions if they pose a threat to your livestock and your livelihood?

Is it acceptable to kill wolves because you cannot live with them?

Is it acceptable to restrict the movements of bison in some areas to save the land for cattle grazing?

Is it okay to build dams that destroy or damage wetlands, fish habitats, ancient burial grounds, or people's homes?

What if we need the dam to generate electricity?

What if we justify the existence of the dam because it provides electricity for thousands of people when, at the same time, it is destroying the lives of thousands of other beings?

What noble cause would justify the extinction of wildlife or the destruction of the wilderness?

What is your shade of gray?

China, Recycling, and Experiments

If you were born into a technologically advanced part of the world, you enjoy inherent advantages that are envied and resented by people in other parts of the world. In large part, your life situation is an accident of birth, not unlike your religion.

What responsibility do you have to ameliorate, make better, or improve the life circumstances of others?

Do you buy goods that are made in China?

Do you agree with the work ethics and labor laws in Third World countries?

Do you recycle and at the same time drive an SUV?

Are you willing to pay higher prices for handmade goods or locally produced items?

Do you participate in the perpetuation of extremes, or do you live in some gray place in the middle?

Is animal testing okay?

If so, when and for what reasons?

Medicine. Health. Cosmetics. Research. Science.

Who decides? How do you decide?

Are animals less valuable than humans?

How are we any different than Hitler and his experimentation on humans?

GRAY GRAY GRAY

What information do you trust?

Do you believe something just because it is said to be scientific or medically proven?

What do you know that you are absolutely sure of?

Is there life after death?

Does the earth revolve around the sun?

Do you believe in evolution or creation?

Is parthenogenesis possible in humans?

Do you believe in magic?

Do you believe in electricity?

Do you believe in the existence of things that are invisible to the human eye?

Should people be required to take an intelligence test before they are allowed to reproduce?

How do you feel about irresponsible reproduction?

Should disabled, genetically deformed, or mentally challenged people be prevented from having children?

Should we try to keep people alive at all costs?

Should we use extreme measures to support the life of premature babies?

Do we have the right to terminate life with an abortion?

What is your black?

What is your white?

What is your gray?

NIMBY

Would you be okay if your town or city decided to locate a garbage dump in your neighborhood?

Do you generate garbage?

What if your town or city decided to build a freeway, expand an airport, or construct a recycling center next to your home?

Do you drive? Do you fly? Do you recycle?

Would you sign a petition protesting the building of a prison or a drug rehabilitation center in your neighborhood? Are these institutions necessary?

Would you sign a petition objecting the erection of a cell phone tower next to your home?

Do you use a cell phone that requires the existence of cell phone towers?

Is it okay for these things to be near others, but not you?

NIMBY is an acronym used in the real estate industry in the United States.

It stands for "not in my backyard."

Do you have a NIMBY attitude or stance on anything?

LIFE AND DEATH

Finding balance between life and death touches on a gray area, the issue of making decisions, often around the need to sacrifice one life for the good of others. Our ancestors in the far north faced daily issues of survival in harsh climates with limited fuel, shelter, and food. This often meant they had to make hard choices about whether or not a weak, sickly, or deformed child would be allowed to live. These decisions were also necessary decisions with multiple births. Necessity might demand parents to offer up the child or children to the earth by placing them outside to die. Such practices also took place when the older family members offered themselves up in death so the rest of the family could live.

What are your thoughts and feelings about such choices?

Does necessity demand we make such choices even in this modern day and age?

Have you ever had to face such a decision?

Where in your life are you living in opposition?

Where in your life are there shades of gray?

Do you have a tolerance for ambiguity?

Do you find yourself caught between two choices, often opposites?

Are you rigid in the extremes of right and wrong?

Have you ever considered the third way?

As a woman of the always do you live in the middle?

What are your shades of gray?

Crossroads

The Triple Goddess
at the Crossroads

A crossroad, by definition, is a road that crosses another road, or a place where two or more roads intersect. This intersection creates a gathering place, literally and metaphorically.
A center of sorts.
At the crossroads, the only person you ever meet for certain is yourself.
You are standing at one right now.
At the crossroads might be a surprise.
Are you ready to meet the triple goddess?
She dwells there waiting for you to remember her.

Many of us think of the crossroads as a place where one stands to make a decision or a choice, usually one that is important or significant.
What would it be like to think of it also as a place you have been before, as have countless others, and now you are all returning with great wisdom, experience, and knowing, and you are all gathering together o share?
In this chapter, we will be exploring different realities, the crossroads, and the triple goddess, weaving them together for ourselves as we go back to the ancient myths and stories from the time when the goddess at the crossroads was honored as well as feared.

The crossroads can represent many other things.
    A place to part ways
    A place to meet
    A place to gather again

A place to pause
A place to sacrifice or offer propitiation
A place of revelation
A place of manifestation
A place to cross over or pass through
A place to work magic in the silence of the dark

SACRED TO THE TRIPLE

In ancient Greece, crossroads were sacred places, often dedicated to Hecate, the crone aspect of the triple goddess, Hebe-Hera-Hecate. Hecate was the triple mistress of three worlds, Heaven, Earth, and the Underworld. Cult images of her and altars dedicated to her were placed at the crossroads. She was depicted as having three faces or even three bodies.

She presided over birth, she preserved life, and decided when it should end. She ruled the Underworld in her form as Crone, Hag, or Old Woman, and her worship was celebrated in caverns, graveyards, and crematoriums as well as at the crossroads. Hecate was also called the goddess of the third way. Those who passed by offered her money or items of value. Springs and wells were often found at the crossroads. Hecate was considered to be a goddess of these as well.

TREVI TRIVIA

According to the dictionary, the word *trivia* is Latin, plural of *trivium*, a place where three roads meet, an open place, a public place, hence common or a commonplace. Today, the word is more often used to mean something that is unimportant inconsequential, or ordinary. Yet Trivia was the Roman name for the Greek goddess Hecate.

Of course, the coming together of roads or their splitting off in different directions is commonplace and perhaps ordinary.

But are we overlooking something?

Why did the ancients connect a triple goddess to such an ordinary place?

Why would they build shrines to her, make offerings there, and place things of value, money included, into the well located at the place of three things coming together?

Is there something important here for us to consider?

Did they know something that we have forgotten?

Did they value and honor the role that a triple female being played in making decisions and choices?

Did they honor the third way?

Did they always offer something in exchange for protection as they traveled, as well as a safe return?

TREVI FOUNTAIN

The custom of honoring the triple goddess who dwells at the crossroads and guards the springs or wells that are often found there can still be seen today in the practice of people casting coins into Trevi Fountain in Rome, Italy. The fountain was built at a commonplace, at the juncture of three roads, a crossroads sacred to the triple goddess, whose name is Trevi. According to the most current information, approximately 5,000 Euros a day are thrown into the fountain. That amounts to about 1.9 million dollars a year. The coins are gathered each night and then distributed by the Roman Catholic charity, Caritas, to food banks and social programs as well as to support a low-cost supermarket in Rome. Not many tourists, or locals for that matter, are aware of the fact that they are participating in an ancient custom of offering things of value to the triple goddess at the crossroads, asking for safe return home.

As a traveler, when you come to a crossroads, you have to choose, and the choice you make always determines how your life unfolds. Crossroads might be commonplace, an ordinary occurrence, but the choices you make are never trivial.

Does the current definition of the word trivia in some subtle way discount, disregard, or disrespect the wisdom and protection granted to us when we stop, acknowledge, and make an offering to the triple goddess at the crossroads?

NORNIR

Norse mythology tells stories of a triple female presence, Nornir. Her names are Urd, Verdandi, and Skuld. Urd is the oldest, she who remembers all things. Verdandi is the keeper of the present moment that is constantly changing. Skuld is the future that comes into form out of necessity.

The Norns dwell in the roots of the World Tree, guarding and protecting it. They also guard the three sacred wells that bubble up and murmur among three enormous roots.

The Norns have been here since before the beginning. They dispense their wisdom to both humans and the gods. In fact, the gods cannot make any decisions or render judgment in any way unless they gather first at the wells to hear the wisdom of the Nornir and be granted their permission.

Here we have another ancient story about the significance of triple female beings. She is the beginning. She is the ending. She is everything that happens in between, over and over again.

The *maiden, mother, crone* description is often used to describe the triple goddess.

The maiden is viewed as young, innocent, full of newness and vitality.

The mother is the maiden matured, ripe. She is seen as protective and nurturing, as well as fierce and decisive.

The crone is the old woman who carries the wisdom of life. She holds our hand as we walk toward death.

Such descriptions bind her to female biology.

She is also likened to the ever-changing, shapeshifting moon. Fully shining. Half. Fully in shadow.

MYSTERY

As discussed in the Gray chapter, it is best if we don't try to categorize everything. The circle of life is fluid, blending, combining together. It's not a straight line with clearly marked stopping points along the way. All of life is present at all times, in each of us. The moment we are born, death is on its way.

The mysteries of the triple goddess are evident in the spirituality, sexuality, and creativity of women of the always.

All the eggs your mother would ever have were in her ovaries when she was a fetus growing in the womb of her mother. The egg that formed your body was present inside the body of your grandmother. All humans come from an egg that was inside the mother, who was inside the mother.

That is the triple goddess at the crossroads.

DIFFERENT WAYS

There are several different kinds of crossroads. You could come to what is called a T-intersection. That means that the road does not continue forward but stops or dead ends, forcing you to go to the right or to the left. Or, you could turn around and go back the way you came.

A crossroad could have several roads going off in numerous directions, rather like a roundabout.

The crossroad can be the shape of the letter Y. This is commonly described as a fork in the road, the splitting of one main road into two.

It is also known as bifurcation.

In science, in a dynamical system, bifurcation accompanies the onset of chaos. Chaos, meaning complexity rather than disorder.

How complex is it for you when you can no longer continue straight ahead on the path you've been on?

In the past, when someone came to such a junction, they would stop and divine with the triple goddess at the crossroads, asking for her guidance, wisdom, blessing, and protection.

What do you do?

When was the last time you made an offering to the triple goddess at the crossroads before making a decision?

What do we miss when we forget there is a *trivium*, a third way?

Christianity brought with it an evil plague, the belief that death was a result of sin and disobedience. Because the triple goddess represented the endless, natural cycles of birth, life, and death, she was viewed as evil, wicked, and dangerous.

The patriarchal rulers of the conquering desert religions tried to stamp out the worship of the triple goddess, but they could not and have not. They tried to replace her with the trinities of male gods who know life and death, but can never know birth. She alone embodies the endless, natural cycles of birth and life, death and decay.

EXPLORATIONS

Is the triple goddess present in your life?
If yes, where? If not, how can you bring her in?

Think about something in your life right now that you're just tolerating, putting up with, or allowing. Go to the crossroads and offer it to the triple goddess.

> What would the maiden say about it?
> What would the mother say about it?
> What wisdom would the crone offer?

Think about a situation where you lack clarity. Take it to the crossroads.

> What would the creatrix, the female creator or originator, tell you?
> What would the preserver have to say?
> What message would the destroyer give?

Another way to use the wisdom of the triple goddess is when facing a major or difficult decision, or when you find yourself trying to weigh two options. Take the situation and look at it one way, then turn it over and look at it in a totally different way, and then turn it over another time and consider it in a third way, a way that is the opposite of the opposite.

CANDLE RITUAL

Many women have found it deeply meaningful to do a ritual, calling in the wisdom of the triple goddess, using three candles on the altar. Possibly black, white, and red. You can, of course, use any colors you want. Sit in the dark with only the light of the candles. Listen. What message does each one have for you?

Crossroads Meditation

Find a place that is comfortable and safe, a place where you will not be interrupted. Settle in and close your eyes. Begin to breathe slowly and deeply, paying attention to your breath, paying attention to your body, and allowing yourself to sink into relaxation. In and out. In and out.

Imagine you are alone on a road at night.
There is an autumn chill in the air. It is dark.
There is no moon, but somehow you know the path and you are not afraid to walk it.
Far ahead in the distance, you see the ever so slight glow of a fire.
You know the glow. You recognize it.
You continue to walk the path toward the glow. It becomes brighter and brighter until you finally reach its source.
You have arrived at a crossroads, and there in the center, you find an old woman.
She is squatting on her hunches, close to a fire.
A tripod stands over the fire.
A heavy chain hangs suspended from the tripod.
The chain is hooked to a large black cauldron, a cooking pot.
The cauldron is steaming and bubbling.
The old woman stirs it occasionally, and you notice her spoon is actually a bone.
You are not afraid. You know this old one.
You have seen her before in her other forms, the young one as well as the mother.

She recognizes you. She knew you were coming, but she did not get up. She continues to stir even as you stand beside her.

Finally, she turns her head and looks up at you.

You see in her face all that has gone before and all that will come forth. She speaks, and she asks you a question, in a voice that sounds like the flapping of a bird's wings and the grinding rumble of an earthquake.

And in your heart, you already know the question before she asks it, and at the same time, she already knows the answer before you speak.

She continues to stir.

The listening and the speaking are the same things.

The question and the answer are the same.

She continues to stir.

You turn and face the direction you know you must take.

You begin to walk along that path.

Slowly and with sure foot, you find your way back, back into your body, back into yourself, back into the place where you started.

It matters not which path you chose. It will take you home.

You are back into the present moment.

You know that when you met the old woman at the crossroads, you passed between the veils. You crossed a threshold.

You saw the past and the future.

Slowly open your eyes and close them.

Slowly open your eyes and close them.

Slowly open your eyes and close them.

When you are completely ready, open your eyes and leave them open.

You have returned.

You find yourself again at a crossroads.

To access all downloadable meditations, go to page 48 and scan the QR code.

Hearth

Tending the Hearth

Winter was a challenging time for our ancestors in the North. A time of dark and cold. A time when bones rattled, teeth chattered, the soil was frozen, and the water was ice. Nature surrounded them with reminders of the endless cycles of life and death, the endings and beginnings of all things.

The hearth was the heart of home, the source of heat and light, the place where clothing was dried, and food was cooked. But more than that, the hearth was a threshold, a liminal space that provided an opening or passage between the outside and inside. It was a place where the ancestors came and went and made themselves visible and felt.

Tending the hearth was a sacred ritual. It was a matter of life and death.

Who is the keeper of the hearth in your home.

HEARTHS

"A life without love in it is like a heap of ashes upon a deserted hearth." –ANTOINE DE SAINT-EXUPÉRY

A deserted hearth is a powerful image. You can feel it in your body. What is it like to enter a home where the fire has gone out and the hearth is cold?

What feelings do visitors have when they enter your home?

What does it feel like to you?

Tending the hearth, whether literal or spiritual, requires focus, attention, and vigilance. In fact, the origin of the word focus, from Latin, means hearth fire, the focal point of a home.

What is the focus of your life?
Where do your fires burn?
What needs tending?
What has gone out?

Winter in the northern hemisphere was a time when the focus and attention of ancient people turned indoors toward matters of home and family. Winter was also the time for storytelling.

Most activities centered around the hearth, the gathering place within the home, the place where food was prepared and served, the place where matters both mundane and spiritual were discussed, and in most cases, the hearth was the source of light and heat during the long winter months. In some ancient dwellings, the hearth was in the center with a vertical pole that held up the roof and protruded through the smoke hole. In some of the old dwellings I have visited in northern Sweden, the central hearth contains ledges and alcoves where elders dozed, and children napped. In extremely cold climates with long, dark winters, wise families lived communally, sharing limited fuel, sharing hearth space, which could mean the difference between life and death.

The importance of the hearth was more prominent during the winter months, but it held a place of honor throughout the entire year. It was the duty of the hearth keeper to bank the fire at the end of the day in such a way that it would not burn out during the night. Prayers were offered, and songs were sung, asking the ancestors and unseen ones to provide protection. It was the hearth keeper's task in the morning to coax the fire back to life, and it was considered most inauspicious, even dangerous, to have the hearth fire go cold.

In some countries like Ireland and Scotland, people live in homes where the hearth fire has been continuously burning for hundreds of years.

Tending the hearth, however, has a much broader meaning than just the literal daily experience. In most modern-day homes, the hearth and its fire are no longer the focus of attention. Our heating systems are hidden, our stoves and ovens are ignored when not in use, and fireplaces tend to serve more as decoration than function. Our dwellings have changed, our lifestyles have changed, but we humans have not. We still require light, heat, and food. We thrive upon companionship and a sense of wellbeing, so hearth-based beliefs and customs can still have relevance and value for us today.

We can strike a match, flip a switch, or use a lighter to start a fire. This was not always true. The ability to start a fire was considered a sacred act, a ritual in fact, one in which the gods, the ancestors, and the fire beings were called upon to assist and bless. There was acknowledgement that one could not perform this magical function alone. The honoring of the fire was as vital as the fire itself.

If you don't have a wood stove or a fireplace, you might want to designate a central area in your home where you can gather and engage in meaningful activities and conversation, perhaps around a table with a candle burning. Consider creating a place in your home, an altar, shrine, or alcove for a hearth guardian. Inviting a fire guardian or spirit into your home and honoring it can contribute greatly to the quality and tranquility of the life within.

WORK OF GREAT VALUE

Home is the foundation of security for individuals as well as societies. Our mental, physical, emotional, and spiritual health are all dependent upon a love-filled, smooth-functioning home. Clean sheets, delicious food, a peaceful haven, all these things inspire a sense of safety and wellbeing. The hearth was revered and honored throughout history, for it was the hearth that turned a dwelling into a home. The thought of tending the hearth might bring to mind the expression *woman's work*. This expression encompasses all the domestic chores that have been traditionally associated with women: cooking, cleaning, spinning, weaving, and child rearing, as well as hearth keeping. Unfortunately, the expression *woman's work* has come to carry a negative connotation.

The more we return to honoring the value and importance of hearth tending, no matter who does it, the deeper our understanding will be of the truth that it was and still is the work of tending the hearth that makes all other work possible.

GODDESSES OF THE HEARTH

> "Hestia, in the high dwellings of all, both deathless gods and men who walk on earth, you have gained an everlasting abode and highest honor: glorious is your portion and your right. For without you mortals hold no banquet where one does not duly pour sweet wine in offering to Hestia both first and last."
> –HOMERIC HYMNS 29:1

Hestia is a Greek goddess who has always been connected to the hearth, the center of every ancient Greek home. She never left the home's threshold. She ruled over domestic life. The Greeks believed that Hestia, whose name means hearth or fireside, dwelt in the flames of every altar and fireplace.

In modern times, some women might find her dull, placid, boring, rather like a spinster aunt or old maid sister who never ventures into the village or the wide world.

We should not be fooled. Hestia is fire, and it is her spirit that has the ability to hold fire in a tranquil manner so humans can use it. She is not tempted by the thought of power because she is stronger than the weapons that can only be forged by her power. When someone chooses to serve Hestia, they are in service to her fire.

Hestia held a place of honor greater than the gods of love and marriage or even those of fertility and harvest. She was the center of all houses and buildings. Every family started their day with prayers to her as the hearth fire was stoked and ended with prayers as the fire was banked. She was honored as the inventor of architecture and a patron of these arts, and her symbols were the circle and the perpetual flame.

Brigid is another honored and revered hearth goddess, beloved by the Celts. Traditionally, she was associated with healing, poetry, and smith craft, inspiration and all skills associated with fire. The fires of creativity and sexuality, the fires of home, and the fires of the forge are all seen as the same in the presence of Brigid.

The sword was forged in the hearth of the goddess herself. It is believed by some that women who were in service to Brigid and her fires initiated young men into manhood, not only as warriors but sexually as well. Through the ritual of sacred, sexual union, Brigid's creative fire and parts of the ancient mysteries were transmitted. She tended the fires of love as well, for a home filled with love is indeed a home with a glowing hearth fire.

In Norse mythology, the goddess Frigga governed the hearth, home, love, marriage, and childbearing. Habondia, an Anglo-Saxon goddess of hearth and home, ensured the fertility of the marriage bed, tranquility among family members, and the blessing of domestic chores, especially the magical arts of cooking, bread baking, and brewing.

OUT OF CONTROL

When fire spirals out of control, it can undermine entire civilizations. There is wisdom in anchoring its energies in the central hearths of homes and sacred places within cities. We all must eat, so we gather daily in the presence of fire. We all need the warmth and light that fire brings to the heart of a family.

The hearth was such an honored and sacred place, no young bride would venture with her husband into their new home without carrying a coal or an ember from the hearth fire of her own family. It would be used to start the hearth fire in their new home.

Another practice in ancient times was for the fire in every home in each new colony or village to be started from a coal or ember that had been carried from the fire of the founding city's central hearth. This tradition kept the connection between all those with related origins or shared pasts.

THE ABSENCE OF SACRED HEARTH BEINGS

Modern societies have lost connection with the sacred beings of the hearth. We eat fast food in noisy restaurants, or worse yet, we eat in our cars. Instead of honoring the sacred fire at the heart of our homes, we sit in front of the television or computer screen, staring unconsciously while eating our food. Add to that the more recent addiction to cell phones at the table.

We are no longer connected to each other on the inside of our homes, but rather connected to others on the outside. Our homes are no longer safe havens of rest and respite. Instead, they have become home to all manner of strangers, violence, atrocities, and faraway places, way beyond the heat, warmth, and light of our hearth fires.

In fact, most of us have no anchors in the simple, earthy, daily rituals. Hestia, Brigid, Frigga, Habondia, to name a few, weep as the hearth-fire flame grows dim.

What a great and terrible psychic cost are we paying for removing ritual from hearth and home and replacing it with fast food and electronic devices?

What are some symptoms of the absence of sacred hearth fire in our society?

Where is this absence evident in your personal life?

One of the challenges we face is finding a way to balance and temper the overwhelming need for speed in so many activities. We no longer feel the need to pray or to call in the blessing of the gods because all we have to do is strike a match or flip a switch.

One of the ways to bring sacred hearth fire back is through ritual. The external world of work and responsibility must be combined with the inner work of hearth tending and family-relational union.

Have you ever been in a situation at work, in a gathering, or within a group dynamic outside the circle of your own home and family where you could have benefited from support by calling upon the ancestors and the spirits of the hearth?

Hearth Heart Earth Home

What is the heart of your home? And where is it? Do you practice any rituals around the fire that burns in your home's center?
Who or what has taken the place of the ancestors and guardian spirits of your hearth?
Who has taken up residence in your home, demanding tribute?
Is it your television?
Your computer?
Your cell phone?

To be sure, modern technology and secular culture have changed our relationship with home, but perhaps even more so is the fact that, for the first time in history, more people live in cities than in rural communities. Few of us still live on land where our ancestors lived, worked, and were buried. Many of us have moved again and again and again. In some ways, we have lost our connection to our hearth as well as the earth and the land on which we live.

When was the last time you gathered around a fire, fireplace, hearth fire, or wood stove and sat in silence with others, watching the flames and listening to the wood crackle and hiss?
Can you do this with a central candle perhaps, or in another way that symbolizes the same experience, even if you do not have a fireplace or wood stove?

Women of the always are hearth keepers, and hearth keepers are keepers of the home. Someone who tends the spirit of the home is a keeper of the heart of the home as well. It is a safe haven, a place closed off from the outside world, a place of peace and rest. Home is a place of hospitality. The energy in our home, around the hearth, affects our state of mind, the peacefulness of our heart, and the peacefulness of our family.

If your home is full of clutter and junk, where is that energy reflected in your life?
If your home is full of strife, where else in your life do you see evidence of the same?

What are some things you might wish to do to honor the hearth in your home?

KEEPERS OF THE HEARTH

Set the intention of having regular hearth time.

Ask your family to share in this, contributing ideas and suggestions.

If you don't have support for this, you can do it yourself.

As keeper of the hearth, you would ask for the hearth space to become sacred, keeping it free of outside influence.

Remember that your hearth is a place of hospitality.

Who might you consider inviting to share in your wealth and prosperity?

Who do you know who might not have a place to go for sharing hearth space?

Turning to the wisdom of the runes and their connection with this topic, Othila is the rune of ancestral home, and is associated with the hawthorn, a tree that holds special healing powers as a heart tonic. Our ancestors knew the connection that existed between the home, the hearth, and the heart. When you lose connection with hearth tending, you suffer illness of the heart.

When you move, do you carry with you the coals of the hearth fire you are leaving behind so you can start the fire in your new surroundings?

What would such a ritual look like?

Even in our transient culture, homes have a hold on us. The places we live have an impact on our lives, and the houses we yearn for reveal something of our inner nature. This is heart and hearth longing.

Do you consider yourself to be a person who tends the hearth?

How do you do that?

Do you have a sacred relationship with fire?

Have you ever thought about the connection that exists between your hearth fire and sexual passion, or the fertility of your family and your land?

Where might the fires have gone out in your body, your home, your life?

Do you observe a separation between fire in your home and fire outside your home?

LIMINAL SPACE

Another aspect of the hearth is in connection with liminal space and liminal experiences. Liminal means a threshold, or the place between two different planes of existence.

The hearth is a liminal space. It provides an opening or passage between the outside and the inside. In some traditions, such as the Celtic, the hearth was the place where the ancestors came through into the home and made themselves visible or felt. It held the energy of all the elements: the fire, water, earth, and air. These, too, connect us with the seen and the unseen.

HEARTH BUNDLE

How might you use a hearth space or a hearth altar to connect with other realms of being, as well as with your ancestors?

Some indigenous traditions include the practice of carrying what is called a medicine bundle or, in Peruvian practices, a mesa. It is a portable altar used for healing, ceremony, and ancestor connection. Could you create a hearth bundle, a bundle of special items you carry with you in your daily travels, things that connect you with your home, your hearth, and your heart?

It could even be a small pouch you wear around your neck.

Women of the always are hearthkeepers. We are in service to one of the most vital roles in human existence.

Hearth Meditation

For this meditation, you may find it helpful to cover your head with a scarf or a shawl. Have a candle and a lighter or matches ready for when you have finished.

Find a place that is quiet and peaceful, a place where you will not be disturbed or interrupted.
Make sure you are warm and comfortable.
Close your eyes when you are ready and begin to take long, slow breaths, in and out, in and out, paying attention to your breath and your body. With each breath, relax and allow your mind to soften.

Imagine yourself in a comfortable chair, drawn up close to the hearth fire. You have a shawl wrapped round your shoulders; a woolen blanket laid across your lap. Your feet are snug in your warm, woolen socks tucked inside your shearling slippers.
Everyone in the family has gone to bed, and you have been sitting here alone for a long time, listening to the sounds of the house as it creaks and groans, settling in for the night.
You are listening to the sounds of the fire as it crackles and hisses, softly gazing into the flames, watching them dance, some blue, some red, some orange, and slowly, as the peat has burned down, the flames have become less and less until there is just the glow of the embers.

For you, this is not the end of the day but rather the beginning. You are the sacred hearth keeper of your home, and your day begins at dusk. This quiet time is special and vital for you, for it is in the flames and the fire and the silence that you connect with your ancestors, those who have gone before, those who have kept the fire going in this same hearth for hundreds of years. It is here that you also connect with your sacred hearth guardian, keeper of the flame, keeper of the fire of life that burns within your body as well as in your home.

Much is asked of you. Much is expected.

You are the one who, at the end of the harvest, takes stock of what provisions are in the larder and the pantry.

You are the one who must keep account of how much fuel there is to provide heat and light for the family.

And it is you who must prepare for the long, cold, dark winters as well as times of drought and pestilence.

You are the one who pays attention to the turning of the wheel of the seasons.

You are the one who cleans the house from top to bottom, marking the cross-quarter points between each solstice and each equinox, clearing away those things which are no longer needed, making way for what is coming into form.

In all of this, you call upon your guardian of the hearth to bless you in your activities, for the work you do is vital to the survival of the entire household.

Slowly, you rise up from the chair and bend over the hearth. Using the fire poker, you gather all the still-glowing coals and smoldering peat, and cluster them together as close as you can in a circle, and then you cover them carefully with the ashes, making sure you leave space for air. You are banking the fire for the night. You must not smother it. It is dangerous for it to go out.

Singing quietly as you engage in this timeless ritual, you carry out this sacred obligation. There must be live coals in the hearth come dawn.

You are singing to your ancient hearth being, asking for her blessings. When you are finished, you lean your poker up against the stone. You turn and walk toward your bed, and climb in. You gently drift off to sleep, knowing that your hearth guardian will come and keep the coals alive.

You will look for her footprints in the ashes in the morning.

As if in a single beat of your heart, the dawn arrives, yet in your sleep, you have traveled far and wide. Half asleep and half in dreams, you rise up from your bed and carefully, in the half-light, you find your way back to the hearth. You rekindle the flame and use it to light a candle. As you do, you ask for the blessing of the ancient hearth keeper upon your house, your home, your family, your land, and your people.

You also ask for her blessing upon something special that you desire and are longing for in your heart. And you ask that she burn away any obstacles that might be in your path. You look down at the hearth and you see her footprints in the ash. She has visited during the night.

You thank her as you sit again in the comfy chair beside the hearth fire. You begin to pay attention to your breath, the slow in and out, the rise and fall of your body. You pay attention to the place where you are, and when you are ready, you slowly remove your veil and slowly open your eyes, and with a soft gaze, you glance around the room.

If it feels right, you may wish to light a candle to honor the guardians of the hearth fires, to honor your home and your family, to honor yourself and your dreams.

To access all downloadable meditations, go to page 48 and scan the QR code.

Veil

When the Crone Pulls Back the Veil with Her Crooked Finger

The breeze at dawn has secrets to tell you.
Don't go back to sleep.
You must ask for what you really want.
Don't go back to sleep.
People are going back and forth across the doorsill where
the two worlds touch.
The door is round and open.
Don't go back to sleep.
—RUMI

Once, not so long ago, people believed that places, times, and events existed where the mysterious and the ordinary touched each other, and the curtain between the spiritual and the material was so thin you could see through it. It was easy to see into the other side. It was easy to cross over the sill. It was also spoken of as the time when the veil was thin.

For those of us who live in the Northern Hemisphere, the thinning of the veil can be strongly felt at the halfway point between the autumn equinox in September and the winter solstice in December. This time is celebrated as Halloween or the Eve of All Hallows.

In order to understand this expression, this thin place, you must come from a spiritual rather than a material perspective, a perspective which allows you to sense the existence of a world beyond what we are able to experience through the five senses.

This thin place can indicate a time, an event, or a unique space where our seen and known world comes near the realm of unseen others. They seem to touch each other. A thin time, event, or place allows for the connection of these two realms to be effortless and ephemeral. It can be sensed, felt, and experienced.

A thin place is where the worlds meet, the seen and the unseen, the known and the mysterious.

There are thin places and thin moments, thin things and thin locations.

This thinness goes beyond the boundaries of thinking, time, and space.

BEYOND THE VEIL

There are Others who live and exist beyond what we as humans consider the ordinary. If you have been raised in a climate of monotheism, such a notion can be frightening, or perhaps even denied. Unseen beings cannot be simply relegated to the realm of angels, demons, and a singular god. Such an oversimplification is both disrespectful and ignorant. There are gods and goddesses, land wights and mound dwellers, ancestors and grave guardians.

We have forgotten that there are entire worlds, realms of experience, unseen places where all manner of beings dwell, beings that are not and never have been human and are certainly not in the category of angel or demon.

It is time for us to remember that there is not just one god, but many, not just a singular, all-encompassing spirit, as is so often spoken about in the New Age community, but many spirits, none superior or inferior, just individual and unique.

It is human arrogance to deny the existence of beings who have dwelt in locations and places far longer than we have, whose presence is often ignored or demonized.

Why would we be so quick to imagine that we have the power or even the right to clear space, or smudge things away with a wave of smoke or incense, when we are dealing with beings much older than we are, perhaps more powerful and in all likelihood, who have been in the space long before we came on the scene?

A Thin Time of Year

For those of us who live in the Northern Hemisphere, this thin veil time of year, autumn, is an ending and a beginning. We enter into the dark half of the year, the season of frost, fallen leaves, and bonfires.

The veil is thin.
The door swings open.
It is summer's end.
It is the time of the ancestors.
It is the time of mystery.
It is the time of the dark.
It is the time of separation.
It is the time of death.
It is the time of allowing.

All things must die.
It is the time for us to align with the cycle of death.
It is the in-between time when our ancestors and the beings of the other worlds pass easily and effortlessly back and forth across the threshold, back and forth between the veils.
In pre-Christian Northern Europe and the British Isles, it was a custom to light bonfires on hilltops this time of year. Perhaps they served as reminders for the people that the gift and presence of fire was a necessity for continued life through the long, dark winter.

The Old Woman

It is not surprising that the ancient ones started their days and their years with darkness. It is the dark that was there from the beginning and will be there at the ending, which is also the beginning, for the light comes forth from the dark, only to be extinguished. All things come forth from the dark, the fertility of the womb, the soil, the cosmos. We all must touch and embrace death and darkness in order to remain in balance. This is why we must honor the crones, the hags, the stone mothers, the ice mothers, and the bone mothers, all our ancestors, and the endless cycles of death and life that have no beginning and no ending.

Death is connected to fertility because it is the rot and decay of death that allows for new life. So, honoring the hag is the only way to ensure the return of spring. We have to kiss death, embrace it, so that something new can come forth.
People have forgotten this truth, and they don't even realize it.

When the crone pulls back the veil with her crooked fingers, what do you see?
What does she see relative to you?
Are you willing to honor old age, death, dying, rot, and decay?
How do you do that?

In Ireland, this dark time of year was the time when the new king had to embrace the sovereign earth goddess, thus ensuring that the land would prosper and produce in the coming spring. But the one he had to kiss was not the lovely, fresh, and youthful maiden of spring. No, he had to turn and embrace, accept, and kiss the old woman, the so-called hag, for it was she who had matured and ripened during the year and was now in the process of dying. She held the seeds of new life.
If the soon-to-be king refused her or was repulsed by her, he would fail the test and could never attain the throne. Often, such refusal was a death sentence for him.

It is only by embracing death, the old, and the dying that we can truly understand the gift of life. It seems that very few men today could pass this test. They are not strong enough to be rulers in their own lives when they are so easily fooled by appearances and seek only the young and pretty.

Do you know any men who would fail the kingship test because they don't know how to kiss the hag?

This is just one of the things that is revealed when the crone pulls back the veil.
What part do we as dark moon women, as women of the always, play in this ritual?
Have we believed the lies of eternal youthfulness?
Do we pretend that we are not growing old?
Do we dishonor and push away, as so often the men do, the old woman we must become?
Have we forgotten that death is the beginning place of fertility rites?

THE SACRED YEW

There was an interesting custom in the British Isles that centered around the sacred yew tree, a tree of life and death, a tree that gives off vapors that are mildly hallucinogenic. The branches of yew trees grow up and then curve down, growing back into the ground. They form enclosures around the trunk large enough for people to gather in. In these enclosures of ancient yew trees, rituals of birthing, sexual intercourse, and dying occurred, often all at the same time.
Is this a part of deeply rooted wisdom we have forgotten?

The crone or hag aspect of the sacred female is present in the form of the triple goddess, who is found in so many of the earth-based, spiritual traditions. She rules over winter, the time of the dark, of fierce storms and shrill winds. She rules over death. She is terrible to behold when she pulls back the veil between the seen and the unseen and opens the gates to let the floods pour forth. Ignore her. Disrespect her. Dishonor her. Deny her. You do so at great peril. Youth obsessed, take heed.

BELIEFS ABOUT THE DEAD

In the pre-Christian, Germanic/Norse worldview, the boundaries between the self, the environment, and death and life were blurry.

Parts of yourself served different functions and went off in various directions at the time of death. Some part of you lived in the mounds, the earth, the place of horizon where the sun disappeared at the end of each day, and the place where we buried the dead.

The part that lives in the burial mounds is familiar and recognized, and this is the one who is called an ancestor, the one we can connect with and who communicates with us, the living. There is another part that is called the hamingja, something rather like luck, that seems to be a being all by itself. It follows along with families and often is reborn into a family member, especially if a new baby is given the name of the ancestor. There was also belief in the presence of a fylgja, a word that means follower which was seen as something similar to an animal spirit (not necessarily an animal guide) that greatly influenced a person's character and personality.

Throughout time, there have been and still are countless beliefs about death and dying. None of them are true. All of them are true. It is important to be open to different ways of thinking. Life continues on, but not in the simplistic way that so many speak of when they use expressions like "life is just a transition" or "only the body dies." Rather, it is about the eternal process, the endless cycles in which all that we are, all that anything is, continues on as parts, nourishing and feeding the whole, always being reused.

THIN PLACES ON THE EARTH

Throughout time, people have acknowledged thin places where the mysterious and mystical happen. They often marked them with mounds and stones. Some thin places have their own markers, things such as sacred wells or springs, or a hill or high place. Such places transcend the senses and the boundaries of space and time, and if you are someone who has had the good fortune to stand in such a place, you no doubt have experienced communion and connection with those who have gone before and those who live beyond the veil.

In ancient Ireland, it was believed that people who passed through the veil and were taken into the land of the fairy could return to the world of humans as poets and storytellers, seers and prophets. The sacred mounds and stone circles were believed to be doorways where the gods, and spirits, and humans could pass back and forth between this world and the other.

For some of us, this is still true. It's not just ancient history. Passing through the veil is about connection to such holy places and the power of transformation. The more often you allow yourself to experience such things, the easier it will become.

> "We gave ourselves up in old times to mythology, and saw the Gods everywhere. We talked to them face to face....
> Even today our country people speak with the dead and with some who perhaps have never died as we understand death; and even our educated people pass without great difficulty into the condition of quiet that is the condition of vision."
> –WILLIAM BUTLER YEATS

As we become more aware of how thin and permeable the veil actually is, the more we will begin to have a sense of connection and relationship with all life. Perhaps the crone will pull back the veil for you, using her bony, crooked finger, and give you a glimpse of the mystery.

LIMINAL OR THRESHOLD HAPPENINGS

Liminal space is that space of the in-between. It is the moment of sunrise. It is the moment of sunset. It is those times when one thing is ending and another is beginning, and it is that exact instant, that blink of an eye, that beat of your heart, when it is not one thing or the other, it is neither. It is the split second of ending and the split second of becoming.

The veil is thin when a woman bleeds.
The veil is thin at the moment a woman gives birth.

The veil is thin with the last out breath of death.

The veil is thin during the sexual act of intercourse, for there is an entering and a surrounding. There is a leaving upon each other the essence of what was inside and now has become outside, and at the same time, left inside.

How would you describe the difference between a thin place and a thin moment?

The Hearth

The hearth is a doorway, a place where the veil is thin. The hearth is an altar, an actual threshold within the heart of the home. There is magic in the hearth. It is the place of fire within the home that holds an opening to the outside. It is a place of alchemy where the elements are mixed and married together. The fire and the air. The water and the earth. Air is necessary for feeding the fire, and it is the element through which smoke moves. Water is present in the kettle or the pot, and the earth is present in the turf, or peat, in the wood and coal.

Do you have a hearth space in your home, a place where the veil is thin?

Halloween or the Eve of All Hallows

Very few practicing Christians give much thought to the origins of the holiday called Halloween. To most of them, it's just a commercial event that marks the beginning of the winter holidays. Parents allow their children to dress up in all manner of costumes, some horrifying and frightening. Children wear masks and clothing that looks as if they are missing limbs and dripping blood. There seems to be a strong presence of violence mingled with the smell of death and decay. Spectral forms of ghosts and goblins, the undead or the long dead, decorate yards and pathways, windows and gates, together with gravestones, skeletons, and skulls.

What do such images and practices teach our children about the ancestors and their place of honor?

Why is this holiday celebrated at this particular time of year?

What are its origins?

What is the meaning and energy behind it?

How does the current commercialization of this time of year actually dishonor the dead?

It quite obviously did not originate in Christianity. In fact, its roots are much deeper and much older. They come from a time and a place when the people of the land, the pagans, knew and understood that the Eve of All Hallows was a liminal time of year, a threshold time when the veil was thin and the spirits of the dead, as well as all manner of beings, could easily pass between the worlds. The power present in the celebration was so strong that Christianity could not remove it from the lives and psyches of the people.

Why was the Christian Church not able to eradicate such a celebration, a practice that seems to be rooted in evil and demons and perhaps devilry?

Because it holds the ancient truth of death.

Death is not always a result of violence or torture.

Dying from old age is beautiful.

Do we teach our children about that?

Do we teach them to remember and respect our dead, asking them for guidance, assistance, and support?

Do we embrace that truth ourselves?

Or do we dishonor this time of year with cartoon images of old women and pointed black hats, plastic bones and tombstones, and sickening amounts of candy?

PERSONAL EXPERIENCES

What are your personal experiences with passing through the veil?

Are there any particular places or locations where you find the veil to be thin?

What are your beliefs about the Otherworld?

Are you afraid of the dark or of the other side?

How has this information been forgotten or hidden, and what value would there be in bringing it back to common awareness?

ALTARS AND RITUALS

Recognizing when and where the veil is thin would be one of many ways to reconnect with our ancestors. They have much to teach us, and they are longing to do so. For those of us who live in the Northern Hemisphere, the end of October and beginning of November is a perfect time of year to create ancestor altars and engage in rituals and ceremonies that support us in reconnecting, remembering, and reclaiming our own traditions. Perhaps creating a celebration where you invite the ancestors to join you, preparing a meal, and setting out food and drink for them to enjoy.

Remembering your ancestors does not mean that you have to know their names or know who they are. You don't need to worry about that. They know you. And often when you begin to work with them, they will come forward and tell you their names. Don't be surprised if some of them are very, very ancient, having lived in their northern areas at the time of the great ice.

As a woman of the always, what does it mean to you to pull back the veil, or pass through it?

What is your relationship with the crone, hag, old woman?

What is your relationship with growing old and dying?

What deep-rooted wisdom have you forgotten or has been forbidden to you up until now?

How might you live your life differently now that you've reconnected with this forgotten wisdom?

As Rumi's poem says, *"The door is round and open. Don't go back to sleep."*

Veil Meditation

Imagine you live in a small cottage out on the moors, perhaps England, Scotland, Ireland, or Wales. Or some isolated place farther north.

Summer has ended; it is autumn.

Most of the leaves have turned color and have fallen.

The air is different. There is frost at night. Everything is dying.

You have kept track of time by paying attention to the ever-changing phases of the moon.

The moon will not be visible in tonight's sky. She is dark.

She is the dark moon closest to the halfway point between autumn equinox and winter solstice.

You have prepared yourself.

This is the time of year when the veil is the thinnest; perhaps there is no veil at all. It is the time when you can not only *feel* but also *see* the ancestors in the realm of the Others.

This is the time of the threshold, and tonight, just at the moment when the sun sinks into the earth, you will set out on the path to the sacred grove of yew trees, where you will step inside the womb of the most ancient of trees in the grove.

It is a holy place where birthing, and dying, and the creating of new life have all occurred.

This is a sacred place, an enclosure created by the root-bound branches of the ancient yew tree.

Tonight, inside the womb of this sacred tree, you will connect with your ancestors, those in your lineage who have passed through the veil.

It is here that you will experience your birthing into the coming new year, the coming dark of winter.

You ponder this magic as you wind your way along the path that leads to the sacred grove.

You know the path, and yet each time you walk it, it is new.
The sky is almost dark now, and you hurry along, both excited and afraid.
There are spirits about this night that are often bent on mischief.
Arriving at the grove, you walk slowly toward the most ancient tree.
You bend down low, crawling between the branches that are rooted into the earth. Once you enter the center of the enclosure, you can stand upright.
And as you do, you look around and bow slightly to the being who is the tree.
You take in her presence.
You place your cloak on the ground and sit down, ready to receive all that the tree has to give to you and ready to give all that the tree asks in return.
Some of your ancestors have joined you.
You sit in silence and darkness, listening to your breath and to the breath of the tree. In the darkness, you sense the presence of a small stone on the ground in front of you.
You hear a whisper that tells you to pick up the stone and turn it over.
You do so, ever so gently.
There is a message written on the underside.
You realize that in the dark you cannot read what is written, but you do not need to.
You already know what is there.
You have heard it in the silence of the tree.
It is a message from one of your ancestors.
There is much that has been written on the stone.
It is exactly what you need to know at this time.

You stay inside the tree for the entire night, listening, remembering.
Time passes quickly and time passes slowly, and soon you sense the dim light of the coming dawn through the thick overlay of the branches.
You rise up, still holding the stone.
You wrap yourself in your cloak and, bending low, you move through the opening out into the new day.
You slowly find your way along the path back to your cottage.

As you gently push open the door, you find yourself back at the place you began.

You take a long, slow, deep breath in and release, and as you do, you slowly open your eyes and then you close them. You take another long, slow, deep breath in and release.

You slowly open your eyes, and then you close them.

You do this several times, each time gaining more focus.

You breathe.

And when you are ready, you leave your eyes open.

You still have the stone.

It is blank now, but you remember.

To access all downloadable meditations, go to page 48 and scan the QR code.

Endings

Endings and Beginnings

"There will come a time when you believe everything is finished. That will be the beginning." –LONELY ON THE MOUNTAIN, LOUIS L'AMOUR

"It is the nature of beginnings that something new is started which cannot be expected from whatever may have happened before. This character of startling unexpectedness is inherent in all beginnings."–HANNAH ARENDT

"You're searching, Joe, for things that don't exist; I mean beginnings. Ends and beginnings—there are no such things. There are only middles."–ROBERT FROST

"If we have been pleased with life,
we should not be displeased with death,
since it comes from the hand
of the same master." –MICHELANGELO

How do you know when something has ended?
How do you know when something begins?
Is there a difference?
Have you ever been in a place in your life where you were not sure?

What began for you during the last year?
What ended in order for it to begin?
What ended for you today?
What began?

FEELINGS

Take a moment to consider how opposite your feelings and thoughts can be.

In one instance, you may be devastated or overwhelmed by the ending of something.

In another instance, the end could actually bring great joy and relief.

You may grieve deeply at the beginning of something, or you may be inspired.

There can be a great deal of sadness, depression, and grief, a sense of loss, anger, even rage that overwhelms when something ends. The same emotions and feelings can just as easily arise when something begins.

And you can experience joy, happiness, delight, or a sense of peace and calm at the beginning of something just as easily as you can at the ending.

Not everything in life is happy, nor should we try to pretend it is. We don't need to always be looking for a silver lining, the good side, the positive, the sun shining through. It's vital that we allow ourselves to feel whatever we are feeling and not try to fix it or whitewash it or try to make it pretty.

There is much written about being happy, looking for the good, being positive, searching for the blessings or the gifts, but such thinking often causes us to bypass the truth of an experience. There is also the strong possibility that if we do not try to find the good, the happy, or the positive, we will be judged, criticized, or even shamed. Sometimes we do this to ourselves.

Life is made of endings and beginnings.
Feel whatever it is you are feeling.
No need to apologize, justify, explain.
Sometimes there is no upside, only pain and sadness.
Perhaps what matters most is that you allow yourself to have the experience by allowing yourself to have the feelings.
When you don't allow yourself to feel, eventually you become

numb. If you stop yourself from feeling sadness, grief, anger, rage, regret, eventually you will no longer be able to feel anything, not even joy, happiness, celebration, and love.

Do you associate negativity with endings more often than with beginnings?
If so, why do you think you do that?

The Beauty and the Challenge of the Circle

"The world is round and the place which may seem like the end may also be only the beginning." –Ivy Baker Priest

Is life a circle?
If so, how can there be beginnings or endings?
By believing that something starts and then ends, what do you miss?

If time is a circle of never-ending cycles, rather than a straight line, perhaps beginnings and endings are tiny markers on the circle, placed there to remind us of times, places, events we wish to remember or possibly desire to forget.

Unique to Women

What beginnings and endings do women experience that are unique to us?
What things happen automatically to us and our bodies, things over which we have no control?
What wisdom do we gain from such happenings?
What experiences have you personally had that might be unique to you?
Have these experiences created bonding or separation?
Are there any experiences unique to men that they consider beginnings or endings?
If so, can we as women relate to them?

SPIRITUAL AND RELIGIOUS

Did you have a beginning?
If so, where did you begin?
Where were you before that?
When will you end?
What might that look like?
Will any part of you continue after the ending?
How does your belief or non-belief in a god, or the gods, affect your beliefs about endings and beginnings?

Answering these questions may require that you get down to the bare bones, the structure or framework of your beliefs. Doing this is not always easy.

ORDINARY TIME AND SACRED TIME

"None of the clocks are right in this rambling old house. Each room you enter becomes a different time. Days mean nothing. Time seems to have no substance. Perhaps this is the way it needs to be. Only the sense of day or night, nothing more. Falling into the natural rhythm that belongs, instead of the one manipulated and contrived by men. Is the earth asking us to remember? Remember where we come from. Remember where we will return to. We are not the masters of our domain. We are beautiful servants and partners. Caretakers." –TRISH COWLES, PARTICIPANT

Is it possible that our view of time and how we use it affects what we believe about beginnings and endings?
Or perhaps it is the other way around?

Thoughts and questions about time can bring us to the ancient Greeks and their gods of time.
Most of us view and experience time from the place of Chronos, the Greek god of ordinary, chronological time, the god of calendars and schedules, of timelines and deadlines, and all things chronic. But the Greeks had another god for time, Kairos, the god of sacred time, good timing, the fleeting moment, and opportunity.

Chronos is sequential and quantitative.

Kairos is qualitative and can be described as the time in between time.

Some of the differences between Chronos and Kairos can be seen in daily activities.

If you live, eat, work, and sleep by the clock or on a schedule, you do so chronologically.

If you eat when you are hungry, sleep when you are tired, and work when you feel like it, you can be said to live kairologically.

EXPRESSIONS OF TIME

Have you ever heard someone use the expression *killing time*?

If it is possible to kill time, is it also possible to create or birth time?

And in so doing, are we affecting beginnings and endings?

Have you ever killed time?

Can you steal time, and if so, do you have to give it back or hold an accounting for what you did with it?

Who did you steal it from?

Is it possible to slow time down or speed it up?

Is it possible to borrow time, waste time, or stretch it?

Have you ever had the experience of time passing so quickly that you were surprised?

Or so slowly you could hardly wait for something to be over?

These sayings have a connection with our beliefs about starting and stopping points, which affects how we handle deadlines, pressure, the need to hurry up or slow down.

Do your beliefs and attitudes about time and endings and beginnings color your view of aging and ultimate death?

How often do you hear the expression, "My time is running out?"

How often do you put off doing something you long to do, or dream of doing, saying you will have to wait until you retire, have more money, or have more time?

Do you live your life waiting for beginnings and endings in order to do things?

The truth is, we all have the same amount of time each day.

The difference is how we choose to live it.

Kairos, the god of the fleeting moment, that flash of opportunity that so quickly passes us by, was portrayed as having a hank of hair falling over his face, that way you could grab hold of the moment. But the back of his head was bald, because once he had passed by, no one could recapture the moment. There was nothing left to grab. A missed opportunity, a neglected occasion, an ignored inkling, those are things that can never be recovered.

Have you ever grabbed hold of Kairos's hair as he sped past?

TIME AND CREATIVITY

Kairos can be found in the timelessness of creativity, imagination, and play. Such things tend to be more spiral or circular in nature. When we are creating, we can perhaps feel we live outside of time. We are not on the clock, so to speak, and we are not worried about endings and beginnings.

Creativity is woven together with intuition, imagination, and our ability to live in the realm of magic, mystery, wandering, and wondering.

Creativity affects our view of time, whether we live inside or outside of it. And it shapes our beliefs about beginnings and endings. Do women live outside of time more often than men?

Do you spend more time living with Chronos, chained to the calendar and the clock or do you live with Kairos, fluid, intuitive, in touch with your cycles, grabbing hold of the moment?

GATES, DOORS, AND HINGES

The Roman god Janus ruled over gates and doors, beginnings and endings. His consort, Cardea, was the goddess of door hinges.

This is something interesting to consider. In order for a door to swing open or shut, there has to be a hinge of some sort. It is the hinge that determines whether the door swings in or out, or even possibly both ways. It seems to be most common that doors swing open into a room or dwelling, but there are instances where the doors swing out. Some of it has to do with the amount of space, but there are times when there is an awkwardness to the way a door swings, like when you have to step back or step down to pull the door open.

The word hinge has the same root meaning as the word hang. The door hangs on the hinge, and if it does not hang properly, it is hard to open and close.

If opening and closing require a hinge, is the same true for endings and beginnings?

What do your doors hang on?
What are your hinges?
Are they rusty, worn, or broken?
Do you have any hinges that swing both ways?
Why would the Romans think of doors and gates as being related to a god of beginnings and endings?
Why would hinges be considered female?

The Norns of Beginnings and Endings

In Norse mythology, the web of life is said to be created, guarded, tended, and fine-tuned by the Nornir, an ancient triple being. Urd is the oldest. It is she who foretells the past. Verdandi is the middle, and it is she who experiences the present moment. Skuld, the third, remembers what must come into being out of necessity. The weaving they tend is the intertwined, intricate tapestry of life, the threads of which hold the entire universe together for those living, those who have lived, and those who are yet to become. She is the *all*.

The threads of each person's individual tapestry are woven into the warp of the universal loom. The warp threads are all that presently exists from all that has gone before. The life you live is determined and created by what you weave into the threads that are already there.

According to this mythology, the Nornir are so great that they actually control the so-called high gods of the Norse pantheon. They are older and more powerful than the gods themselves. They are beings who bind and unbind the very fabric of life. For them, there is no beginning and no ending, only the weaving, unweaving, and reweaving. When anything in life meets or interacts with someone or something else, it is the coming together and touching of the threads that weaves and knots the formation of a pattern, and these patterns hold the shape of your life as well as mine.

In the present moment, we experience the energies and effects of our past choices, as well as the choices of everyone else. These choices create energy fields that become layered around us and become bound into our pattern. We are not controlled by outside forces but rather participate in a living, vibrant force of life that is a woven web. This web is not only ours but contains the patterns of all living things, the gods, the planets, the stars, all of the worlds and all who inhabit them, the entire Universe.

So what we might consider to be our own beginnings and endings take on a much larger and grander meaning and significance than what we might consider from our own small perspective.

NEW YEAR'S RESOLUTIONS

New Year's Day, an arbitrary date on the calendar, does not relate to anything that is happening in nature or with the seasons. It's just a date we have all agreed upon to be the beginning of a new year. Having a set date provides a way to count time. Marking dates also serves the purpose of giving us pause, to take stock, to reflect, to plan ahead, set goals, regroup, start over, prioritize.

There are and have been cultures that ended and began the year at harvest. It was the end of the growing season, a time to gather things in, and it was the beginning of the dark, cold time of the year, a time of quiet and stillness. It seems to make more sense to mark beginnings and endings as they relate to the seasons and nature, rather than a month and a number on a calendar.

It is not uncommon for people to make resolutions on New Year's Day. A resolution can be defined as a firm decision to do or not do something.

Some statistics show that about seventy-four percent of Americans make at least one New Year's resolution. They tend to focus on things like losing weight, saving money, stopping smoking, eating better, or getting more organized. Supposedly, less than twenty percent of the seventy-four percent are successful at accomplishing what they say they want to do.

Why would anyone, yourself included, have a sudden urge to make changes or solve problems beginning on a particular day, at a particular time of year?
Once you make a decision, why would you wait?

STRIVING FOR GOALS
Setting goals and then striving to reach them also plays a big part in the New Year's resolution scene, where you make a firm decision to accomplish something or attain something. But setting goals often sets us up for disappointment, if we tend to look at them as all or nothing; succeed or fail. And when we focus on just those things, we forget to experience the experience.

It is like the mother who wants to take her toddler to the park. That's the goal. Yet the toddler, as might be expected, is more interested in experiencing the journey to the park, stopping to examine every leaf, poke small rocks into holes, splash in puddles, pet neighborhood cats, and if all these experiences are allowed to happen, the mother and child may never get to the park.
There is a big difference between a purpose-driven life and meandering.

It is not uncommon to hear people talk about reaching enlightenment or arriving at an ultimate state of being, as if somehow they are going to make it to an end destination.
It's wise to remember that enlightenment is not a destination. It is part of a continuum, like the infinity sign. The moment you attain something, you start your return. Another thing that gets overlooked in striving to reach a goal is that once we achieve it or arrive at it, we

are at the top, and the moment that happens, there is the slightest pause, the still point, and then we are on our way back down.
Something ended, and something began.
Something begins because something has ended.

Like fruit hanging on the tree. There is only the ever-so-fleeting moment when a piece of fruit is ripe and then begins the process of rotting and decaying.
Like human life. We strive to grow up and gain maturity, but the moment we do, we begin to grow old and die, because death begins in the middle, halfway between the beginning and the ending.
The beginning is the ending, and the ending is the beginning, which is the ending again.
Round and round, an endless loop of eternity.

What might shift for you around beginnings and endings if you decided to live from questions instead of goals?
Instead of setting external goals for a New Year, why not ask yourself some questions and use your answers as your guidelines?

How do I want to feel this coming year?
What do I want to taste, smell, see, experience?
How do I want to use my body to move through life?
What is longing to rise up in me, to swell, to ripen, to unfold?
Who or what inspires my creativity?
What am I hungry for?

Such questions come from the longing of the soul, not the mind.
Let the answers arise from your heart. The outcome can be very different when you live from the questions rather than from goals, plans, and resolutions.
Our world needs more visionaries and dreamers, more of us who are willing to live from the images and the senses.
Live in the questions and answers that come from the heart instead of living only from the mind, the calendars, and appointment books.

What is ending in your life right now?
What will take its place?
What is beginning for you?
What needs to end in order for that to happen?

TASKS

- Review the past year and make a list of things that ended for you. Then take each thing, one by one, and ask the following question: When this ended, what began in its place?
- Make a list of all the things that began for you during the past year. Then take each thing, one by one, and ask the following question: What ended in order for this to begin?

When you reflect over the past year and look at your endings and beginnings, be honest with yourself.

Allow yourself to feel whatever it is you feel, without judgment.

BARE BONES AND SKELETON TREES

Getting down to the bones of something can also be about beginnings and endings.

Bare bones are a stark reminder of the circle of life. All things return to the place from which they came, only to start the cycle over again.

All beginnings demand change.
All endings demand change.
Something must end in order for something to begin.
Acceptance of change is acceptance of life.
Acceptance of change is acceptance of death.
Life is not frozen in time. It moves like a river, changing everything it touches, just as it is changed.

Trees have skeletons, hidden and exposed. The branches and the roots. It is through the skeleton that the tree is fed from the roots down below to the branches above, the energy and nutrients flowing endlessly up and down the trunk. Skeleton trees play a part in the image of the endless cycles of nature. Endings and beginnings. There are times when the leaves are budding and opening in spring. There are times when the leaves are full, vital, and alive, and there are times when the leaves change color, let go, and fall to the ground, thus exposing the skeleton.

There is nothing that can be done to stop this cycle of letting go.
There is nothing anyone needs to do to make it happen, either.
Leaves fall to the ground, only to be reused, recycled into nutrients that the tree will use to grow new leaves.
When the tree is bare, you can see the structure and patterns of the branches and limbs. You can appreciate the massive root system that lies hidden beneath the surface, deep in the earth.
The root system mirrors the skeleton of the tree above.
Bare branches mirror the roots.
Endings mirror beginnings.

PROBLEM SOLVING

What situation or issue in your life, at this time, needs to be stripped down to the bare bones?
What would this issue look like if you stripped away the flesh or outer layers?
Try to imagine the skeleton or framework that holds this thing in place.
Because stripping away can symbolize death, you can often find a solution by remembering that what dies is used to feed or fertilize the new things that will grow from the choices and decisions you make during the process.

Remember, leaves fall from the trees without interference or intervention.

Are there any challenges you are facing that will reveal their inner framework in due time, without you needing to do anything?
What would it look like if you just allowed the leaves to fall off?
What is possible if we don't try to interfere with endings and beginnings?
What are your bare bones?
What are your skeleton trees?
What do they reveal that has been hidden inside as well as down below?
How are they part of your endings and beginnings?
What has died and what is coming forth as new life?

Endings Meditation

If it feels safe for you, close your eyes and begin to breathe slowly, taking in long, slow, deep breaths, holding them for a moment, and then slowly releasing them.
Long, slow breath in.
Long, slow breath out.
And again,
In and out.
Quietly relaxing into your body.

Imagine that it is early morning, just about dawn.
It is still and quiet.
It is the first day of a new year for you, the ending of one, and the beginning of another.
You quietly slip from your bed, dress warmly, and before you open the front door, you reach down and pick up a bundle that you carefully and lovingly wrapped up the night before. You place it under your coat.
You take one last look around the room, then you open the front door and step outside.
Everything is magical.
During the night, a heavy fog settled in, and all around the air is swirling with mist. There are dewdrops caught in the spiders' webs, and the shapes of trees are ghostly.
You make your way down the path to the river's edge.
All is silent except the gentle lapping of the water on the bank.
You stand there wrapped in the fog and mist and you ponder the wisdom of the river and the water.
There is no beginning and there is no ending to the cycle of the water.
It is a circle.

All water flows to the ocean, only to rise up, or sink down and return again.

This water in the river that is flowing past you now is the same water that flowed past your ancestors.

And it will flow past those who come after you.

Again and again.

As you stand still and silent, watching the river, you begin to see, just barely visible in the fog, a boat moving slowly toward you, coming down river, carried by the flow.

You watch, and as it gets closer, you see that there is a single person in the boat, and they have taken up the oars and are rowing toward the place where you are standing on the bank.

You watch.

The boat touches the shore, and the person steps out of the boat. Someone you have never seen before, and yet someone you have always known.

This person hands you a bundle that has been carefully wrapped and quietly whispers to you,

"Take this. It is what you long for in the coming year."

You reach out, take the bundle, and gently set it down at your feet. Then, carefully, you reach inside your coat and take out the bundle that you have carried with you down to the river's edge.

You hand your package to the stranger you have never seen before, who is also someone you have always known, and you say,

"Take this with you, please, as you travel down the river. It is something I no longer need."

Taking the package, the stranger steps back into the boat, pushes away from the edge, rows out to the middle of the river, and is soon caught up in the flow.

Within minutes, the boat, the stranger, and the bundle have all disappeared into the fog and mist.

You bend down, gently pick up the bundle you were given, turn, and walk back toward your home, carrying the gift that was given to you by the stranger you have always known.

When you arrive, you lift the latch and the door swings open. You step inside, anxious to unwrap the package.

You take a deep breath in, and as you exhale, you open your eyes.

To access all downloadable meditations, go to page 48 and scan the QR code.

Silence

The Sound of Silence

Noise can be dangerous to our health, both physical and mental. Scientists have discovered connections between chronic noise, also known as noise pollution, and high blood pressure, increased heart rates, sleep loss, and stress.

Noise pollution signals a lack of respect for others, perpetrated by individuals and corporations.

According to an article by Candice Gaukel Andrews, *Hearing The Sound Of Silence,* posted in Natural Habitat Adventures,

> "Silence provides a space that promotes a sense of mental clarity, peace, and tranquility...A period of silence each day provides an opportunity for relaxation and a reduction in stress levels."

She lists several benefits of silence. It enhances concentration, boosts creativity, improves learning, cultivates patience, increases productivity, and heightens self-awareness.

Silence is a powerful state.
It is more than an experience. It is not merely the absence of noise; the same way sleep is not the absence of wakefulness. Silence is a presence. It is a being. When we come to know it as a being, we can be with it without needing to do anything. We don't need to empty it or fill it up. It invites us to experience it as itself.

One of the best ways to do this is in nature.

"In the silence of the wild, we find the home we lost in the city." –John Muir

---

Very few of us live in the wild. Most of us live in towns or cities. Modern life is noisy. Traffic, airplanes, machines, construction, sirens. Most of the time, we have no choice about the noise. Sometimes we do have a choice, but rarely consider silence as an option.

SILENCE IS VANISHING
According to some sources, there are only a handful of places left in America where silence pervades, and there is nowhere in Europe.

Silence, according to audio ecologist Gordon Hempton, refers to "the complete absence of all audible mechanical vibrations, leaving only the sounds of nature at her most natural."

Silence is an endangered species. Taking this into consideration, should we perhaps be as concerned with the extinction of silence as we are with the extinction of animals?
Is it possible that silence could be used for healing?
Could the lack of silence be contributing to people's feverish, nervous temperaments and high-strung excitability, or the fact that people no longer know how to wait and be still?
Many, perhaps most, of the people alive today have never truly experienced silence.
Is silence important?
Should we be concerned about preserving it?

A BOUNDARY ISSUE
The lack of silence is a boundary issue.
One of the ways this boundary issue is evident is the constant bombardment of music in public places, waiting rooms, the doctor's office, toilets, restaurants, coffee shops, the taxi to the airport,

and elevators. The list is endless. Music is even being played while you're pumping gasoline. We are so accustomed to this intrusion that we've come to consider it normal. It's even considered normal to automatically play music while getting a massage or a facial, or having your hair cut. I've found that most massage therapists seem to be genuinely surprised when I ask them to turn the music off. Have you ever requested no music?

I enjoy going to coffee shops to write, but it's become increasingly difficult for me to do that because of the noise. Not the sound of people's voices or the clattering of dishes. No, it's the endless loop of music.

Imagine you're sitting in a restaurant having lunch. Music is playing, not in the background but more accurately in the forefront. People are speaking loudly so they can hear each other. The louder the people talk, the louder the music is played. Eventually, there is only noise.

I recently attended a seminar where participants were given a period of time to write answers to questions and jot down their thoughts and ideas. The moment the assignment was given and the instructor stopped speaking, the music started. During a question-and-answer session at the end of the day, I asked about the lack of silence during the writing time.

Was the music necessary?

What value did it serve?

Why were we not given a choice?

The answer: "Oh, it's normal to play music. It's done at all the retreats and events."

Normal?

Is it normal not to have silence, to believe that there must be music playing in order to think?

How might our experiences be different if we were given the option to choose silence?

What would it feel like to actually request it?

Even more radical. What if silence was normal, and if you wanted music, you'd have to play it for yourself using headphones or earbuds?

How long has it been since you spent any length of time in silence, other than sleeping?
Do you get anxious even thinking about it?
Do you have a daily practice of silence?
Do you consider silence sacred or spiritual?
Does silence have to be meditation?

EXPLORING SILENCE

"I fear silence because it leads me to myself, a self I may not wish to confront. It asks that I listen. And in listening, I am taken to an unknown place. Silence leaves me alone in a place of feeling. It is not necessarily a place of comfort." –CIRCLE OF STONES: WOMAN'S JOURNEY TO HERSELF, JUDITH DUERK

I invite you to set aside time each day, an hour if possible, to experience the joy of silence. It doesn't have to be as formal as meditation, sitting on a special cushion in front of your altar. It can be walking outside in nature without earbuds or headphones. It could be doing yoga without music. It could be sitting on your porch or in the garden watching the clouds or the sun. It could even be driving in your car in silence.

What would it be like to claim for yourself an entire day of silence? Once a month, perhaps, or even once a week.

If you are addicted to noise and sound, as so many people are, you may have to start very gradually. It can be almost shattering on an emotional and spiritual level to spend time with yourself. Endlessly listening to music, news, and podcasts can be an escape from yourself and your own thoughts.
Try silence. You will discover things that can change your life.

One woman shared her experience of creating, with her partner, a new family ritual. They dedicated one day per month to silence. They found it to be more fun and less difficult if they wore all black and pretended they were in a monastery and had taken a vow of silence. They did not isolate themselves from each other; they just did not speak.

What might happen for you if you chose to have such an experience for a day or chose to do it on a regular basis?

During times of chosen silence, pay attention to the sounds you do hear. Is there a mixture of sounds of nature and manmade sounds? Is it noise?
How are you affected?
What feelings come up?
What thoughts or memories?

CHOOSING A LOW-INFORMATION LIFE

Creating a life that includes periods of silence can be challenging. We live in an age of information overload, a life of constant input and stimulus. Often, there is a surprisingly intense level of resistance to intentionally seeking silence. That resistance can be a pretty good indication of the level of addiction. If you have resistance to such periods of silence, you might ask yourself, "what am I trying not to hear?"

Herbert Simon, an American social scientist and Nobel Prize winner, states that information consumes.

> "In an information-rich world, the wealth of information means a dearth of something else: a scarcity of whatever it is that information consumes. What information consumes is rather obvious: it consumes the attention of its recipients. Hence a wealth of information creates a poverty of attention and a need to allocate that attention efficiently among the overabundance of information sources that might consume it."

That is a rather interesting observation. A wealth of information creates a poverty of attention.

You might wish to explore the possibility of becoming selectively ignorant. That might look like learning to ignore information and interruptions that are unimportant or irrelevant, even if they are interesting.

In his book, *The 4-Hour Workweek: Escape 9–5, Live Anywhere, and Join the New Rich*, Timothy Ferriss states,

> "Most information is time-consuming, negative, irrelevant to your goals, and outside of your influence."

He challenges us to think about what we read, watch, and listen to each day and ask these questions:

Is it time-consuming?
Is it negative?
Is it irrelevant to my goals?
Is it outside of my influence?

Asking these questions might actually be a good measuring rod to use when considering how you fill your time and your mind at the expense of silence.

Take some time to consider various forms of silence, not just the absence of speaking.
Imagine experiencing silence with all your senses.
Your eyes and ears.
Your heart and mind.
Your entire body.

Explore how that could manifest in your life.
Can silence come from closing our eyes?
Is our heart silent when we are content?
Could silence of the mind support us in letting go of fear and worry?
What benefits might come to you from practicing such forms of silence?

NATURE

What experiences have you personally had with silence in nature?
Where were you?
Who were you with?
How long were you able to enjoy the experience?
What broke the silence?

If you were to draw a picture or make some artistic representation
of silence, what would it look like?
What color would it be?
What shape?
Would it have a taste or smell?
Can you feel silence?
Is it palpable?

Once you begin to experience silence as a part of your life, or even
a way of life, you will become sensitive to noise and less tolerant.

Silence is primal, it is a being, an entity, just as darkness is a being.
It existed before humans and will continue after we are gone.
Silence was there at the beginning. Then came sound. Then came
the word. Then came noise. Then the silence came again.
There is silence in the deep earth, in the depths of the ocean, and
in the darkness of space.
Silence is not the absence of sound or the absence of anything.
Silence *is*.
Darkness is not the absence of light. Darkness *is*.

In silence, you can hear the voice of the child in your womb, the
song of the universe behind a waterfall, the heartbeat of a tree, and
the breath of a cloud.
Silence is necessary so you can hear your inner self, hear your
ancestors, hear the land speak.
We need silence to remember who we are and our connection to
the earth.

Because we live in the middle of noise, the land of no choice in
public, we must find ways to allow for silence in our personal space

and then create a longing for it. Claim the right to silence. We shouldn't need to ask permission from those around us. Rather, they need to ask permission to intrude with their noise.

Noise pollution eats away at our well-being, and very few have given thought to the truth that noise is a consequence of commercialism, consumerism, capitalism, technology, and greed.

Thinking is silent. Intimate connection is developed and nurtured in silence.

In his *Manifesto For Silence: Confronting the Politics and Culture of Noise*, Stuart Sim reflects the thinking of the Romantic poets when he writes,

> "The ability to think, to reflect and to create are all to a significant degree dependent on our being able to access silence... It is an absolute necessity of existence, which the trend towards a 24/7 society is rendering more and more difficult for many of the population. Its loss would seriously impoverish our lives."

Another interesting insight regarding silence is shared by Sara Maitland in *A Book of Silence: A Journey In Search Of The Pleasures And Powers Of Silence.*

> "As time passes, I increasingly realize there is an interior dimension to silence, a sort of stillness of heart and mind which is not a void but a rich space. What became obvious to me as I thought about this is that for me there is a chasm of difference between qualities like quietness or peace and silence itself... In my personal vocabulary the difference is similar to the one between happiness and joy."

SILENCE, SOUND, AND NOISE

Silence does not mean there is no sound.

Sound is everywhere.

Sound is all the things you can hear.

Sound becomes noise when it is unpleasant, irrelevant, incomprehensible, unwanted, too loud, disruptive or disturbing.
Noise has a negative effect on health and well-being.

Do you find it challenging to experience silence in your personal life? At home, at work, in public. It is becoming more and more difficult. The world is noisy. The day-to-day operations and functions are noisy.
Do you contribute to the noise in your own life when instead you could seek silence?
Is constant sound so common that you no longer even think about it?

Women of the always, take heed. In solitude, we can find silence.

> "Certain springs are tapped only when we are alone. Women need solitude in order to find again the true essence of themselves; that firm strand which will be the indispensable center of a whole web of human relationships."
> –GIFT FROM THE SEA, ANNE MORROW LINDBERGH

> "The breath of life is in the sharp winds of change mingled with the breath of destruction.
> But if you want to breathe deep, sumptuous life breathe all alone, in silence, in the dark, and see nothing."
> –THE BREATH OF LIFE, D. H. LAWRENCE

Silence Meditation

∾

Begin the meditation by closing your eyes.

Pay attention to your breath. Long, slow, deep breaths in. Long, slow exhales. Keeping your eyes closed, continue your rhythmic breathing, noticing the sounds you hear around you, inside the room, outside the room, even inside your own body.

Imagine you are walking along a path in a flower-filled meadow, birds singing, bees buzzing, the warmth of the sun on your face. This meadow is in a valley circled by high mountains. The path you are on wanders along following a small stream.

You continue to wander beside the stream and as you do you begin to climb a bit and soon find yourself out of the meadow and among rocks and then boulders and as you round a bend on the path you see up ahead a glorious waterfall cascading down the side of a rock wall, filling a pool at the base and the pool opens out into the stream.

Curiosity calls you to climb a bit higher around the slippery, moss-covered rocks, glistening in the sunlight. You are rewarded by discovering a ledge, not too high up. It juts out from behind the waterfall, and as you climb your way up onto the ledge, you discover it forms a shelf that extends back into a cave. You carefully step into the cave and discover a hidden world of mist and water and darkness and the sound and the silence of the waterfall.

You are called to sit down upon a large flat stone, and you close your eyes. Eyes closed, you slowly become aware of not only the sound of the waterfall but of the silence within the cave. You listen. You begin to hear what sounds like music.

You realize that what you are hearing is the song of the universe, the great song spoken of by the Celts as the Oran Mor.

You linger, entranced by the music you hear within the silence. It is a short time. It is a long time. It is in between time.

The great song tells you it is time to find your way back. Slowly, you climb down off the ledge, going carefully over the slippery rocks and boulders, down the slope, back into the meadow. You wander along the stream, winding your way to the place you began. When you are ready, you can open your eyes and close them. Open your eyes and close them. Open your eyes, and you leave them open. Quietly take time to reflect upon what you heard.
The sound of the universe that lives within the silence.

To access all downloadable meditations, go to page 48 and scan the QR code.

Dark

The Dark Will Remain

The universe, the void, Ginnungagap, outer space.
No matter the names or words we use to describe what is out there, it is dark.
Pinpoints of light visible to the human eye come and go.
The stars. Luminous gases.
They are transitory.
Dark remains. It has always been, and when all the lights go out, it will still be there. Dark.

> "Light thinks it travels faster than anything but it is wrong. No matter how fast light travels, it finds the darkness has always got there first, and is waiting for it."
> –TERRY PRATCHETT

The dark lacks nothing.
We do not need to bring light into the dark any more than we need to bring dark into the light.
They exist separately from each other and yet are connected.
They exist whole and complete in themselves.
We experience darkness here on earth because the body of the earth shields us from the light of the sun. We have named this experience night.

Night is a shadow. It allows us to see the dark.

SPEAKING THE WORD

We are living in a time of great imbalance.

People are afraid. People are seeking.

The marketplace is flooded with workshops, seminars, online and in-person events. Gurus and life coaches. All focused on enlightenment, white light, high vibrations, raising consciousness, positivity, perfect health, and perpetual youth.

It seems that everyone everywhere is seeking the light, wanting to shine light into the darkness.

Do you ever consider endarkenment?

How often do you use the word dark?

Is it possible to use the word dark without thinking of or referencing something bad, negative, evil, or even simply less valuable or less important than the light?

When darkness is maligned, extreme imbalance occurs.

There's an old story that goes like this,

> One moonless night, a man lost the only key he had to his house. He was down on his hands and knees searching for it under a streetlamp. A friend came by and, after learning that the key was lost, he too got down on the ground to search. After a long time of searching and finding nothing, the friend asked, "Are you sure you lost it here?" The man replied, "No, I lost it over there." He pointed to the darkness. The friend then asked, "Why are you looking here?" The reply, "Because this is where the light is."

We have been severed from our roots, disconnected from the earth, the body of our mother. We can't find the missing key by searching in the light. Balance can only be restored by going to the dark. We must go to the dark, the roots, the well, the places where the dragons dwell. There we will find the answers to what has been lost.

To go in the dark with a light is to know the light. To know the dark, go dark. Go without sight, and find that the dark, too, blooms and sings, and is traveled by dark feet and dark wings.

—WENDELL BERRY

The only way to get rid of a shadow is to turn off the light.

LIGHT POLLUTION

Ever present in our modern society is the artificial illumination of the night. Most of us have never experienced the wonder and grandeur of the night sky, studded with stars and streaked with occasional meteors. For this to happen, we must take ourselves away from the cities into the wilderness or to the tops of mountains. The closest I have ever come to this experience was camping in the forest in a remote region of Yellowstone National Park in the State of Montana.

Seeing such a night sky is truly awe-inspiring.

Have you ever had such an experience?

Perhaps this lack of night caused by light pollution has contributed to our disconnection from and understanding of the necessity of the cycles of life.

We are unwilling to be affected by the ending of daylight.

We don't like that we are limited by darkness, so we always leave the lights on.

This puts us out of balance, out of harmony.

It creates disease.

We ignore the dangers of perpetual light.

We ignore that it is a form of pollution.

If we don't allow ourselves to be stilled by night, fed by it, nurtured by it, loved by it, how can we truly embrace its darkness?

Have we gone too far?

OUTSIDE IN THE DARK

Imagine living at a time when the only man-generated light was from fires, candles, or small oil lamps?

In times past, were people more conscious and aware of the scarcity and finite nature of fuel sources? Did they appreciate their preciousness? Would they have imprudently left the lights on?

Any person living at such a time would surely have been aware of the intensity of a fully reflecting moon and the ability it gave to see at night. And they would have also known the total darkness of a night when the moon was fully in shadow.

We know that humans in times past spent endless hours in the dark, studying the night sky, the movement of the stars and planets. What they observed and learned is still evident in what they left behind. Enormous standing stones, burial mounds, monuments that are perfectly aligned with events that happen in the heavens. Events that can only be seen when it is dark.

FINDING SOME DARKNESS

How difficult would it be for you to remove or block out all sources of light from your sleeping area so you can sleep in total darkness? Check around your home and notice how many things you have that glow or shine in the dark. The face of a digital clock, the glow of the instant-on button of the television, the light on the smoke detector.

Sleeping in the dark might require using blackout curtains on your windows because most often we have light coming into our bedrooms from the ever-present streetlights or other forms of security lighting.

Be creative with your solutions.

How difficult is it for you to experience the dark?

SEASONS OF THE DARK

My favorite time of year is autumn.

Restless currents of air blow clouds across the face of the moon. Dry leaves swirl along the shadowed garden paths. It's a time of gathering in and a time of letting go.

It's the time when we who live in the northern hemisphere start our return to the dark.

Life begins in the dark and ends in the dark.

Many ancient cultures began their year by going into the dark. Many of them began their days with the setting of the sun.

When my ancestors speak to me about this autumnal time of year, they remind me that we reap what we sow. They remind me that going into the dark means we must gather and harvest, prune away and plow under; that it's the time when things begin to rot and decay, the time of dying and letting go. The season of going into the dark is also the season of slowing down, of preservation, a time of necessity.

Could much of the illness, stress, and depression that affect so many people in autumn and winter be directly related, not to the dark and cold, but to how out of balance we have become with nature and how out of touch we are with the rhythms and cycles of life?

Do you or does someone you know always get sick in the fall and winter?
Do you blame it on the weather rather than the possibility of imbalance with nature and the seasons?
This is a time of year when the days grow short and nights grow long, a time when nature becomes still and rests, when leaves have fallen to the ground, when acorns have been buried by the squirrels and the bears are in their dens.
Do you embrace this dark time of year, or do you leave all the lights on?

Winter holiday season is anything but still. The music, the decorations, the advertisements. People rush around after work and on weekends, spending long hours in crowded stores, with bright lights and frantic shoppers, perhaps spending money they don't have on things they don't need, often buying gifts out of obligation and a sense of guilt. This may seem like a harsh observation. Perhaps it is not.
How out of balance do you become in wintertime?
How do you honor the dark?

The next time you experience the arrival of autumn with winter close behind, why not give yourself the gift of slowing down?
What if you give yourself the gift of pruning, culling, of letting go, of removing from your life things that no longer serve you or cause stress?
What if you listen to the wisdom of nature, pay attention as the wheel turns, and be still?
What if you embrace the dark?

DARK AND NIGHT

In Norse mythology, there is a giantess whose name is Nott. There are some who say this giantess named Nott is Night, and she is the mother of Jord, the Earth.

I have a strong sense that the giantess Nott is Darkness rather than Night.

There is a difference.

Night is the name earth-dwellers give to the experience of being in the Shadow of the body of Earth.

If the giantess whose name is Nott is Darkness, then she is the one who gave birth to Jord who is the Earth.

The body of Jord gives birth to Night, over and over again.

Night is a Shadow created by the body of earth, and this Shadow provides a place of shielded protection from the light of the Sun.

Does that mean that Shadow is a being?

A Shadow can only be created when there's a light source, such as the Sun. The Sun sends forth her rays, and those rays come in contact with something that has form and substance.

Light cannot pass through the body of the Earth.

Does Light create the Shadow, or does Shadow dwell inside the body of the Earth?

What then is the meaning of the expression, "cast a shadow?"

The Shadow we call Night is not the same as Darkness.

It is not the absence of Light because Light must be present in order for Shadow to appear.

Darkness is not the same as Night, because Darkness exists without Light.

If humans are suffering and ill because of Darkness deficit, who or what are we missing?

Are we missing Darkness as well as Night?

In Paul Bogard's book, *The End Of Night: Searching For Natural Darkness In An Age Of Artificial Light*, David Saetre states we are obsessed with a kind of false clarity, the idea that everything can be brought into some kind of pure light.

"...night is a time of liberation, the time and the place where we are set free from the overbearing presence of light. Or, in other words, sometimes light keeps us from experiencing the deep truth of things."

When we can no longer see the night sky because we are controlling and manipulating nature, we close our window to the universe. We lose sight of our place as humans. We forget the scale of who we are. When we can no longer see in the dark because there is no night, we have truly lost our way.

Women of the always embrace the dark. We know it in our bodies.
Life comes forth from the dark and returns to the dark.
We are cyclical in a world of orchestrated straight lines.
We honor Darkness, who gave birth to Earth.
We honor Earth, who gives birth to the Shadow we call Night,
over and over again.
We honor Shadow.

Moon

The Moon is Always Full Even When She's Dark

Women of the always are intimate with the moon.
The nature of the moon is dark.
She does not shine.
She is dark when she is herself.
And she is always full, whether she is in the shadow of the earth or is reflecting the light of the sun.
The moon is always full, even when she's invisible.

When I refer to the dark moon, I find that many women don't know for sure what I am talking about. That's because it's common to call the dark moon a new moon. But they are not the same. There is a difference. We cannot see the dark moon because she is completely hidden from us by the shadow of the earth.

The new moon is a tiny sliver in the sky, barely peaking out of the shadow. When the earth is positioned between the sun and the moon, the side of the moon facing the earth is unlit so she is not visible to us. Does being in the shadow of the earth allow us to know her more intimately? She is fully present but she is unseen.

I believe that the main reason we rarely hear anyone speak of the dark moon is because we are a society of people who often attach words like evil, bad, or negative to the word dark and because of that, we're afraid to even use the word. We skip over this aspect of the moon and miss some of the power and potency that exists when the moon is showing us her true nature. We are so afraid to call the moon dark, it is rare to find a dark moon indicated on a calendar.

As we learn to connect more intimately with the moon, we may begin to notice how closely our bodies and our energy follow her rhythms. She is a visible manifestation of a cycle. Fully in shadow, gradually waxing, emerging from the shadow of the earth until she is fully illuminated. Then waning until she is fully in shadow again. This can be likened to birth, living, dying, and then rebirth. Ignoring the dark phase, we actually skip a section of this cycle.

If you are a woman who is still menstruating, you may find that as you pay more attention to the moon, your monthly cycles will change. For many women, a regular cycle occurs approximately every 28 days, with bleeding occurring during the time of the dark moon. Women who live together in close proximity often bleed at the same time. This is evident today in living situations such as dormitories, barracks, and shared housing.

By paying attention, we might begin to notice that the dark moon is a time when we long for more contemplation or perhaps a time we experience profound dreams or waking visions. This is a great time to set intentions for the new beginning that arrives with the appearance of the crescent. We might notice a need or desire to be quiet, alone, altered, or still.

Many people equate the expression "going into the dark" with soul searching, looking inside for things that might be negative, or things we refuse to look at, so we have hidden them away, or things we do not want to admit. This kind of thinking perpetuates the belief that the dark is connected only to what is negative or bad.

It's time to set such thoughts aside and consider going into shadow, following the moon, to explore the richness and depths of your inner wisdom. Use it as a time to connect with your creativity, your intuition, those subtle ways of *knowing* that have nothing to do with the light or the mind. Use it as a time to receive messages that often cannot be heard due to the constant noise and busyness of our everyday lives. Use the time when the moon is fully in shadow to practice your ability to see in the dark, to see the hidden things that cannot be seen when we are being blinded by too much light.

On a seasonal scale, the time when the moon is fully in the shadow of the earth can be compared to the time of winter solstice in the northern hemisphere. It's a time to slow down, go inside, and be still. Try exploring and paying more attention to how you feel emotionally, physically, and spiritually when the moon is fully in shadow, as well as at winter solstice when the sun stands still.
If you are a woman who still bleeds, take note of how this awareness might change or affect your cycles.

Consider creating alternating altars, one for going into the dark and the other for going into the light. This could be done daily as evening and morning rituals. Monthly, following the moon cycles. Yearly, following the seasons. Be creative. Tune in to your body. Select objects and colors that express how you feel.

If you make a commitment to follow the moon cycles for an entire year, you may want to notice how dark moons feel during the winter months and how they feel during summer months.
Is there any difference for you? If so, what?

Male or Female
It's somewhat common, especially in the pagan and witch communities, to refer to the moon as female or she.
In Norse traditions, as well as several other cultures, the moon is considered to be male.
Have you ever thought about the gender of the moon?
What does it feel like to think of the moon as male?
If you do, how does that affect the way you view the moon's influence on your menstrual cycle?
What reasons or explanations would you give for one culture honoring the moon as male and another one honoring the moon as female?

The same thing is true regarding the sun. Some cultures see the sun as male. Others as female. In Norse mythology, the sun is female and her name is Sunna. In the earliest Japanese literary texts, the sun is Amaterasu, and she is the ruler of the heavenly realm.

FEAR OF DEATH

There is a connection between fear of the dark and fear of death. The womb and the tomb are the same. They are places of transition, transformation, and mystery. Is our hesitancy to speak of the dark moon somehow subtly linked to our fear of death?

Another piece of this discussion involves the use of the word or concept of shadow. You may hear people talk about doing shadow work or dealing with the shadow.

Stop a minute and think about it.

The existence of shadow is dependent on the presence of light.

As Wendell Berry said in his poem, *To Know the Dark*, we must be willing to go into the dark, without light.

Step away from the fear of the dark. Acknowledge the dark, be willing to speak about the dark, be willing to do work in the dark. Explore and embrace the dark, without light, so you can truly know it.

ARE YOU A DARK MOON WOMAN

Dark moon women are passionate, fierce, and courageous.

We are eager to explore, study, and discuss the wisdom that abides in the dark, wisdom that has been hidden from us, forbidden to us, and in some cases, all but forgotten because of obsession with the light.

We are willing to ask questions and participate in discussions that are thought-provoking, controversial, challenging, and perhaps disturbing. Discussions that focus on topics specific to women.

Is the dark moon a beginning or an ending, or both?

How do you live in relationship with the ever-changing appearance of the moon?

Does she play a part in what you believe and how you feel about endings and beginnings?

The sun is always in the sky, shining, casting light upon the moon and the earth.
The moon is always in the sky, round and full.
The earth is there too, round and full, always creating a shadow.
A shadow that the moon moves in and out of.
Full moon. Crescent moon. Dark moon.
We see her differently depending on where she is in the shadow and the light.
She is always full.

A woman of the always is herself a moon.
Always full. Always whole and complete. Not missing, lacking, or omitting anything.
And just like the moon in the sky, she moves in and out of shadow.

When there is no light source, there can be no shadow.
A shadow is its own being. It's not darkness. That's because dark is not created by something eclipsing a light source. Dark is a being that exists without light.

In his book *Becoming Animal: An Earthly Cosmology*, David Abrams speaks of shadows as actual beings. They have form and presence. They have substance and temperature and feeling.
It is the actual shadow being that is created by earth that we see interacting with and affecting the moon.
Recognizing shadows as beings changes how we see the moon.
It is a matter of perspective. Earth is always throwing, casting, or creating a shadow that extends out into space because the earth is always in the presence of the light source we call the sun.

Shifting our perspective of the moon, the dark, night, and shadow might be radical. And radical is such a great word to use here.
Radical, from Latin, meaning roots, originating in the root or ground.
Women of the always are radical.
We travel to the crossroads to meet the old woman.
We find wisdom there that is sourced from the dark, originating in the roots.

Shifting our perspective means we are willing to wander, to leave the purpose-driven life.
Willing to live with two left hands.
Willing to be circles instead of straight lines.
We reclaim our mysteries. We remember who we are.

Women of the always embrace the shadow we call night.
We are intimate with the darkness of the void as well as the darkness that exists in all those places where light never goes and does not need to go.

Death

Death is Always Waiting. She Means No Harm.

No one ever died because they were willing to talk about death.
It is a dreaded topic.
It is a much-needed conversation.

What are your first memories of someone dying?
Was it a family member or someone close to you?
Did you witness an accident or a killing?
Do you have any early memories around the death of someone famous, such as a president or a monarch, a film star or a sports hero?
When you were a child, how did the adults around you deal with death?
Were children included in the conversations, discussions, arrangements, and funerals?
What beliefs does your family have around death and dying?
What are your beliefs?
If your beliefs are different from your family's, when did they change?
How often do you talk about death with others?
How often do you think about it?
Do you have a will?
How old do you have to be before you write one?
Have you clearly spelled out your wishes regarding your death, funeral, and burial?

In her book *Hagitude: Reimagining the Second Half of Life,* Sharon Blackie reminds us that the punch line of everyone's life is the same: we die.

What happens to a culture that is fascinated and entertained by violent, bloody, catastrophic death?
What happens when we deny and try to hide from the inevitable, the death none of us can escape?
What special connection exists between women and death?
How do common funeral and burial practices reflect our obsession with beauty and eternal youth?
Death means no harm.
Death is always waiting, and the only thing that separates any of us from the already dead is time.

BIRTH IS DEATH
All mothers are birth.
All mothers are death.
All women know this in their bodies.
All of us are alive today because of our ancient mothers.
Women are not the cause of death, yet they bring forth death when they give birth.
They are part of the endless cycle.

For a woman, sex is surrender, but perhaps not in a way you might think. As Terry Tempest Williams writes, a woman can never forget that she faces death when she has sex. With sex, her life may become two or more. When she bleeds each month, she must decide to celebrate or mourn.

When a woman gives birth, she always faces death.
When a woman gives birth, she always gives birth to death.
That which comes forth always returns.
Men, in spite of all their power and aggression, cannot give birth.
They may take away a woman's freedom.
They may take away a woman's name.
They may take away a woman's children.

They may take away a woman's life.
Men can cause death, but they can never give birth.

Dying is a necessary aspect of the human condition.
Aging is a natural process leading to death. It's not a disease that needs to be cured, nor should it be.
It has been stated that humans are the only animals who know they are dying.
Is that a true statement?
Can we prove it?
Is it possible that all living things have the same knowing, but we humans are the only ones who try to stop death or believe that preventing it is possible?
We are obsessed with youth.
We are obsessed with beauty.
We pretend we're not aging.
We pretend we're not dying.
This pretense of artificial, perpetual youth is a lie.

When people surgically alter their faces trying to look like the person they used to be instead of who they have become, their faces can no longer be trusted.
Our children deserve to see real people, to see the truth.
We all need to see the truth of death in the faces of each other.
The lines and wrinkles of aging are the hallmarks of a life fully lived, a life that will end.

Fear of aging is, of course, woven and knotted together with fear of death, and most of us are not comfortable with the thought of dying, even though there's no way to avoid it.
Many of us are still tainted, perhaps unknowingly, by the Bible's teaching that death is not part of the natural process of life but rather a punishment, the result of sin and disobedience, and the finger is always pointed at the woman as the cause.

The message of the current culture is, you must not age. It's found in advertisements for creams and lotions, pills and potions, surgery and health clubs. There are books devoted to

the subject and websites dedicated to the concept.
How is this obsession with anti-aging woven together with our beliefs about death and dying?

Sadly, we are often so preoccupied with trying to stay or appear young that we place no value on what's actually happening to us. Aging is a natural part of living. And dying.

It's okay to glance in the rearview mirror, but you can't drive forward by always looking backward.

As I am writing this book, I am nearing the age of eighty. I love that I have lived long enough to truly be myself, an eccentric creative. To be irreverent. To be opinionated and judgmental. To be a wise storyteller and a troublemaker. All at the same time.
I like that I can take a nap in the afternoon if I feel like it. I can sit in my small garden and watch the birds and drink whiskey in the middle of the day. I like that I don't have to remember everything. All the little details of all the unimportant stuff. I like that I can choose what I want to remember, forget what I want to forget. I love having lived long enough to become the character I was born to be. I know that I am dying. There is a bittersweet contentment with this knowing, but no regrets. I know that I am not alone. We all face death. We all have the same end.

We are fascinated by death as entertainment, the bloody, violent death that happens in conflict and aggression, accidents and war. We watch, entertained, or perhaps numbed, imagining that such a thing will never happen to us.
The kind of death we do not find interesting is the inevitable death that none can escape, the slow aging and degeneration of the body and mind. This is the death we try to hide with all our anti-aging creams and cosmetic procedures, so widely advertised as the solution to all our fears. We are obsessed with this to such a degree that we embalm corpses with toxic fluids, dress them up, apply makeup, and fix their hair, so they appear not to be dead but wonderfully peaceful and well instead. And then we have the viewing of the lovely body that appears to be sleeping.

FEMALES OF DEATH

In times past, women were associated with goddesses of death and fertility, sexuality and old age, because they go together. The Fates, the Nornir, the Morrigan, they spun new life from raw wool in the basket. With this spinning, they determined the life of a newborn, and they held the death as well, measuring the thread and deciding when to cut it.

The Greek giantesses, the Titanides, not the gods or the goddesses, were ancient, active, powerful beings, the ones most closely connected to nature and the earth. They were most connected to death because it is death that feeds the earth so it can give birth again.

This is the cycle.

Females as birth.

Females as death.

Females giving birth to death, because all things that come forth must return.

The women seers were the ones consulted by the gods about the dead.

In older, earth-based religions, there was an acceptance of death that was perhaps more realistic than what we experience today. It was believed that it was one's duty to realize and accept the ugliness, corruption, and decay that are always present in nature, just as one accepts the beauty, growth, and bloom that are also always present. Death was accorded the same value as birth. They held equal importance as two passages through the same doorway, the coming and the going. That is why, in some myths, the incoming king must willingly embrace and lovingly have sex with the old woman, not the young maiden. It was required that he kiss the hag. If he refused, he was not fit to rule.

A spirituality that is intimate with nature and the earth reminds us that death is natural. It's impossible to ignore. It is not the result of sin. It is the gift of life.

This truth is present in all things: the anticipation and the emerging, the unfolding and the ripening, the rot and decay.

The old death goddesses of matriarchal society were not only connected to death, which was a result of war, violence, and murder.

They were the guardians of death which was the natural consequence of life and aging. It was honored that the mother was the giver of life, and within life was buried the seed of death.

All forms of life are recycled in death, so all forms of life can be nourished.

Many of our beliefs and ideas of death come from the patriarchal concept of life being linear, not cyclic, an eternal stasis in either heaven or hell. Cyclic is about reabsorption.

As Barbara Walker says in *The Crone*,

> "The patriarchs' choice between 'good' and 'evil' is irrelevant to the symbolic archetype. The real choice is between the (phallic) line and the (yonic) circle; between death as a mere passage in time to a mysterious imagined world that can never change, and death as a real dissolution according to the law of nature, where change is the only constant."

Existence is about becoming, not being. Life is perpetual transition. Everything is always changing. Form, color, qualities. Even when something appears to be lifeless or dead, it will eventually become part of something that is living, and everything that is living is in the process of dying.

Our denial of death as a culture necessitates our dismissal and removal of the old woman.
This removal is part of the lie.
It *is* the lie.
Death is always hanging around.
At the foot of the bed.
In the face of a stranger.
Reflected from the mirror on the wall.

We can never remove the old woman because we are always going to be a dying person.

FEAR

Sometimes our fear of aging is connected to regret, and sometimes that can be quite painful. We come face to face with the fact that we have often settled for less, given ourselves away, perhaps compromised our true self, and have even in some cases just not paid attention.

Worry about growing old seems to be starting younger and younger, especially for women.

The cosmetic and fashion industries play an enormous role, marketing and selling eternal youth even to the twentysomethings.

The rich, multi-faceted experience of growing old and dying has come to be viewed as a disease, something we not only fear but also are ashamed of. It's easy to get hooked into the lies about aging that are sold to us by sophisticated advertising.

What activities or practices do you engage in that are directly related to supporting anti-aging or the imagined appearance of eternal youth?

Don't use the question to judge yourself.

Use it as a way to take stock of some of your own feelings, fears, and challenges.

There's a difference between taking care of yourself in an effort to remain healthy and active, and pretending you are not growing old.

To pretend that there is such a place as Never Aging Land disconnects us from our bodies, from all of life, from the earth, nature, and all the mothers.

She who gives birth does so from the realm of death.

PERPLEXING

Why would we use expressions such as *I don't feel my age*?

How can you know what your current age should feel like if you have never been that age before?

Another puzzling expression is *You don't look your age*.

What is my age supposed to look like?

And here's another one that's often found in personal dating ads.

I'm 40, or 50, or 60...but I feel and look 20 years younger.

Who are you trying to fool?
Do you honestly believe that you've lived the last 20 years and haven't changed?

WOMEN'S BUSINESS

> "As among the gods, so among the mortals was death everywhere woman's business. A woman is said to have invented the wailing for the dead...women cradle the infant and the corpse, each to its particular new life."
> –THE FEAR OF WOMEN, WOLFGANG DEDERER

Sadly, a common lie that is still taught in many churches and believed by millions is that Eve, said to be the mother of all humans, is not only responsible for birth but is blamed as the cause of all death. According to the Bible, death was the result of sin and disobedience, and Eve, of course, is the culprit. In fact, the entire Christian belief structure hangs on the gallows of a need to be saved. And if you don't think that this belief still influences our ideas about death, think again. The Bible is still one of the most widely read and believed books of all time, and the United States is still considered to be a Christian country.

Woman is not the reason humans die; she is the portal through which life and death come.

As stated by Elizabeth Cady Stanton, a leading figure in the Women's Rights Movement of the nineteenth century:

> "Take the snake, the fruit-tree and the woman from the tableau, and we have no fall, no frowning Judge, no inferno, no everlasting punishment—hence no need of a Savior. Thus, the bottom falls out of the whole Christian theology. Here is the reason why in all the Biblical researches and higher criticisms, the scholars never touch the position of women."

Black Widows

> "The collective unconscious of man holds a secret that
> women seldom realize...the secret is this. In the hidden
> depths of men's minds, images of women are often iden-
> tified with images of death."
> –The Crone: Woman of Age, Wisdom, and
> Power, Barbara G. Walker

In some cultures, men connect death with women's devouring
sexuality, blaming them for the diminishment of the penis after
climax.

Lies were built up around widows. They were often blamed for
the man's death. It was believed that she somehow used up her
husband's life force, and that's what killed him. The widow was
dangerous. She had to kill someone every year just to stay alive. She
became the black widow spider who kills the male after mating.

Big Business

It's really quite shocking how little most of us know about what
happens to or is done to the body after death. Few of us are aware
of what is legal and what is not concerning the disposal of the
body, the care or preparation necessary or required, or even the
laws around transporting the dead.

Do you have the right to take a body from the hospital or care
home, and can you transport it in your own vehicle?

Does a body have to be embalmed?

Is a casket or coffin necessary, or can you place the body directly
into the ground?

Is it legal to bury someone in the backyard or to dispose of ashes
wherever you want?

What purpose does a funeral home serve?

Are the things you are told about the law and what is required
always true?

Or are you being lied to because it's big business?

YOUR BELIEFS

What do you believe happens at death?

Do you separate the soul, and spirit, and body?

Do you think of the self as different from the animals?

Does a part of you go into the mounds like our British Isles and European ancestors believed?

Do some of us come back into the family?

Do you think our ancestors believed in a past life?

Based on your beliefs, who do you think the ancestors are?

Did the idea of heaven or going to the light come from Christianity?

Why would the ancestors imagine life after death as being different from the life they were living?

Why would some cultures place elaborate items in the grave with the dead?

Why did the Vikings place some of their dead on a ship and then set it on fire?

Why are bodies placed in the Ganges River in India?

Could all the experiences that were imagined and written about in ancient texts occur here on earth, perhaps just in other dimensions or layers of existence?

How does your belief about what happens after you die affect how you live your life right now?

How does this belief affect your attitude and ideas about aging and growing old?

What are the symbols of old age, dying, and death present in your culture?

What symbols do you personally associate with death?

How do you, as a woman, support and honor the hag who sits at the crossroads?

ALLOWING FOR DEATH

William Stafford's poem, *Traveling Through The Dark*, provides us with an interesting challenge regarding our view of death.

Traveling through the dark I found a deerdead on the
edge of the Wilson River Road.
It is usually best to roll them into the canyon:
that road is narrow; to swerve might make more dead.
By glow of the tail-light I stumbled back of the car
and stood by the heap, a doe, a recent killing;
she had stiffened already, almost cold.
I dragged her off; she was large in the belly.
My fingers touching her side brought me the reason—
her side was warm; her fawn lay there waiting,
alive, still, never to be born.
Beside that mountain road I hesitated.
The car aimed ahead its lowered parking lights;
under the hood purred the steady engine.
I stood in the glare of the warm exhaust turning red;
around our group I could hear the wilderness listen.
I thought hard for us all —my only swerving—,
then pushed her over the edge into the river.

"No one is finally dead until the ripples they cause in
the world die away – until the clock he wound up winds
down, until the wine she made has finished its ferment,
until the crop they planted is harvested. The span of
someone's life is only the core of their actual existence."
–Terry Pratchett, Reaper Man

Tasks
- Research what is true and lawful about funeral practices in the area where you live. What is and is not allowed. What is the law and what ideas are being sold to you about: Embalming. Transporting. Burial of the body. Dispersing of the ashes.
- Write your will or update your current one.
- Research goddesses such as Freya and Venus, who are both sex and death goddesses.

Witch

No Day of Remembrance

DISHONOR AND DISRESPECT

Witch hunts were some of the most monstrous attacks perpetrated by men, primarily on the female body, and sanctioned by the religions of the father.

Rather than being outraged, we have been duped.

Sadly, we have created cartoon characters out of the victims of these atrocities. Witch hunt tourism and entertainment is lucrative. It is sometimes labeled Witch Kitsch. We model Halloween costumes and decorations after our perception of these victimized women. We create tourist attractions in the cities where they were tortured, hanged, burned alive, or torn apart. We profit from the sale of trinkets, greeting cards, and souvenirs.

Such activity "perpetuates the idea that the so-called witches...were not victims of a terrible persecution, but were fictional figures," says Silvia Federici, author of *Caliban and the Witch*.

> "I do not think the tourists who buy these dolls realize that these were women who were charged with fictional crimes, and then horribly tortured and most often burned alive."

Imagine the outcry if we did such things around the victims of the Holocaust concentration camps in Europe. What if we sold souvenirs, and greeting cards, and key chains with images of diseased and emaciated bodies, and then paraded on a certain day in costumes that resembled prison rags?

"No 'day of memory' has been introduced in any European calendar," writes Federici in the introduction to her 2018 collection of essays, *Witches, Witch-Hunting, and Women.* The victims' history can't "be buried in silence unless we want their destiny to be repeated, as is already happening in many parts of the world."

No days of remembrance for tens of thousands of women who were tortured and killed.
Why are we not outraged by this?

Have you ever participated in celebrations that included cartoon representations of witches?
Have you ever dressed up as a witch at Halloween?
Is it not shamefully dishonoring of our tortured, brutally murdered sisters when we parade in the streets with brooms, wearing pointed black hats, flowing capes, striped stockings, greenish face makeup, and nose warts?
A rather romanticized enactment of what it means to be a witch is often played out in rituals and ceremonies, with the prerequisite pentagrams, candles, skulls, goblets, tattered black clothing, cauldrons, and moon circles. Some self-proclaimed witches have embraced clothing and jewelry styles from the Goth subculture. There are even some who attempt to overlay these rituals with the currently popular ideology of vegans and vegetarians. *We only burn soy candle*s. *We don't eat meat.*

Our foremothers killed things. They ate meat. Their lives depended on their intimate relationship with life and death. They burned candles made from tallow, a stinky animal product, and on special occasions, they burned beeswax.

MODERN DAY PRACTICES

Much of what is presented as modern-day witchcraft is not rooted in ancient, pagan practices of Old Europe but is rather an interesting and somewhat troubling mixture of Greek and Roman mythology, Masonic rites, Eastern mysticism, Jewish Kabbalah, with a few bits and pieces of lore and legend from the British Isles.

It is not uncommon in the witch community to hear references to the right way and the wrong way.

> You must place things on your altar in a specific location.
> You must move around your altar in a certain direction.
> You must go to the right, not to the left.
> You must stand on one leg and whistle, and wear black.
> [I made up that last part.]

In actuality, somebody made all of it up. We have no idea what they did or did not do.
There is no one right answer.
A woman of the always steps into her own center and trusts herself to know what it means to be a witch.

We see this same *right-way/wrong-way* energetic ideology present in other modern spiritual practices. The belief that you must do something a certain way to make it real or acceptable. Meditation, for example.
The cushion, the position, the stillness, the silence.
But what if my meditation is knitting or weaving?
What if my meditation is chopping wood, or walking, or singing, or chewing gum?
What if my spiritual practice as a witch is smoking, or drinking, or eating meat?
What if I'm a witch and I look ordinary?
Are there good witches?
Bad witches?
Green witches?
White witches?
Who has the right to determine such a thing?
How much of what we hear, believe, practice, or shun comes from the taint of the rule of the fathers?
It's possible that this pollution can be found in our drinking water.

In past centuries, during the time of the witch hunts, women were accused of being witches for many reasons. Some were targeted because they were outspoken against the feudal lords and the new enclosure laws regarding the use of public lands, or the injustices of loss of property and home that came with the death of a husband. It was easy to use accusations to stir up madness, to label women as heretics, agents of the devil, baby killers, evil herbalists who poisoned men in power.

Opinionated, radical, disobedient women were a danger to the patriarchy. Based on what we see happening today, in the twenty-first century, not much has changed.

The women accused of being witches were wise healers, herbalists, midwives, death doulas, sin eaters, cunning women, workers of magic, seers, knowers, enchanters, and diviners. They were disobedient wives, women who dared to live alone, old ones who questioned authority. The widows.

Remember, these atrocities were being perpetrated in the name of Christianity. This allowed for all the accusations to be lumped together as heresy and blamed on the devil.

And the magistrates in the towns and villages worked closely with the Church fathers.

So what is it?

Woman *as witch*, or woman as *a witch*?

Has the concept been objectified?

When you claim the word witch, is it who you are?

Is that your being or is that your doing?

Are you pagan or are you a pagan?

Is there a difference in the way we speak about it?

Do you need to look a certain way or dress a certain way so you can be identified by others?

Is there an element of shock factor present in the way you look or what you say?

I cast spells. I do magic. I dance naked under a full moon.

Are you playing a part, even if it is unconscious, in the perpetuation of a stereotype that was actually used by the witchhunters to identify and justify killing our foremothers, tens of thousands of them, at times systematically wiping out entire villages?

The witchhunters looked for women who were ugly, women who were sexually unattractive, women who were herbalists or widows, women who relieved the pain of childbirth, who helped prevent pregnancy and facilitated abortions. Women who perhaps showed other women how to poison their abusive husbands. These women were hunted down and killed because the powers they tapped into could not be controlled by the men.

Our power as witches came from doing spell work when we were spinning, weaving, stitching, or singing over the fires as we stirred the cooking pot. Not all of us were herb gatherers, or basket weavers, or cooks. Some had a stronger talent for one thing than another. But we were all witches in our own way, doing magic in whatever form it took, depending on our unique talents.

It is recorded in historical accounts that during the witch hunts, some women turned against their neighbors, accusing them of witchcraft, ultimately resulting in their death.
Were these women duped into believing that they would be safe because they sided with the men in power?
Such betrayals are still going on today.
Do we betray our sisters by our political affiliations?
Are we betraying our foremothers who were witches by how we portray them in our modern culture?
We are all caught up in something that is so insidious we accept it as being normal without stopping to question what ugly thing is hidden below the surface.

It is common to focus on the enslavement of the blacks and the massacre of people of native cultures in the Americas. It is not so common to focus on what happened to the native cultures of indigenous people in Europe. Not that many hundreds of years ago, large segments of the population were still practicing the old ways and worshiping the old gods. When they refused to be controlled, refused to submit, to convert, they were killed by the Romans and by the Church. A connection exists between what happened to the witches and to the pagans and heathens in Europe, and any colonized people around the globe throughout time.

What would it look like if we held a time of remembrance?
What would we do if we advocated for the remembering of the
women who were killed because they were women, because they
were doing death work, life work, herbal work, and because they
had powers to do things that could not be controlled?

Attacks on witches are attacks on women. We are more than half
the population on earth. We have incredible power. We hold the
ability to bring forth life. We are biologically different. We are
containers. We weave things together. We see in the dark. We know
things we have not learned, and we can move between the worlds.

What has happened to us? We have forgotten who we are. We turn
on each other, and we turn each other in. We support systems that
are female-hating, misogynistic, life-hating.

What is Being Asked of Us

Women of the always.
Women as witches.
We must find a way to bring ourselves together, to refuse to be
women of the book, women of the rule of the fathers, but instead
rise up, find a new language, remember our names, and create
something different.
That is really what we are being asked to do. Most of us reading
this book are not in danger. Not in danger like so many women
in the world.
What are you willing to do? What are you doing?

If we take away the modern-day trappings and we take away the label-
ing, we step into the realm of our ancestors. They were animists, they
were polytheists, they were pagans. To them, all things were alive, all
things were equal. Life was about collaboration, cooperation, and
respect, for the gods, the land, the unseen ones, and the ancestors.
We know that in every culture at all times, there have been those
who carried the power and understanding of life and death. We
know this to be true because there have always been women.

The longing and desire of a woman to return to being witch is sourced from inherited ancestral grief. We are striving to remember, to make meaning of, to understand what we carry in our bones and in our blood. It is necessary for us to know where we come from in order to know who we are, where we are, and also where we are going.

When we remember we are witches, we must not come forward with an apology. We must come forward proudly. We must be willing to declare,

> *I am a woman of the always. I am part of the long line of women healers that was driven to the brink of extinction. I am indigenous because I am of the land. I carry the memory of the land in my body. I create from my body, just as the land does. And I give my body back in return.*

Making such a statement allows us to stop pitting ourselves against each other as women and instead make space for each other as equals. We are all daughters.

Reclaiming the witch is remembering who we are.
Wise women
Prophetesses
Seers
Diviners
Enchantresses
Healers
Doers
Makers
Shapeshifters

We know that when we tap into our power and connect with our ancestral line, we become instruments through which our ancestors can speak.
We are the offspring of our ancestors. They fed us and brought us forth, and their bodies continue to feed us because their bodies returned to the earth.

That is what a witch knows in her body. The cycle of life and death. We are fed by our ancestors, and eventually we will become ancestors.

This is what we remember, not because we read it in a book, but because we remember it in our bodies.

Women as witches.

We know that everything is alive.

We know the past and we know the future because they exist in the present moment.

We know that our bodies hold the memory of everything that has happened to us, the food we ate, the food our mothers ate, the joys and the traumas, all of that is held in the body.

We know that we hold the future in our bodies.

We are the future.

Not just because we can give birth. More than that. A witch knows the truth. She will die. All of us do. And our bodies go back to the earth and feed the earth, so the earth can grow the future.

Are you a witch?

Do you identify as a witch?

Do you connect being a witch with belief in your ancestors?

Do you have a daily practice, a special way of dressing, or speaking?

Do you perform rituals or engage in honoring the ancestors in a certain way or at certain times of the year?

Do you honor all women, or do you turn against some because they live or believe a different way?

Are you a woman of the book or a woman of the rule of the fathers?

Are you a woman of the always?

Can you be both at the same time?

TASKS

- Take some time to locate on the Internet a recording of Eivor Palsdottir singing Trollabundin. When you find it, close your eyes and listen. A single woman, singing in Faroese. A single drum, most likely reindeer hide, pegged, not laced. All the strange, amazing sounds are just her voice, singing in a way that is similar to Saami joik. It is haunting. She is singing about the trolls.

- Locate and listen to the song Manaus (Word of Incantation) on the album Wizard Women of the North CD 1999.

Words

Breathing Words
That Are Our Own

As women of the always, we know what it means to stand in the center of our own lives and remember.
Remember what we already know but perhaps have forgotten.
Remember what we know but have no words for.
Remember that what we know is more than language, more than mental.
What we know is in our bodies.

What we know, without a doubt, is that we can stand in the presence of a man and say, without hesitation, *Bow down in awe because you came forth from the body of a woman.* That's what it means to stand in your center.
It's not about power over.
It's about what is true.
Men do not need to be protected from this truth. They do not need to be coddled.
Women don't need to explain or defend our power.
This is the miracle.
The awe.
The magic.
The mystery.
This is life. This is what we remember in our bodies.

The challenge we often face is that we don't have the words for what we remember. We have only patriarchal language, the words of the father, not the mother.
As one woman said in a gathering,

"I appreciate being reminded that the reason I don't have language to talk about the connection to nature that I feel in my body is because the only language that we have is the language of the patriarchy, the conquerors, the winners, those who control us. It's all we have." –SARAH, PARTICIPANT

We need to break the code.

We must stand in the center of our lives and speak the language of our bodies. When we do, we connect with the earth. She knows the truth. Our bodies know the truth.

We are in danger.

We are all in danger because in the language of the fathers, the bodies of women are sinful, unclean, less than, not holy. And what men believe about women is what they believe about their mothers, and what they believe about their mothers is evident in how they treat the earth.

It's time men remember where they really come from.

A CHEST-FEEDING PERSON WITH A CERVIX!

In the fall of 2024, Natalie L. Dinsdale, PhD, collaborated with Dr. Karleen Gribble and a few other women on a project about sex and gender identity in the context of language in science. Their paper was published in the *Journal of Academic Ethics.*

> "The sexed words 'women' and 'mothers' are increasingly being replaced in research and other contexts with alternative terms that either make sex invisible (e.g. 'people', 'parents,' or 'families'), reference body parts (e.g. 'cervix owners') or allude to physiological processes (e.g. 'birthing bodies'). The word 'breastfeeding' may be replaced with terms like 'chestfeeding' or 'bodyfeeding.' Desexed terms like 'person with a cervix,' 'vagina owner' and 'menstruator' disperse women's reproductive system into component parts so obscuring the coherence of women's bodies and reproduction and collective belonging to the female sex class."

We should all be concerned about this.

No, we should all be outraged.

In the House of the Father

The language of the Bible is the language of the patriarchy. This book is believed to be the word of God by over two billion people worldwide.

According to the creation account in the book of Genesis, the first man, Adam, was made by a male god from the soil of the earth.

As the story goes, the first woman was also made by a male god, not from the soil of the earth, but from body parts of the male.

Adam named the animals.

Adam named the woman.

Women are not namers.

Women are the named, and the names we bear are the names of the father.

Because we are the named, the language is not ours.

It is the language that was given to us, and the telling and retelling of this Bible story serves to perpetuate the language of the patriarchy.

Words have power. They are beings. They are alive. They vibrate. They come from our breath.

Women need to breathe differently.

Breathe new words.

Words that are our own.

There are some who suggest that the Bible would be okay if we altered some of the words.

We could change some of the pronouns or even say mother father god.

It's still a patriarchal book, with patriarchal stories.

We can't put a dress on the god.

The suggestion to change a few words is a pat on the head by the fathers to placate the mothers.

It is still the house of the father.

It is not enough to walk away.

We need to step into our center and remember who we are, remember our names, and begin to speak in the language of the mothers.

We have been lied to. We have been threatened. We have been indoctrinated.
We have been told that if we just stay ensconced in the structure of the father's rule, we will be okay. Everything will be okay.
But it isn't.
That's because Christianity is a religion of slaves. Slave mentality. Slave behavior.
We are convinced that we have to stay in slavery because we are afraid. It's how we get our food and shelter. It's how we can be saved. It does not matter the price we have to pay.
We are in fear for our lives if we run or walk away.

Take a look at the interesting story line of the Jesus character who goes to his death because his master told him to.
Was he perhaps the ultimate slave?
In his own words, "Not my will but your will, Father."
Christianity is a religion based on human sacrifice.
A willing sacrifice.
There are many people who become outraged and enraged if you speak of Christianity as a religion of slavery and human sacrifice. But these same people don't hesitate to condemn so-called pagans and heathens, calling them blood thirsty and savage because they practiced human sacrifice.
If you take away the story of the garden, the tree, the serpent, the woman, the command, there is no sin. There is no need for the sacrifice. There is no need for the religion.

How is it acceptable that some man agrees to be hung on a stake, tortured, stabbed, and ultimately killed, because it was his father's will?
Is that not a human sacrifice?
If it is argued that Jesus was born to be killed, the same argument can be used about the human offerings of other ancient tribal people. How do we know that the people who were sacrificed by the Mayans were not also born to be offered up just as Jesus was?

How do we dare criticize those who practiced the same ritual as the one approved of by the Christian god?

Look back at history. What did the conquerors do in the name of a god they called *father*?
They forced people to stop using their language.
When we have our language taken away, we are disempowered, and when we try to use it again, we are accused of being subversive.
That's why it is vital for women to reclaim a way of speaking that is not the language of the conquering male.

A woman of the always shuns spiritual teachings that perpetuate the belief that only one child, a male child, is perfect and that (man)kind needs his blood in order to be saved from the sinful disobedience of the female.
A woman of the always knows that all babies are perfect.
She knows that death is not a punishment caused by a woman's disobedience but rather the brilliant necessity of the cycle of life.
A woman of the always honors the magical, monthly bleeding that issues forth from the bodies of women.
She rejects the lie about the rib because she knows the truth.
She rejects the lie of the life-giving, sin-forgiving blood of the sacrificed male.
She honors the truth that human life comes forth from the body of a woman.
She rejects the words "chest-feeding person with a cervix" and embraces instead *mother*.

Words matter.

Give some thought to how many of our religious holidays [holy days] celebrate the savior son. Even the few days that seem to honor women are based on their relationship relative to a male.
When we decide to walk away rather than try to fix, we are able to recognize that these stories from the so-called Word of God book are just that, stories. They served a purpose.
Look at how much focus goes into trying to make Jesus into a good guy.

What would Jesus say?

What would Jesus do?

The bottom line is, he was a man existing in a patriarchal system. His apostles were men. The angels are male. God is a male. These stories were told by men, using their words, and the words that are written down, by men, are the words of the word-givers, the words of the namers.

STUPEFIED BY THE WORDS

We are obsessed. With the Dalai Lama. With the Pope. With all the other Holy Fathers.

Have we forgotten they were all birthed from the blood and through the body of a woman?

Who made them holy? Who has the right to determine that they are special?

Why would we be excited to repeat the story, '*the Dalai Lama said that the world will be saved by Western women?*'

Does a woman need to be told that by a man?

What words of wisdom would you be able to share...

If your every need was always taken care of by someone else?

If you were always driven around in a fancy car, flying in a private jet, never had to carry your own luggage, never had to worry about paying the bill?

If you never had to go to work, or the grocery store, or cook, or do dishes, or laundry, or stay up all night tending the sick and dying?

What words of wisdom would you speak if you were not afraid of being robbed or raped?

Would you be able to wear a perpetual smile and wave?

Who decides who gets to be called holy?

Give me a grandmother who has birthed children, raised some, buried some, who has lived a full life, one we can all relate to. Why would a woman be willing or even think it was okay to have a man tell her what she can or cannot do with her body, especially a man who supposedly has never had sex?

Who benefits from the perpetuation of the lie that being celibate makes you holy, sin-free? That sex makes you unclean?

Sisters, we need to rise up, find our own words so we can call each other holy because we have lived life, and declare all children perfect because they have come forth from the mother.

May we sit in awe in the presence of each other and listen to words that are rooted in wisdom, sourced from the dark.

Why are we still bowing down to and groveling at the feet of men? Some might object, pointing to the majesty of the late Queen of England, but she was only granted the right to rule by the authority of the male god. She served in the house of the father, and everything was supposed to be okay if she followed all the rules. But everything was not okay and is not okay.

Your Holiness

Who gets to determine what is holy and sacred? We associate these words with some sort of awesome reverence, somehow allowing ourselves to be separated from our own sacred, powerful, beautiful self.

When you name only some things as being sacred, what do you base that on? The religion of the fathers?

Life is about living. Sex and birth and dying. The *all* of it. Erupting volcanoes and blooming daffodils.

Rainbows and cheetahs hunting down gazelles.

Men believe they have the right to control nature, to use it to their advantage, that it should be in service to them.

Such beliefs are not about relationship or connection but rather control, power over, and servitude.

Earth is not here to serve us. It is not ours to tame or control. We are not its guardians. We are part of it, not separate from it.

This belief of God-given right is from the language of the father. It is no accident that earth is most often referred to as female. It fits the story.

It is not our job to control nature; nature does not need to be controlled and neither do women.

Every time you hear or read something about god-given rights, you must ask the question, who does this serve?

Who benefits from the control?

The answer to that question is pretty obvious when we look around the globe at the atrocities being brought upon women and the earth.

Step into the center of your own life.

Claim your sovereignty.

Breathe new words.

Remember you are a woman.

Find new words.

Begin by naming yourself.

Wisdom

Rooted in Wisdom

Women of the always are staff carriers. We are each connected to the World Tree through our staff. The World Tree feeds us. We are nourished by the wisdom that is sourced from the memories held in the rich, dark soil of the earth and drawn up through our roots. We know that it is not possible to have branches without a deeply connected root system.

All too often, I hear women speak about fearing the dark, dreading it, not liking it, feeling like they must push it away or shine light into it, transcend, and raise their consciousness.
When we stand in our center, in sovereignty, holding our staff, we can grow into the dark, learn to embrace it and trust it, value it, and live with its wisdom.
Earth wisdom.
Root wisdom.
Life and death wisdom.

It's January 2025. As I am writing this, devastating fires are burning in Los Angeles, California. People have lost their homes. People have lost their lives. We want to find someone or something to blame. We see ourselves as victims. We look for the cause, the enemy. During times of war, it is easy to name the enemy and place blame there.
But what if we are not at war?
What if there is no one to blame?
What if these events are part of life, the kind of life we humans have created for ourselves here on earth, and the earth is responding to us in her own way?
She is self-cleaning, self-balancing, self-regulating.

What if we speak the truth?

What happens when almost four million people try to live in one small area?

Where does our water come from?

Where does our waste go?

How does the vegetation suffer?

How does the wildlife survive?

What happens to the soil?

Year after year, we prevent fires to save houses when the truth is that nature uses fires to keep the balance. When we poison the mother, she feeds us poison in return. When we use the earth as our toilet, eventually she will flush.

When we dam the river, it will break.

All dams break.

All rivers flood.

All water flows to the ocean.

If we swim in the ocean, it's possible that we might get eaten by a shark.

It is not tragic. It might be sad, but it is not tragic.

The shark is not an enemy. Not savage or blood thirsty. The shark is a shark. It kills and eats things in order to live. When we swim in the ocean, we become an uninvited visitor in the home of the shark. Volcanoes erupt. Eruptions destroy things. Trees, wildlife, humans. Volcanoes create new land. Who does not appreciate the beauty of the Hawaiian Islands?

Ice melts. Deserts form. Sea levels rise. The earthquakes and great fissures open up and swallow things. Species become extinct. Small flowers and lichen begin to grow on the rocky surface of newly formed islands off the coast of Iceland.

We are a people who have lost our way. We have forgotten where we come from, so it's impossible for us to know where we are going. All we need, we can learn by observing and connecting with the earth, her seasons, cycles, and rhythms of life and death. We may imagine how great we are because we can fly to the moon or put men in space, but we must never forget that such things are only possible because we create our rockets and spaceships from the elements of the earth. We humans are only able to stay alive in space because we bring food and water with us, from the earth. The earth is our mother. She gives us life. She feeds us from her body. She takes us back and recycles us.

I have a friend who lives in Australia. She has a close connection with Aboriginal women. They share earth wisdom with her.

> See the tree over there with the bright flowers. It blooms when the sharks are having babies.

Nature gifts wisdom to all of us when we pay attention.
Many evenings, I sit outside my home in the garden. I don't need to worry about what time it is because the crows tell me.
No matter the changing of the seasons.
No matter the clock or daylight saving time.
It's not 7:00.
It's not 8:00.
It's about 20 minutes after sunset when the crows start to fly, at first one or two, then groups. Cawing and calling out to each other as they fly overhead. Always heading in the same direction. West. They tell me the time.

Women are containers. We are holders, keepers of the mysteries of life that come forth from the dark places of our bodies. We are the mothers' daughters, our human mother and our earth mother. The earth is a container. She holds the seeds of new life. Her soil is the story of all that has lived and died. Her stones tell the same story that the ancient trees hold. The glaciers, too, are keepers of history. When they reach the sea, they calve. They give birth to icebergs. They birth memories that have been held frozen in the ice and will now be released as the ice melts into the waters of the oceans. Great wisdom from times past is being given to us as the ice melts. Pay attention.

Humans can plan and study, measure and calculate, but the force of life is so strong it happens in its own time. All water flows to the ocean. All life outside the body of the mother begins with an inhale. All life ends with the last breath. Some men teach that we can control things with our minds. They teach this as fact, but it is a lie. They tell this lie because they are not women. They have never given birth, and because of that, they cannot know what a woman knows in her body. Once a woman goes into labor, she is overtaken by a force greater than her mind, the force of life coming through. The labor overtakes her, and if she is unable to give birth, she will die and the baby with her.

The birth of a baby, the sprouting of a seed, the release of a leaf, the hatching of an egg. There is no such thing as primitive, uncivilized, uneducated, unscientific. Life has its own language and wisdom; it continues with or without us, even in spite of us and our interference.

The bear emerging from its den in spring. The waves of the ocean. The back and forth of the tides. The swing of a pendulum, the evaporating of water, and the silent falling of snow. The in breath and the out breath.
We women innately know such things.
Yet somehow, much of this wisdom has been lost to us.
Not really lost but rather forbidden, hidden away, and forgotten.

Before we had scales to weigh ourselves, we knew our bodies by paying attention to how we felt, how our clothing fit, how we moved.
We didn't have easy access to mirrors. Perhaps the only time we saw a rather blurry, undefined reflection of ourselves was in the still surface of a lake or pond.
We measured time with the moon and our bleeding.
We trusted others to look out for us, and we knew how we looked when it was reflected back to us in the words or the gaze of another.
We could trust a stranger to tell us if our nose was frostbitten or a friend to say, 'You have something green stuck in your teeth.'

There was truth and wisdom in the decisions we made. What to harvest and when. What to leave in the field. What to prune away, and what to cull. We saw the wisdom of nature when a baby bird was pushed out of a crowded nest or the runt of a litter was pushed aside to die. We marveled at the wisdom of survival when we watched a mother, who had just given birth, eat her young.

In the work I do, I find women who don't know what direction to look to see the sun rise, nor which way to turn to see it set. Perhaps such knowing is deemed unnecessary for now. We have GPS or Siri, our navigational systems. But what happens when we find ourselves without the gadgets that do these things for us, or when no electrical power is available to keep the gadgets working? We don't know where to get water when the faucet stops flowing, or where to find fuel when there is no heat or light.

This is not about being nostalgic for the old ways or wishing to live in the past or off the grid. This is about connection.

We are not mere observers.

We are participants. And it is we, the women, who are being called to remember.

We are not lacking.

We are not less.

We are not sinful, bad, broken, or defective.

We do not need to be saved.

We step into the center of our own life, day after day, claim our sovereignty and declare what is true.

I am a woman of the always.

Rooted in wisdom.

Sourced from the dark.

I am creative, sexual and spiritual.

A woman of the always knows that the universe, the void, the cosmos, is dark, dotted with pinpoints of light, stars that burn brightly and eventually burn out.

The dark remains.

Night is the time gifted to us by the body of the earth. She protects us from the light of the sun so we can rest at night. She shields all the earth beings from the light of the sun, the animals, the plants, the soil, the water. We all need to rest.

Night is a gift. Winter is a gift. Dark is a gift.

Women of the always know that darkness is not the absence of light. Darkness is not an absence any more than light is an absence.

Darkness is its own being.

Light is its own being.

A woman of the always knows that she is an archer. She must pull back the arrow first, before she can release it and hit the target. She knows what she needs, and that knowing guides the direction of her arrow.

She knows she cannot cross a threshold or pass through a portal without leaving something behind, and what she leaves is an offering. She cannot step into a new or different place unless she is willing to leave the place where she is.

She knows the price that is demanded from her if she chooses the imagined safety of domesticity. It is the loss of her true nature, wild and free.

She would never stay in a dangerous, abusive, dominating relationship, not even for the sake of the children. She knows that if she were to do that, she would be modeling for them a lie, that it is okay to be abused. And even worse, her children would know that she cannot be trusted to keep them safe.

A woman of the always would never believe the lie that she is the cause of death, that she is sinful and imperfect, and that she needs to be rescued or saved.

This is the lie of the holy book.

This is the lie of the rule of the fathers.

This is the lie of those who claim the right to name us.

This is the lie of slavery.

The list can go on and on, and I am sure you can add to it your own insights, experiences, and wisdom.

From the place of all this remembering I envisioned, conceived, created, and wrote this book. Each topic is an invitation to explore and wonder about a single word. You will find questions woven throughout. You will find statements I've made that resonate with you, and others that you adamantly reject.

None of this matters.

There is room for all of it.

Read the book, but don't be satisfied with just that.

Take the time to do the work.

Answer the questions.

Keep a notebook specific to the journey.
Create a scrapbook from your experiences and insights.

Many of the chapters include guided meditations. You may want to read them out loud, recording your own voice so you can listen to them. You can also go to my website and find access to these meditations recorded in my voice.

You will find a list of books I suggest and recommend. These may become great additions to your personal book collection or you may decide to borrow them from your local library.

There are suggestions for activities you can explore that support and enrich your journey.

Work through the book with a friend or group.
Gather together, perhaps alternating locations.
Bring food and share it.
Bring an open mind.
Be curious about the beliefs and perspectives of other women and learn from their experiences.
Listen with an open heart, even when you might not agree or approve.
Most of all, come on this adventure with curiosity and a willingness to wonder and to wander.
Perhaps you began already by remembering your name.

One could rightly say that humans are a species that lives with post-traumatic stress disorder. And, universally, it is the women who suffer the brunt of violence, degradation, humiliation, and devastation.

We do not always need a label, a diagnosis, or a medication for a condition. We know in our bodies when we are out of balance, disconnected, exhausted, and outraged.

Genetic information from our ancestors determines physical characteristics, and at the same time, this genetic information carries the energy of unhealed wounds, unfinished business, and grief.

People of northern European descent have forgotten that their ancestors were indigenous, that they suffered violence, cultural destruction, and spiritual devastation in the name of monotheistic, desert religions, and the lie of Roman civilization.

Remember your name.
Remember who you are and where you come from.
Reclaim the words you can use to speak about your own life and your body.
Remember that you are a woman of the always, rooted in wisdom, sourced from the dark.

A Wild Woman Is Not a Girlfriend. She Is a Relationship With Nature.

But can you love me in the deep? In the dark? In the thick of it?
Can you love me when I drink from the wrong bottle and slip
through the crack in the floorboard?
Can you love me when I'm bigger than you, when my presence
blazes like the sun does, when it hurts to look directly at me?
Can you love me then too?
Can you love me under the starry sky,
shaved and smooth, my skin like liquid moonlight?
Can you love me when I am howling and furry,
standing on my haunches, my lower lip stained with the blood of
my last kill?
When I call down the lightning, when the sidewalks are singed
by the soles of my feet, can you still love me then?
What happens when I freeze the land, and cause the dirt to
harden over all the pomegranate seeds we've planted?
Will you trust that Spring will return?
Will you still believe me when I tell you I will become a raging
river, and spill myself upon your dreams and call them to the
surface of your life?
Can you trust me, even though you cannot tame me?
Can you love me, even though I am all that you fear and ad-
mire?
Will you fear my shifting shape?
Does it frighten you, when my eyes flash like your camera does?
Do you fear they will capture your soul?
Are you afraid to step into me?
The meat-eating plants and flowers armed with poisonous darts
are not in my jungle to stop you from coming. Not you.
So do not worry. They belong to me, and I have invited you here.
Stay to the path revealed in the moonlight and arrive safely to the

*hut of Baba Yaga, the wild old wise one... she will not lead you
astray if you are pure of heart.*

*You cannot be with the wild one if you fear the rumbling of the
ground, the roar of a cascading river, the startling clap of
thunder in the sky.*

*If you want to be safe, go back to your tiny room — the night sky
is not for you.*

*If you want to be torn apart, come in. Be broken open and de-
voured. Be set ablaze in my fire.*

*I will not leave you as you have come: well dressed, in fine-
ly-threaded sweaters that keep out the cold.*

*I will leave you naked and biting. Leave you clawing at the
sheets. Leave you surrounded by owls and hawks and flowers that
only bloom when no one is watching.*

*So, come to me, and be healed in the unbearable lightness and
darkness of all that you are.*

*There is nothing in you that can scare me. Nothing in you I will
not use to make you great.*

*A wild woman is not a girlfriend. She is a relationship with
nature. She is the source of all your primal desires, and she is the
wild whipping wind that uproots the poisonous corn stalks on
your neatly tilled farm.*

She will plant pear trees in the wake of your disaster.

She will see to it that you shall rise again.

She is the lover who restores you to your own wild nature.

—ALISON NAPPI

WHO IS THE LOVER THAT RESTORES YOU TO YOUR
WILD, CREATIVE, SEXUAL, SPIRITUAL,
TRUTH-TELLING SELF?

Suggested Reading

NAMES
The Creation of Patriarchy –GERDA LERNER
Breaking the Patriarchal Code: The Linguistic Basis of Sexual Bias
–LOUISE GOUEFFIC
The Tongue Snatchers –CLAUDINE HERRMANN
The Guerilla Girls: The Art of Behaving Badly –THE GUERILLA
GIRLS
I Married Adventure –OSA JOHNSON
Pioneer Women: The Lives of Women on the Frontier –LINDA
PEAVY & URSULA SMITH.
Beyond God The Father –MARY DALY

MIRRORS
Ways Of Seeing –JOHN BERGER
The Force of Character: And The Lasting Life –JAMES HILLMAN

BREASTS
A History of the Breast –MARILYN YALOM
*Women's Bodies, Women's Wisdom: Creating Physical and
Emotional Health and Healing* –CHRISTIANE NORTHRUP, M.D.
Vagina: A New Biography –NAOMI WOLF
*Eve: How The Female Body Drove 200 Million Years of Human
Evolution* –CAT BOHANNON

FLESH
*Women's Bodies, Women's Wisdom: Creating Physical and
Emotional Health and Healing* –CHRISTIANE NORTHRUP, M. D.
Cunt: a declaration of independence –INGA MUSCIO

Transcendent Sex: When Lovemaking Opens The Veil –JENNY WADE
The Red Book: A Deliciously Unorthodox Approach to Igniting Your Divine Spark –SERA BEAK
Whores And Other Feminists: A Collection Of Essays And Personal Narratives –JILL NAGLE
Sacred Pleasure: Sex, Myth, and the Politics of the Body –RIANE EISLER
Vagina: A New Biography –NAOMI WOLF
The Urethrovaginal Gland, Amrita & Amritasis: Cultural and Medical Background –VINCENT M. RICCARDI

WHORE
Whores And Other Feminists –JILL NAGLE
A History of the Wife –MARILYN YALOM
I, Claudia: Feminism Unveiled –CLAUDIA
Caliban and the Witch: Women, the Body and Primitive Accumulation –SILVIA FEDERICI
Beyond the Periphery of the Skin: Rethinking, Remaking, and Reclaiming the Body in Contemporary Capitalism –SILVIA FEDERICI

SPINSTERS
The Valkyries Loom: The Archaeology of Cloth Production and Female Power in the North Atlantic – MICHELE HAYEUR SMITH
The Norns in Old Norse Mythology –KAREN BEK-PEDERSEN
Witches and Pagans: Women in European Folk Religion, 700-1100 –MAX DASHU
Charlotte's Web –E. B. WHITE

CREATIVITY
Women Who Run With The Wolves: Myths and Stories of the Wild Woman Archetype –CLARISSA PINKOLA ESTES
Stoking The Creative Fires: 9 Ways to Rekindle Passion and Imagination –PHIL COUSINEAU

The Artist's Way: A Spiritual Path to Higher Creativity –JULIA
CAMERON
*Marry Your Muse: Making a Lasting Commitment to Your
Creativity* –JAN PHILLIPS
Art & Fear: Observations On the Perils (and Rewards) of Artmaking
–DAVID BAYLES AND TED ORLAND
The Courage To Create –DR. ROLLO MAY
The Creative Act: A Way of Being –RICK RUBIN
The Story Of Art Without Men –KATY HESSEL

MONEY
The Woman's Book of Money & Spiritual Vision –ROSEMARY
WILLIAMS
Patriarchy Of The Wage: Notes on Marx, Gender, and Feminism
–SILVIA FEDERICI
Money and the Soul's Desires: A Meditation –STEPHEN JENKINSON
Simple Abundance: A Daybook of Comfort and Joy –SARAH BAN
BREATHNACH
*Web of Debt: The Shocking Truth About Our Money System and
How We Can Break Free* –ELLEN HODGSON BROWN, J.D.

BEES
*The Shamanic Way of the Bees: Ancient Wisdom and Healing
Practices of the Bee Masters* –SIMON BUXTON
The Hidden Hive Of History: The Forgotten God of the Ancients–
ANDREW GOUGH
Becoming Animal: An Earthly Cosmology –DAVID ABRAM
Murder, Magic and Medicine –JOHN MANN

WATER
The Fourth Phase Of Water: Beyond Solid, Liquid, Vapor –GERALD
H. POLLACK
The Hidden Messages In Water –MASARU EMOTO
The Nine Muses: A Mythological Path To Creativity –ANGELES
ARRIEN

The Well and the Tree: World and Time in Early Germanic Culture
–PAUL C. BAUSCHATZ
The Mist-Filled Path: Celtic Wisdom for Exiles, Wanderers, and Seekers –FRANK MACEOWEN
The Water of the Hills: Jean de Florette and Manon of the Springs (a two-volume novel) –MARCEL PAGNOL [MADE INTO TWO FILMS OF THE SAME NAMES PRODUCED BY CLAUDE BERRI]
If Women Rose Rooted: The Journey to Authenticity and Belonging –SHARON BLACKIE

LEFT
Sex, Time And Power: How Women's Sexuality Shaped Human Evolution –LEONARD SHLAIN

SILENCE
Circle of Stones: Woman's Journey to Herself –JUDITH DUERK
A Book of Silence: A Journey In Search Of The Pleasures And Powers Of Silence –SARAH MAITLAND
Manifesto for Silence: Confronting the Politics and Culture of Noise –STUART SIM
Gift From The Sea –ANN MORROW LINDBERGH

DARK
Becoming Animal: An Earthly Cosmology –DAVID ABRAM
At Days Close: Night In Times Past –A. ROGER EKIRCH
Wild Nights: How Taming Sleep Created Our Restless World – BENJAMIN REISS
The End Of Night: Searching For Natural Darkness In An Age Of Artificial Light –PAUL BOGARD
The Darkness Manifesto: On Light Pollution, Night Ecology, And The Ancient Rhythms That Sustain Life –JOHAN EKLOF

DEATH
Die Wise: A Manifesto for Sanity and Soul –STEPHEN JENKINSON

Come Of Age: The Case for Elderhood in a Time of Trouble – STEPHEN JENKINSON
Holding Space: On Loving, Dying, and Letting Go –AMY WRIGHT GLENN
The Good Death: A Guide For Supporting Your Loved One Through The End Of Life –SUZANNE B. O'BRIEN
The Second Half Of Life: Opening The Eight Gates Of Wisdom –ANGELES ARRIEN
Advice For Future Corpses (and Those Who Love Them): A Practical Perspective on Death and Dying –SALLIE TISDALE
Finding Meaning In The Second Half Of Life: How To Finally, Really Grow Up –JAMES HOLLIS
Hagitude: Reimagining the Second Half of Life –SHARON BLACKIE
The Crone: Woman of Age, Wisdom, and Power –BARBARA G. WALKER
The Fear of Women –WOLFGANG LEDERER

WITCH
Witches and Pagans: Women In European Folk Religion, 700-1100 (Secret History of the Witches) –MAX DASHU
Caliban and the Witch: Women, the Body and Primitive Accumulation –SILVIA FEDERICI
Witches, Witch-Hunting, and Women –SILVIA FEDERICI
Witch: For Those Who Are –LY DE ANGELES
Witchcraft: Theory and Practice –LY DE ANGELES

WORDS
The Creation of Patriarchy –GERDA LERNER

WISDOM
Kissing The Hag: The Dark Goddess and the Unacceptable Nature of Women –EMMA RESTALL ORR
The Second Sex –SIMONE DE BEAUVOIR

Acknowledgements

It is not possible to list and name all the amazing, wonderful women as well as the amazing, wonderful men who helped me along the way. With money. With housing. With criticisms and accolades. With listening to my endless rants, my excuses, my frustrations. They recognized my need for solitude as well as friendship. They attended my classes, shared their notes, challenged and praised the material, cheered me on. They traveled with me as well as kept track of me when I traveled.

The creation of the yearlong course, and then eventually the writing of this book, has taken me 20 years. With heartfelt gratitude I thank them all. My daughter, my sons, my brother and my friends. Naomi St. Clare, Daniel Hanych, Christianne Elise Hanych, Dave Hanych, Craig Kincaid, Debbie Kincaid, Jaine Ingals, Toni Tona, Trish Cowles, Kristi Williams, Susan Webb, Tinah Hekman, Dorene Lucchesi, Erin Donley.
My father, Fay Kincaid. He lovingly listened as I asked questions and gave me answers that left me wanting more.
My mother, Sigrid Olson Kincaid. She instilled in me a love of reading and gifted me some of my first books.

About the Author

Ingrid calls herself an Irreverent Wise Woman, a storyteller, a trouble maker, an eccentric creative who has lived many lifetimes by dwelling in the realms of the real and the imaginary. There are no letters after her name. She has earned degrees in wisdom, intuition and determination by being curious, and always asking questions. When others see a wall, Ingrid opens a window. Life for her is an adventure, not a prison sentence. She is an internationally-known author, teacher and mentor, a respected elder in the community who provides spiritual counseling and intuitive guidance, both in person and virtually. When she's not traveling, Ingrid can be found at home in the Pacific Northwest, at the confluence of two rivers, in sight of two volcanos.

IngridKincaid.com

Also by Ingrid Kincaid

LOST TEACHINGS OF THE RUNES:
NORTHERN MYSTERIES AND THE
WHEEL OF LIFE

Lost Teachings of the Runes is an
unexpected adventure into the hidden
meanings and profound lessons held
in these simple markings that are the
signatures of ancient beings.

THE RUNES REVEALED: AN (UN)
FAMILIAR JOURNEY
RECLAIMING OUR HERITAGE HEALING
OUR ANCESTRAL GRIEF

"The Runes Revealed will challenge
you to remove the tainted, distorted
lens of patriarchal interpretation and
start seeing the runes with clearer
vision. Long before Odin, the Vikings
or Christianity, the runes were."
–INGRID KINCAID, AUTHOR

"My work with the runes began with my hand in a leather
pouch held by Ingrid. I drew Raidho, rune of the journey,
and so began a sacred task of reweaving ancient wisdom."
–LARA VESTA, ILLUSTRATOR

(UN)FAMILIAR
Limited edition handmade book
33 copies, 33 runes, 33 words for each poem
handmade paper, handset type, hand cut leather, hand stitched

Red Thread Publishing

About the Publisher

Red Thread Publishing is an award-winning indie press dedicated to amplifying powerful, authentic nonfiction voices. In our first five years, we've published more than 65 books, supported over 320 authors from 30 countries, and celebrated 38 book awards, proof of the impact and quality behind every title we produce. Our passionate team is committed to guiding authors through every step of the writing and publishing journey so their stories not only get published but make a lasting impact. Visit **www.redthreadbooks.com** or email **info@redthreadbooks.com**.

@redthreadbooks
/redthreadpublishing